Praise for *Amor and Exile*

"If there is one enduring truth it is that love of family will always drive human decisions. Through the stories of these American families, *Amor and Exile* exposes how immigration policies undermine the family unit and enforcement practices have little to no relationship to national security or safety. This book will explain why the immigration system makes it nearly impossible for people to attain legal status in a reasonable amount of time and how American families suffer through blind application of existing immigration laws."

—**Maria Andrade**, immigration attorney, American Immigration Lawyers Association National ICE Liaison Committee, National Immigration Project board member and advisor to American Immigration Law Center Legal Action Center

"*Amor and Exile* is a highly gripping, personal and accurate account of the tragedies of our current immigration system, especially as they impact American families. It is particularly timely given Congress' current focus on immigration reform."

—**Michael Davis**, immigration attorney, Chair of USCIS International Operations Liaison Committee and Co-Editor, *The Consular Practice Handbook*

"I thought I knew in broad strokes everything there was to know about illegal immigration until my path crossed that of Nicole Salgado and other women who have followed their deported husbands into exile. I was wrong. Salgado and Hoffman have provided me and others who care about illegal immigration in all its harsh complexity another "dot" that needs to be brought into clear focus and connected to all the other dots on the immigration spectrum including free trade agreements, migrant deaths and the United States' burgeoning for-profit prison system.

In her compelling, spare prose style, Salgado introduces us to her Mexican husband, Margo, and to the adjustments their love in exile has required of them both. Hoffman broadens the cast of characters to Susie and Roberto, Carlos and Beth, Ben and Deyanira, Juan and Veronica, and J.W. and Gabriel, a same-sex couple. None of them set out to fall in love with someone who had no lawful status in the U.S., but they did.

None intended to face the agonizing decision to follow their loved one into a more or less permanent exile, but that is what happened.

Salgado and Hoffman do more than sketch personal stories. They do more than ask Americans to consider the humanity of illegal immigrants. What they do engagingly and significantly is ask Americans to consider what it means to be an American who loses his or her political voice, who technically becomes a legal stranger, who lives for indefinite periods in personal and political limbo—all because she or he fell in love.

Hoffman asks [us] to consider that the reality of love in exile does not square with Americans' (erroneous) understanding that the immigration system is wide open to family members, our genuine regard for families and our deep cultural belief in marrying for romantic reasons.

Amor and Exile is important, timely and deserves a wide readership."

—**Ellin Jimmerson**, Ph.D., historian, theologian and writer/director of "The Second Cooler," an award-winning migrant justice documentary, narrated by Martin Sheen

See back cover for more endorsements.

Amor & Exile

True Stories of Love Across America's Borders

~

By Nathaniel Hoffman and Nicole Salgado

This is the new civil rights!

Thanks

Nathn Hfm + N.R.S

Boise 10/2014

Cordillera West Books
Boise | Querétaro

Cordillera West Books
Boise | Querétaro
First Edition, 2013

Cover Design by Gilad Foss.

Permissions/Sources:
Cover image remixed from "The Wall…" by Wonderlane / Flickr under Creative Commons Attribution 2.0 license.

Excerpt at end of Chapter 1 from "St. Cesar of Delano" in *Darling: A Spiritual Autobiography* by Richard Rodriguez. Originally appeared in *The Wilson Quarterly,* Winter 2010. Used with permission.

Excerpt at beginning of Chapter 7 from "The Sicario" by Charles Bowden originally published in *Harper's Magazine,* May 2009.

Lyric at end of Conclusion from "Love Coyote" by Bright Eyes.

Library cataloging information available upon request.
Library of Congress Control Number: 2013909745
ISBN-13: 978-0615824062
ISBN-10: 0615824064

amorandexile.com | facebook.com/amorandexile | @amorandexile

Contents

Authors' Note

Everything you are about to read is true. It's the truth of journalism, the first draft of history. And it's the truth of memoir, self-documentation and survival. It is reporter and source in a modern-age mash-up. Nathaniel Hoffman writes of *amor*, love, and exile starting in Chapter 1. His account of lives rocked by border politics continues in subsequent chapters. Nicole Salgado tells her own story starting with her arrival in exile in Chapter 2. She later continues her account of her life's limbo between Mexico and the United States. Two narrators, each in search of truth, transparency and justice, lead you on this journey across America's borders… and back.

Chapter 1

Love in the Time of Deportation

~

Nathaniel Hoffman

CHAPTER 1

Susie & Roberto

Susie Fischer did not want to be a wallflower. But it was her first time and someone had to watch the purses. At least Susie stood as she held those purses—only dead people sit when the band takes up a merengue. Some older white people might sit out a salsa, but Susie was not old and she was sort of ethnic. Her people dance in circles with their hands up in the air, kicking their legs. They don't use their hips, their core. By the end of the evening Susie would feel her hips. She would hear the merengue steps in her calves, her ankles. She would start to mimic the complex body movements of the salsa.

It was a generic Latin dance club with a large dance floor, spinning lights and live band, but in a western city like Denver, La Rumba was high class. The clientele was shockingly *sofisticado* and well dressed. The salsa notion is so international in Denver—not even New York international, beyond New York. There were Argentines and Colombians there, maybe some Italians. It's hard to tell, especially if it's your first time.

There were definitely some hip Mexicans there because one was about to chat Susie up. She made feeble attempts at resistance; he had an answer to every excuse.

She had to watch the girls' purses. *Dance with the purses then.*

She did not know how to dance. *Follow me then.*

I don't even know what you are saying. *I have no idea what you are saying.*

Susie put down the mess of handbags and allowed Roberto to lead her to the dance floor. After one or two songs she began to relax. Then she began to smile. Then she got the giggles. After an hour, all of her friends went home and she stayed at the club, dancing the night away with Roberto.

Latin dance is more about attitude than movement. The steps are secondary to the gaze, the touch. Maintain eye contact and body contact at all times. Keep moving and even in moments of stillness, keep moving. That's the first thing to do.

It does not always work.

The second rule: Learn… no, you don't learn. Just allow yourself to move from the center, from the hips. Hear the music with your core first, that center that we seek in trendy incarnations of yoga. Dance with your core power.

According to Roberto: "Americans don't know how to dance... you have to learn to coordinate."

See, it's easy, he said.

But Roberto doesn't know *everything*. He didn't know how to order breakfast the next morning when they met up again. They tried to go for Chinese, but it was closed, so they ended up at Peeps around lunchtime—that's Le Peep, a well-known American breakfast chain in Denver. He'd never been there before. He'd never been to a restaurant where you sit down and order. His food came fried up crispy—not at all what he wanted. He used to hand cashiers twenty bucks in those days and pray it was enough; he didn't really know his numbers in English yet. He'd only been north of the line for two or three years.

The conversation made Susie's brain hurt. She thought he said he knew how to make hot cakes, or pancakes, but he was trying to tell her he had worked as a cake decorator for a cousin in Washington State. She had to really focus on what he was saying. They couldn't talk about movies or politics because he could not express his deep thoughts in English.

Roberto asked her to give him three months. He took some English classes. She took him to yoga and they went skiing. They dated other people—at least Susie did—but they had a really good time too. He met her mother, bonded with her father. He took back the five years he had added to his age that October night at La Rumba. In the summer he moved in to her place, a newish, suburban townhouse that she had kept after a brief first marriage ended.

It has a piano and a gas fireplace.

Ben & Deyanira

Ben and Deyanira had a lot more in common with one another when they first met than Susie and Roberto did.

Ben's mother kept bugging the hell out of him to meet this girl because, well, she speaks Spanish too. Benjamin Reed speaks Spanish professionally. He is a tall, balding white guy who hosts his own local public affairs show on Spanish radio in south-central Idaho. His radio persona is *El Chupacabras*, the mythical goatsucker, a creature that comes in the night to steal your livestock. Ben Reed is very famous among Spanish speakers on the dairies and in the potato fields of Rupert, Burley and Paul, Idaho, and in little towns in central Mexico that no one has heard of either. But he got even more famous in 2005 when he made an appearance in Héctor Tobar's book *Translation Nation*, a journey through Spanish-speaking America. Ben described himself then as a Latino trapped in an Anglo body.

Ben's mother thinks him somewhat famous as well. So when she heard Deyanira Escalona speaking Spanish in line at the Social Security office in Idaho Falls in late 2004, she kind of hit on her.

Deyanira recalls the first thing her mother-in-law, Beverly, said to her: "I have a son who speaks Spanish all the time." So Deyanira gave up her phone number. Then she thought about it: "I would never give my number to a stranger."

But no matter, there are few strangers in a town like Idaho Falls, and Deyanira's scholarship was expiring at the end of the semester, so she had to make the most of her time. The problem was Ben lived in a small town a few hours west of Idaho Falls, where he worked in radio. At the time, he was in and out of the hospital with an unexplained illness. Beverly put Deyanira on the phone with him but she got voicemail, which opened with a larger-than-life, "*Ay, buey ... *"—a mildly vulgar Spanish greeting that shocked the sweet Deyanira, who had come to the United States as a Mormon missionary, serving two years in Oakland.

Within a few months, Deyanira and Beverly were good friends, but Deyanira had not even spoken to Beverly's mythical, Spanish speaking son over in Burley. Deyanira's attempts to stay in Idaho were falling short. She didn't get into a master's degree program at BYU; her visa would expire when her scholarship expired. But Beverly had a master plan: She asked Ben to accompany her, her daughter and Deyanira down to Salt Lake City for a day. Ben's sister had a doctor's appointment, and Ben was to take Deyanira to an immigration attorney to see about extending her visa. They walked in holding hands and the attorney immediately asked if they were getting married.

"No way," Deyanira responded. "We just met."

The lawyer told her to just find a guy. She said that was not an option. So they left and found that Beverly had left them alone with quite a bit of time to kill, so they wandered around downtown Salt Lake City together talking.

"I had a hard time believing she was *mexicana*," Ben said.

Deyanira is tall and fair skinned with prominent cheekbones and a charming smile. Her mother is Honduran, but she grew up middle to upper class in Mexico City, attending good private schools and earning a degree in marketing from one of Mexico's top universities. She is named after Hercules' third wife, Deyanira—destroyer of men.

Ben perfected his Spanish in Argentina, where he went on a Mormon mission in 1989, but he later employed it when he allied himself with the Mexican population of southern Idaho. Mexicans settled in Idaho more than a century ago, but their ranks have swelled in recent decades with migrants from the countryside, rural people who come from the abandoned fields of central Mexico to work in the fields and factories along the Snake River. Ben's Spanish is precise and elegant but infused with the slang and sarcasm of the working class. It is also politically charged and very much in tune with local Idaho Latino politics, which lean to the left in an otherwise very right-leaning part of the country.

Deyanira was somewhat impressed. Their first meeting, the road trip to Salt Lake, earned a mention in her diary. Their second meeting was recorded again in her journal and then they started emailing back and forth. Deyanira returned to Mexico when her visa ran out, and they did not see one another for more than a year.

But that year of separation provided both Ben and Deyanira a new perspective on their relationship. There was a spark and then an ember, forming the type of dense, burning material that will lay quietly under a cold fire, under a blanket of coals, stoked by a minuscule air pocket for hours at a time, only to erupt in flame when inevitably stirred with a poke stick.

They were not teenagers, but Deyanira did that thing that teenagers do when they are not sure, when they feel some pull, but can't quite place it. She stirred the fire to life. She took the tourist visa that she'd had since 2001 after a canceled New York City trip, hopped on a plane and went back to Idaho. He thought she was moving to Cancún and he'd never see her again. She thought she heard that thing in his voice. They had six months to try it out.

They dated for a few months. They got serious in October 2006 and then engaged in December 2006, as Deyanira's visa ran out again. Ben flew down to Mexico City to meet her family, Deyanira furiously planned the wedding and her family prepared to travel to Idaho for it.

But something bad happened. This love story was interrupted by an agent of the government, by a close—some might say flawed—reading of the law. The invitations and the bunches of artificial flowers went to waste. All her castles came tumbling down, as Deyanira puts it.

Beth & Carlos

Beth and Carlos met at school. No, Beth Kelly was not his teacher. She was *a* teacher and he wanted some "*intercambio*," as they say, to "practice his English." The head of their fly-by-night English academy in Denver introduced them in the lobby one day.

Here's how Beth describes the meeting: "He wasn't my student—no scandal. He asked me if I would be willing to work with him on his conversation skills outside of school. I wasn't very interested because I had just broken up with someone. We exchanged phone numbers, but never called each other. I ran into him again about a month later at the school. He asked me why I didn't call him. I asked the same question of him. We set up a date for that weekend and have been together since. Not a very exciting story."

Well, it was actually a pretty exciting ride for Beth. Carlos Corona did not have papers when they met. Many people might call him an "illegal immigrant" or an "illegal alien" or just an "illegal." Thoughtful people would call him "undocumented"; demographers and some lawyers would refer to him as "unauthorized." But Beth did not have any problems describing her boyfriend. She called him Carlos, though that wasn't actually his real name either. She called him "honey" and "sweetheart."

She called him her husband, the father of her children.

These two don't have a "spark" moment, or at least not one they talk about. Their first date certainly did not beget that spark. They went to see *El Crimen de Padre Amaru* at a Denver movie house, a fairly erotic tragedy about two generations of priests and their lovers in a small Mexican town. Beth cried and then hushed Carlos during the movie.

During the next four years their relationship was forged in the stressful crucible of life without papers in the United States. Carlos wasn't completely undocumented—he carried a Mexican voter ID card and a Mexican driver's license. But he did not have the "papers" that really matter: a valid U.S. immigration visa in his passport. He did not even have a passport. And the driver's license that he had was about to expire.

Exhausted and teary, Beth Corona—née Beth Kelly—sat at one of the five or so Mexican restaurants on Main Street in Othello, Washington. She was on a Spring Break road trip with her boyfriend, Carlos Corona, and it was not going well. Some eighteen hours prior, the couple had left Denver, Colorado, and driven through the night across the vast open plains of southern Wyoming and Idaho. They took turns driving, stopping only to fill up the tank.

They arrived in Othello for lunch. Othello is in the irrigated farm country of southeast Washington State, a town of nearly 7,000 people that has been majority Hispanic since the 2000 U.S. Census. In 2006 it was still a destination for noncitizens from surrounding states who needed driver's licenses, as Washington was one of only three U.S. states not requiring proof of immigration status for driving privileges. (In 2010, Washington tightened the law to discourage out-of-state driver's license applicants.)

This was their first trip together and at first they were in a good mood, fueled by the optimistically melancholy mariachi refrains of Vicente Fernandez and Estela Nuñez. But it was not a normal kind of road trip for Beth. Beth Kelly grew up on a tree-lined street in the northeast Denver neighborhood of Park Hill. Her father was a prominent and liberal attorney, and her mother ran the local League of Women Voters. Beth had a comfortable upbringing, though she was not unfamiliar with how the other half lived.

After college, Beth served as an AmeriCorps Vista volunteer, working for a homelessness prevention program in Salt Lake City before joining a newly founded economic justice organization called JEDI Women. At JEDI, she worked with low-income women and learned about nonprofits. But Beth was not very happy in Utah, so after three years there, she moved back to Denver and started her own nonprofit organization called People United for Families. She worked to involve low-income families in the public assistance agencies that they were accessing, such as the Denver County Department of Human Services.

After about five years, Beth left the group she had founded and went to Mexico to study Spanish, landing at a popular language school in Cuernavaca for a while where she fell in love with education. In the ensuing years she returned to Denver and became more involved in the immigrant community, helping to organize day laborers and teaching English as a second language to parents of school children and at the night school where she met Carlos.

Eventually, Beth would go on to earn a master's degree and teacher's license, but at 37 she was living with a man who was in the United States illegally and driving across the West in her 2003 Subaru Outback, hoping to score him a driver's license.

The trip to Washington State was out of Carlos' comfort zone as well. In a way he was an accidental long-term immigrant to the United States. Carlos had had a good job in Mexico, working as a lead industrial mechanic at a paper products plant in San Juan del Rio, in the state of Querétaro. He crossed over in October 1999 during a two-week vacation from his job to see if there were any better options north of the border. He had told his mother that he was going to visit his grandmother in Mexico City but headed for California instead. He worked for Labor Ready, a temp agency in Santa Ana, for two months but did not like it. Then he temped in Las Vegas for a short time and considered going home; he even called to see if he could get his old job back. But someone told him there was work in Denver, so in the snowy December of 1999 he headed to Colorado and quickly found steady work installing molding for six months. It was entry-level work and still not what he wanted, but he soon found another job working for a plumber, a contractor who took a liking to him, giving him as many hours as he wanted and trying to teach him English. Perhaps taking it a little too far, the man even offered to adopt Carlos to get him papers. Carlos became a skilled plumber and pulled in a decent wage.

Then, in 2004, he met Beth and fell in love. Two years later, his Mexican driver's license was about to expire, making driving to work an even riskier venture. And their driver's license mission to Washington State wasn't going well.

Carlos had the phone number of a Washington man willing to outsource his address—for a fee—so that a few undocumented people could get at least one document. But the guy wasn't answering his phone or returning calls that Thursday in March 2006. So they stopped for Mexican food and Beth had a small breakdown.

That restaurant in Othello was pretty quiet. A group of construction workers finished up and two ladies spoke quietly in the corner. Carlos struck up a conversation with the two women, putting out feelers.

Hi. We're from out of town. Do you know of any cheap hotels? Can I put down your address on my driver's license application?

It worked. One of the women—she was from Michoacán, in Mexico—offered a local address. Beth and Carlos finished their meal and ran down to the Department of Motor Vehicles to take the test.

Carlos failed.

The next day was Friday and the increasingly harried couple moved onto another town, another DMV. This time he passed, after studying the Washington driver's manual all night. He had been studying the New Mexico version for some time, but they drive differently down there, and it was not quite as easy to play the system. Carlos was pleased, but it was not over yet. He still had to do the driving part of the test and it was getting late.

They managed to pressure the lady at the DMV to schedule a driving test for Saturday morning. They unpacked the car and covered the Colorado plates on the back bumper because it would be weird to show up for a driving test in Washington State with a fully packed car from Colorado. They even made an appointment at a local medical clinic using the local address just to get the confirmation slip—another piece of paper oddly accepted as proof of residence by the Washington DMV.

Carlos easily passed the test Saturday morning, so they repacked the car and headed home ecstatic. A few weeks later the *michoacana* from Washington sent along his new Washington State driver's license.

Carlos had done this thing, this crazy drive followed by a bending of the truth and a reliance on the kindness of strangers. And it had worked.

But Beth was with him all along the way. Beth Kelly, who just had to take a utility bill and go down to the local DMV during her lunch break if she needed to renew her license. Now she was a partner in a multistate driver's license running scheme for one, an accomplice of sorts? Maybe a protector, a harborer of aliens? She felt the highs and the lows of the adventure even more than he did. All he wanted was a little laminated card so he could keep driving to and from work in Denver. All she wanted was not to have to worry about him getting caught, getting kicked out of the country.

With Carlos, Beth saw other things that most Americans don't see, or choose not to see. She saw how hard it was to cash his paychecks. The corner store would only do up to $900, so if he worked overtime he'd have to go to the boss and ask for two separate checks and the boss didn't like that so much. She saw her own elected officials clamping down on illegal immigration in Colorado and in Washington, D.C., and how it affected Carlos and his friends. And how it affected her.

She saw that his name was not even Carlos. It was Rogelio. His mother named him Rogelio. But he'd been a plumber named Carlos in the United States for so long that everyone just called him Carlos. At one job, he forgot he was briefly a Puerto Rican named José Torres and was quite surprised when they had a cake for his birthday and handed him a hundred dollars.

She saw how all this obfuscation, these white and grey lies, stressed him out and then how it stressed her out, so they put their names in the hat for a green card and all of the attendant hoops that come with it.

J.W. & Gabriel

The relationship began as a class project of sorts.

For Gabriel, it began a bit earlier. He first met J.W. Lown at a party for the international students at Angelo State. J.W., then in his third term as mayor of San Angelo, a mid-sized city in West Central Texas, was the guest of honor.

Gabriel met J.W. briefly at the party and became good friends with the mayor's assistant, a fellow student. Gabriel is not his real name and some details of this story will be left out to protect the privacy of his family.

A semester later, in February 2009, Gabriel took a speech class and one of his assignments was to interview someone whose job he might like to have. He thought of J.W. and emailed the former mayoral assistant, who had since transferred to another university. Gabriel asked for a phone number for the mayor but got an email address instead. He emailed a request for the interview and within a few days, J.W. called him.

"One day when I was walking to my room he called… and he's like, 'I can't do a personal interview but we can have it over the phone.' So I'm like, OK," Gabriel recalled.

Gabriel asked the mayor to give him a few minutes, ran up to his room and opened his notebook, where he had already outlined his questions. They got through the questions but it did not go that well.

"Throughout the interview I felt that he was not very comfortable," Gabriel said.

Gabriel sent a thank you note to the mayor along with a photo from the party the semester prior, to remind J.W. that they had once met. J.W. wrote back thanking him for the thank you note.

This exchange may seem very formal and awkward, but for Joseph "J.W." Lown it was just the way things were done. J.W. grew up quickly in San Angelo, taking charge of his family estate as a teenager, after his mother got sick with cancer and died. He learned how to manage money and properties and other society skills as well: golf, how to sit on antique chairs, how to work a room. On the other hand, J.W.'s youth was not completely sheltered. His family experienced some hard times in the 1980s and he spent two and a half years in the Peace Corps, living in impoverished rural Bolivia. When he decided to become the mayor of his hometown at twenty-six years old, J.W. sought out constituents on both sides of the river in San Angelo.

J.W. keeps a bank of file cabinets in the shop on his ranchito in Christoval, a small town twenty minutes south of San Angelo. The cabinets are full of correspondence from his six years as mayor. He saved every note from every gadfly, second grader, clergyman and critic who wrote to him. And he wrote back to every single one. J.W. maintained a mayoral calendar that took him to more than 1,500 civic events a year.

And he was just a ceremonial mayor, with a salary of $600 a year.

J.W. says he dislikes politics, but he is a natural-born politician. He liberally dispenses hugs and handshakes, remembers random anecdotes about his constituents and genuinely cares about his neighbors. And so when a Mexican student from the college asked for an interview, it was not strange in the least that J.W. agreed and then followed up with a note.

The next weekend after the interview, when he called Gabriel again, he may have been pushing it, but J.W. insists it was still common courtesy or a form of Southern hospitality. He just wanted to know how the project had turned out, but Gabriel had yet to turn it in.

J.W. recalls that it must have been on Sunday because someone had canceled a dinner date with him and he suggested that Gabriel join him at Cheddar's, a Texas comfort food franchise, and ask a few more questions. J.W. picked him up at his apartment and they went to grab a bite—just to talk.

"That wasn't a date, that was just taking an interest in how his project unfolded," J.W. said.

Gabriel was interested in politics and had considered becoming a politician in Mexico. He asked J.W. a few more questions for his homework assignment. Then J.W. asked him what he was doing to help the community. Gabriel actually did a lot of community work, in part out of gratitude for the multiple scholarships that allowed him to go to Angelo State. He worked with a faith-based drug and alcohol abuse program and he volunteered at the multicultural center at the college. He also gave free salsa lessons and mentioned this as well. J.W. grew animated, talking about his time in Bolivia and his taste for Latin music.

Gabriel thought the mayor was interesting and he was happy to get to know him a bit. J.W. and his sister Alicia showed up at the next salsa class and had a good time. They went out to eat again after that class and started spending more time together. J.W. told Gabriel that he was attracted to him and Gabriel took some time to think about it. He did not think about it very long.

"It quickly became quite a pressure cooker," J.W. said. "We probably spent two to three weeks together and really felt a relationship."

In some ways the relationship was a first for both of them. J.W. realized he was gay while in the Peace Corps and had dated men for a few years, though he never had a serious relationship. Gabriel was attracted to men but had always dated girls—he was struggling with his sexuality when he met J.W.

"I didn't see any reason to tell everyone, 'Hey I'm gay,'" Gabriel said. But that was before he met J.W.

"When I met Joseph and we started dating then I was like, 'OK, so I won't be lying to anyone about my sexuality,'" Gabriel said. He told his friends, mostly other international students, and they supported him.

As J.W. and Gabriel fell more deeply for one another, they were both fully immersed in their respective worlds as well. Gabriel was a serious student and athlete who had midterms coming up and lots of extracurricular activities. J.W. was in the midst of a re-election campaign. It was his fourth and he did not face any real opposition, but he took running for public office very seriously and had lots of work to do.

A few weeks into their relationship, J.W. confided in his political mentor that he was dating someone, but gave few details. Gabriel had told J.W. that he was living in the United States illegally. He had crossed the border at fifteen years old in order to further his education—to finish high school in Texas and maybe go on to college. Texas is among a handful of states that allow undocumented students who graduate from state high schools to attend college at in-state tuition rates, so Gabriel went on to study at Angelo State.

J.W. knew this was a huge piece of information. He was a public figure, an official who swore an oath to uphold the Constitution. He went back to his mentor, Mario Castillo, a San Angelo native who had introduced J.W.'s parents to one another and then went on to work on Capitol Hill. Castillo is now a very well-connected Washington, D.C., lobbyist and he made a few calls for J.W., including to an immigration attorney. They were told that J.W. could not do anything about Gabriel's status and that the mayor could face charges for "harboring an illegal alien" or other offenses.

"At that moment I realized I had to make a decision—politics or Gabriel," J.W. said. He decided to break off the relationship before it became public.

It was a week before the election. J.W. went to Gabriel's apartment and told him they couldn't see each other anymore. It felt like sticking a knife in his own heart, he said, but he did not see any other way.

Gabriel was crushed as well. He called some friends from the city a few hours away where he had attended high school and they picked him up. He laid low for the weekend, read a good book and sent J.W. a text, congratulating him on his fourth win.

When Gabriel got back to San Angelo, there was a letter waiting for him. J.W. wrote and told him that he wanted to be with him but that it was very complicated. In all, he mailed three letters that week between the election and his swearing in.

"In the letters I said please work with me. I'm in the middle of a very difficult situation. I love you. I care about you deeply… I can't be an official and be with you," J.W. recalled.

Gabriel wrote back and told J.W. he trusted him and that he knew he had to figure out what to do.

"It's his decision—just like when he broke up with me," Gabriel said. "I cannot think for him. We each have to make our own decisions."

"It was like we were oceans apart, and we were in the same town," J.W. said.

By the third letter the two had hatched a plan. It was tentative but it was a plan. J.W. continued to make inquiries about getting a green card or student visa for Gabriel. He told his childhood friend what was going on but no one else. He did not see Gabriel, but Gabriel was the only thing on his mind that week, despite the headlines and the speeches and the post-campaign wrap-up.

They would have to find a way to be *together*.

Juan & Veronica

No one is sure how this story will turn out in the end. It starts in Mexico where it's possible that Juan Diaz never sleeps. Every morning he sits on his bed in the dark, maroon USC hoodie pulled tight around his head, feet hovering over the cold, concrete floors of his father's house. If he sleeps, he wakes surrounded by the trappings of what should have been his normal life: a sturdy wooden baby crib holding several crisp Steelers caps, a laptop case, a stack of cold blankets, dresser tops lined with Talco and baby sunscreen and Vero's hand cream.

A plastic highchair gathers dust in one corner of the extra bedroom. Bags and suitcases full of kids' clothes pile up along the walls.

But there are no kids or women in this house. It's just Juan and his youngest brother, Oliver, who stops by only to sleep or eat. It's usually just Juan, alone with a dubbed sci-fi movie on the snowy TV, a bag of tacos for one, a cup of Nescafe in the morning or a Modelo Especial in a bottle in the evening when there is a little extra cash. Vero had been here for about ten months last year and everywhere Juan goes elicits memories of her stay: climbing the crumbling steps to Juan's grandmother's house across the street, eating ceviche under a tent in Zacapu, walking past the elementary school, Juan's aunt's house next door, the park, the internet cafe.

For three days Juan and I plod around the village—La Virgen—checking in with Juan's old friends and relatives, sampling tacos and soups at his regular spots: Leti's fried intestines, Rogelio's beef cheeks. He introduces me as a friend, a reporter from *allá*—from "there," which is the United States. *Acá*, here, is the village, and if one is not here they are there. But the people here in West Central Mexico are intimately familiar with the geography *allá*, so I specify Idaho and they nod down the street mentioning a son in Pocatello, an uncle in Marsing. They are towns known to only a handful of Americans, but known here as sister cities of sorts, places that Michoacanos have been settling for two or three generations. *Acá* and *allá* are not absolutes. Notions of here and there have merged from 1980s, when the dads all came back from *allá* flush with cash and stuck around for a few months or years to now when the brothers and nieces and nephews visit for ten days and return *allá*, which for them is now *acá*.

The town of Nampa, Idaho, was almost *acá* for Juan two years ago, until he got caught and sent back here. Now he's not sure where is here and where is there. His wife and two baby girls and step-daughter are there and he is here. He has never met his youngest daughter. He misses his job there, his friends, his family—they are all there in Nampa, in Los Angeles, in Denver—except Oliver, who has been trying to get there for a year now. Only Juan is here, stuck with his memories of there, stark and immediate, his recollections of a childhood here having slowly faded over the course of two decades there.

Here, Juan Diaz lives like a monk in his father's house in La Virgen, a tiny village in the rural Mexican state of Michoacán. The house consists of three cluttered bedrooms and a sitting room, graced with two sagging couches and a wooden entertainment center. The bathroom and kitchen are out back, in separate structures along the west wall of the yard. An uncle's minivan with Colorado plates sits in the backyard near a burnt trash heap and the vestiges of a small vegetable garden. A rusted hoe and its disassociated wooden handle lay about, perhaps awaiting spring, perhaps not. Juan lives like a monk here, distracted only by moderate amounts of American football and drink.

The night I arrived in La Virgen we met Juan's friend Nicolas at a convenience store to stock up on orange juice. We walked to Nico's house, along the quiet stone streets that the pair once prowled nightly for girls back in the olden days when the streets were dirt, before they were cobbled with gold from the north. Nico is an aberration here, a 34-year-old man who never left. His memory of *acá* is not polluted by the life *allá*, and his considerable efforts to salve his friend's pain tonight include a bottle of vodka and a satellite dish.

It's third and 19, and most of the Oso Negro and OJ is gone. The guys are Steelers fans, semi-unemployed, mostly beer drinkers. They cheer the latest touchdown. It seals the game for Pittsburgh, which will go on to win the 2011 Super Bowl a few weeks later. We just met and I'm still awkwardly sober and quietly rooting for the Ravens in these playoffs, as Juan and Nicolas drain glass after glass of cheap Mexican vodka mixed with OJ. We lean up against Nicolas' king-sized marital bed, surrounded by quality wood furniture, his wife's face creams and a well-stocked shoe and boot cabinet. Just beyond the bedroom door, rebar sticks out of the unfinished second story landing, the concrete staircase descending precipitously to the kitchen without the comforts of a railing or opposing wall. Nico holds his cigarette out the window.

Juan speaks in a soft undertone, his melancholy eyes downcast behind wire-frame glasses. He delivers a steady stream of facts and stats about the players gleaned from an NFL history book that he left in the United States. He drinks slowly, offering excuses in Spanish and English as he pours another: "In Mexico we drink away our problems and then we sing." His wife, Veronica, had warned me he might need a bottle to get through all of my questions.

Up on Nico's roof, where Juan helped install an outdoor grill and seating area, the sun sets over the fields of La Virgen. They are recently harvested cornfields, the dried stalks stacked in lumpy cone shapes, ready for processing. Along the twisting, green byways of Michoacán, similar fields abound. But just beyond the highway lies Mexico's marijuana basket. The scene from Nico's roof—red sun refracting off church bells, shadowy cobblestones, amber waves of grain, the sound of children laughing and women whispering is at once communal and isolating. It could be 1911 or even 1811, except for the sound of the footballers below, the occasional truck driving slowly up the road, Juan's lonely reality.

We are probably not the only guys watching the 2011 NFL playoffs in this rancho. The NFL has surely rubbed off on others in this soccer-crazed province with its double life in the States. But Nicolas has enough TV channels to make it happen for us. His parents had the means to send him to college where he studied veterinary medicine, but he scored a job at a bank after school, making good money until he screwed up some paperwork and got fired. Then he worked at a rent-to-own store and has a decent entertainment center and stereo to show for it. For the last year he's been selling off a truckload of auto parts that a friend sent home from Texas, but it's not a good business. He's never been North, unlike nearly all of his friends. Instead he married a local girl and built this house. All the essential parts of the house are done: the sturdy metal door, the kitchen, bedroom, bathroom. He has a large dining room table for family meals with his wife, brothers, parents. Occasionally Juan joins them for supper. Usually Juan eats alone.

There has always been trauma in leaving La Virgen. But over the years the trauma of northward migration, a special form of exile invented again and again by millions of rural Mexicans throughout the latter 20th Century, became normal. Juan went North for the first time in 1990, seeking a nest egg to attend college, to study medicine, or maybe animal science, like Nicolas. But he liked the nest egg better than the idea of furthering his studies, so he kept going North—six times in 19 years. He crossed the porous border like everyone else, rebuffed again and again by the Border Patrol—he's forgotten how many times—until he made it to the interior where he was welcomed with paid work, with freedom of movement and association, with the NFL and college ball on TV. Where his brothers and sisters and father were eventually welcomed with papers.

Juan worked as a breakfast cook and housekeeper in Mammoth Lakes, California, and in a wood products plant in Nampa, Idaho. He worked and he went home to La Virgen to renew his ties with his mother, to his mother country. But his exile—this uniquely Mexican form of emigration—was slippery. At first he left home out of economic necessity, unable to find the kind of salary he desired in La Virgen. He followed the example of his father and left home seeking his fortune abroad. But as the fruits of that fortune grew and the economy in La Virgen further stagnated, he accepted this economic exile as his new reality, in many ways giving up on La Virgen. His life abroad—eventually more than half his lifetime—became just his life.

Now Juan is exiled back to his own hometown, banned from *allá*, prevented by U.S. immigration law from settling down with his family, getting a work permit and eventually citizenship and living the American dream.

While we watch the game, Veronica is in Nampa at a friend's house waiting for Juan's call. She is on Facebook, posting hundreds of pictures of her babies. She posts them for Juan and for all of her friends who are supporting her in his absence and for herself, for on Facebook her family is complete, her status, "Married to Juan Diaz," broadcast to the world. I had spoken to her by phone on the bus into Zacapu earlier in the day, but once I arrived we forgot to call her back. Now she is home wondering what we are up to: guys night out in La Virgen, NFL playoffs supplanting wife and kids in an almost normal marital dynamic.

Veronica is a California girl but child of Idaho. She has the natural demeanor of a caregiver and has worked as a nursing assistant. She's the kind of woman who looks at the bright side of her own personal tragedy. She still smiles after having two babies alone, after dealing with earaches and night nursing and dirty diapers alone. She smiles when she talks about how much she misses her Juan. She posts YouTube videos of love ballads on his Facebook Wall on Valentine's Day: Lalo Mora's *El Hombre Que Más Te Amó*, about a child separated from his father; Joan Sebastian's *Me Gustas*, about a woman's most precious features; Allison Krauss' sweet, sweet *When You Say Nothing at All*. She stays with her mom or visits her friend in Nampa, closer to Juan's family, not sure where to settle. Not settled at all.

I first met Veronica on a cold December evening in 2008. A few dozen people gathered at the Anne Frank Memorial, a beautiful stone plaza in downtown Boise set with quotes from Martin Luther King, Jr. and Mahatma Gandhi. The full text of the Universal Declaration of Human Rights is on display in the plaza, asserting the rights to work and make a living, to choose a partner and begin a family, to a fair trial and a presumption of innocence.

The group of immigrant rights supporters, attorneys, Mexican consular officials and liberal clergy had gathered to bring attention to the plight of sixteen Mexican men arrested earlier that week in an immigration raid on a factory in Nampa. Many of the men had family locally, American kids who needed them, American wives. Three of the sixteen had unspecified prior criminal convictions, according to an Immigration and Customs Enforcement, or ICE, spokeswoman at the time.

Veronica stood up at the hastily organized candle-light vigil, held up a small, black and white sonogram printout of the little girl she was going to have with Juan and told the assembly that she had not even been permitted to see her fiancé.

The next day Juan and Veronica were married by telephone, through the bulletproof glass at the jail.

"I blew him a kiss," Veronica told me that day. "We'll get plenty of kisses in later."

That sonogram image that Veronica brandished at the vigil was very fresh. The day of the raid Veronica had an appointment with the obstetrician and Juan had considered taking off work to go with her. In fact, rumors had been swirling around town for months that the plant where

Juan worked was under investigation. In August 2008, Juan moved in with Veronica and her first daughter and the couple went to see an immigration advisor—not an attorney but a legal advisor at a nonprofit immigrant aid society in Nampa who gave some good advice and some suspect advice. She told them that getting married would probably not help Juan stay in the United States—the good advice—and that the couple should flee Nampa before the expected raid at Juan's workplace, which was a bit more suspect. They did not take her advice on either count, not quite ready to wed, not wanting to flee.

After he was detained, an attorney who was working pro bono on his defense team confirmed for Juan that marriage would probably not help his case but offered to arrange a jailhouse ceremony if they wanted.

The Rev. Ed Keener, a retired Presbyterian minister and prominent figure in Boise's interfaith community, performed the ceremony on Dec. 10. A brief mention of the jailhouse nuptials appeared in the *Boise Weekly*, where I worked at the time. And on Jan. 5, 2009, ICE flew Juan to Ciudad Juárez and he took a bus to Morelia, Michoacán, and then on to La Virgen.

As Juan settled into his new exile, Veronica quickly realized what had happened: She was three months pregnant and her new husband had just been deported and banned from the United States for twenty years. Ever the optimist, she immediately began planning her trip to La Virgen.

Nicole & Margo

Nicole Salgado raised backyard chickens before it was cool, more than a decade ago, when I could still visit her without a passport. Back then, she was living in a small cottage on a communal landholding a mile from the Pacific.

Nicole and her college boyfriend had headed straight to California to work in the environmental movement after an early graduation from Cornell University. A few months later, I drove up the coast with a buddy, rendezvoused with Nicole and a few other Cornell people and ended up sitting down to a backyard chicken feast.

Of course Nicole Salgado, at 21 years old, knew how to barbecue homegrown chicken.

Even in her teenage years, Nicole knew stuff that her peers didn't know. She could name the flowers and trees. She knew how to make herbal teas from plants she found on her way back from class and how to bake pies. She knew the alignment and significance of the constellations.

Nicole was unselfconsciously bohemian when I met her at Cornell University in the late 1990s. We lived in a big old house off campus during our senior year, near the famous Cornell Plantations. The head of the house was an older Venezuelan botanist who lived in the largest room with his artsy Chicana girlfriend. Across the hall was a young marathon runner who would stash beers along his training route. Then there was a self-effacing and spaced-out gymnast who was dating a much older Alaskan hunting guide. Nicole—sometimes joined by her college boyfriend, who was equally precocious, though a bit more self-consciously so—was the *de facto* housemother. I joined this motley crew, moving into the old laundry room downstairs and contributing $90 a month to the rent.

I had met Nicole through my off and on involvement with the Cornell Greens, the campus environmental club. I went to a few meetings. Nicole was the president and crusading leader her sophomore year. She pulled off a regional conference for college environmentalists that spurred several lasting activist campaigns.

Nicole made it to the Ivy League from a working class, Italian and Polish suburb of Syracuse, a former industrial town in upstate New York that has been in decline since 1950. She had a Hispanic surname and a Chicano dad who was born and raised in San Diego eating *enchiladas* and surrounded by Spanish, though he was not keen on speaking it. But Nicole's family was thoroughly assimilated in Upstate New York. Her dad was stationed there in the Air Force and her mom's family had been there for generations. Nicole was not really forced to consider her Mexican ancestry until she started filling out college applications.

I was very aware of race and ethnicity in college, gravitating toward black studies and allying myself with the Afrocentrist movement on campus. But I never thought of Nicole as Latina nor attributed any racial identity to her whatsoever—though she did travel to Mexico, Venezuela and the Dominican Republic during college to do research and got a first real taste of her Latin-American roots.

She was hard to stereotype in other ways as well. Nicole put a lot of stock into horoscopes and naturalism without sounding at all New Agey. She hung out with the greenie crowd without giving off too many hippie vibes. She made Chiapas seem no more exotic than Binghamton.

And she kept that down-to-earth activist spirit after college, landing a job teaching organic gardening to juvenile offenders at a boys' ranch south of San Francisco.

A 2001 *San Francisco Chronicle* article on the program described Nicole well: "She has the gleam of the proselytizer in her eye when it comes to native plants and she clearly loves spreading the gospel of gardening and ecology."

Nicole worked for four years with gang bangers who did not really appreciate being sent to the boonies to garden. They turned out 50,000 to 100,000 nursery plants a year. While it was a frustrating and difficult job, Nicole felt that she reached some of the young men. She was simultaneously promoting indigenous plants, helping reform the justice system and making a living. There is something about the Pacific Coast that brims with potential and big ideas. As you crest the hills of San Francisco and catch a glimpse of the sea, all vestiges of self-doubt dissipate and anything seems possible. Nicole was drinking it all in. She took advantage of San Francisco as the tech boom morphed into a permanent cultural phenomenon. She went to clubs and restaurants in the city on the weekends, but lived forty minutes south in San Gregorio, a rural crossroads along a creek that flows its final mile to the Pacific Ocean where it sloughs off under one of the oldest nude beaches in the area. There was plenty of work to do and she had access to old college friends and many new contacts.

It was the same ferment of creativity and opportunity—that same American optimism—that drew Margarito Reséndiz to the Bay Area. Margo arrived in Northern California from Querétaro—a colonial-era city full of students and retirees fleeing Mexico City—at about the same time Nicole landed there.

Margo grew up in a large family in a big city, but also worked on his father's farm from a very early age. He took care of a small herd of milk cows after school, from the time he was five years old, and sowed and harvested corn with all of his siblings, using traditional agricultural methods. Margo's father had a stake in an *ejido*, the communal land holding system that is now being privatized and eliminated across Mexico. Margo's father also worked the night shift at a cannery for twenty-five years in order to make ends meet.

Margo did not have much time for play as a child. At eleven he joined a neighborhood soccer team and his father trudged out to the field to tell him he had work to do and could not play. He did manage to play basketball for one year after school. He was not a very social kid because he felt different than the other students at his school, most of whom came from upper middle class homes, the sons and daughters of engineers and architects. They always had new clothes and new shoes. Margo wore old clothes and painted his shoes and could not afford school trips. His parents and older siblings didn't support him academically; he never became a great reader. But Margo had natural precision and a good eye and became a very skilled builder and craftsman.

After finishing *secundaria* (ninth grade), Margo left school and went to work full time in a metal shop making doors and windows. "I liked it because it was interesting, it was more interesting than taking care of cattle," Margo said. He went on to a job in industrial maintenance, working with metal and learning plumbing and electricity and other systems. Margo also started going out more, drinking with a few friends and meeting girls.

Some of Margo's contemporaries went off to Argentina to work and more went to the United States. Margo was happy in Querétaro. He had good work, was close to his family—half of his salary went to his mother, to help out with household expenses—and he was a little scared to leave home.

"When you don't leave the place you grew up you don't have the vision of how to live somewhere else," Margo said.

He certainly didn't want to go north and tend to cows again or work in other people's gardens, even though he would have made a lot more money. But eventually he was drawn northward by the opportunity to build homes in California. He viewed it as a learning experience and a way to see how people lived in another place.

Margo had a cousin who had been working for a contractor in Northern California, building and restoring houses—nice, fancy houses—and flipping them or renting them out. The contractor had a job for Margo so he slipped into the U.S. with the aid of a coyote, or human smuggler, nervously flew to Oakland, spent $85 of his remaining $100 on a cab to Half Moon Bay and started from scratch.

Since he had no money, Margo lived in the house he was remodeling for the first two weeks. He traveled to California with another cousin, but was otherwise alone in the United States. The contractor for whom he worked had a stake in the San Gregorio property where Nicole was living and after two weeks, Margo moved into one of the rooms in the historic Bell Hotel, across the yard from Nicole's cottage.

Nicole may have noticed Margo, but she was not single and he was focused on work. Margo spent just a few weeks at the old hotel and then moved several more times, crashing on the couch of some acquaintances from Guanajuato state and then moving into a run-down trailer with a moldy outdoor shower. The rent was cheap. He would occasionally visit San Gregorio to pick up tools or materials that his *patrón* stored there. Then he left for a while, returning to his family in Mexico with cash.

In May 2001, Nicole was pulling out of the driveway and saw Margo and his brother. She rolled down the window and invited them to her Cinco de Mayo party. They had a bonfire and drumming and Nicole remembers speaking with Margo.

"I remember finding it interesting to talk to him but I wasn't particularly taken with him at the time," she said.

Nicole's college boyfriend had left for good a few months prior, after an extended breakup, and she was still on the mend. Margo doesn't really remember much about that May evening except that someone got drunk and said something to his cousin's wife and their verbal altercation broke up the party. Five months later Nicole spotted Margo again in the backyard. She went over to chat. Her housemate, one of the property owners, had been talking up Margo and Nicole recalls checking him out that afternoon.

The afternoon ran into the evening and everyone got hungry again. There was some negotiation for seats in the pickup trucks, mostly in Spanish. Nicole ended up in Margo's truck, listening to Santana and driving to a *taquería* in Half Moon Bay. Margo says now that the conversation was strange. Nicole spoke some Spanish, but she spoke like a foreigner and Margo had not learned to slow down and use clear language to make his point. Margo only spoke a little English and was shy using it.

He ordered *carne asada*. She got a *quesadilla*, which he thought was weak. They exchanged numbers. She waited for a call, but it never came.

Margo couldn't figure out how to dial the number, or he missed a digit. Whatever the case, they did finally arrange a date with the help of his cousin. Nicole brought a Cornell friend along, another biologist named Sara, and the threesome headed into San Francisco to go salsa dancing at Café Cocomo. They drove around in the rain for a while and finally found the club, but there was no salsa that night. So they ended up eating tacos in the Mission District and driving back down the coast. They dropped off Sara, got coffees at the 7-11 and went back to the second-story verandah of the old hotel. The sound of San Gregorio Creek burbled in the background.

The Ivy League educated, upstate New York girl and her new Mexican builder friend talked for a long time. Nicole became enamored, as she puts it, and they made a second date a week out. But Margo called sooner, and Nicole got worried. She didn't want to move too quickly, but she didn't know how to explain that either. She actually said to him something like, let's just "*hasta la fecha*," which means setting a date on the calendar, rather than just dating, as she meant to say. Margo came over and they sat in the old, formal library at the hotel and carried on a slow conversation, much of it, literally lost in translation.

Over the next few weeks, the two spent more and more time together. They finally went dancing in San Francisco. They went to the beach. They dressed as Bam Bam and Pebbles on Halloween and went running around the city looking for a party, jumping freeway underpass fences.

"He was so compliant with me in those early days," Nicole recalls. "Margo would never do that now."

Margo, who is stocky and strong from working with wood and metal and concrete, made a striking Bam Bam. When they first started dating, Nicole was vaguely aware of Margo's immigration status. She had not asked him a lot about it and she was only somewhat conscious of the semi-underground shroud that covered the large population of mostly Mexican laborers living in the area. Margo was part of that underground community, but also a bit aloof, staying focused on accomplishing the goal of his mission north: making money to build a nice house back home. But he knew that his status was precarious and that if picked up he could be deported again.

They dated for four or five months and in early 2002, after an informal engagement—he did not get down on his knee or anything—moved in together. At this point, Nicole was concerned for Margo's safety but confident that her American citizenship would help him if it ever came to that.

"I just assumed that whatever it was, that once we started getting really serious that anything could be resolved with marriage," Nicole told me by phone in the summer of 2010, as she drove back to her home in Querétaro, Mexico, after a morning of errands. Nicole and Margo self-deported in 2006, leaving behind friends and family, promising and lucrative careers and the Bay Area version of the American Dream, to wait out at least a decade of U.S. government-imposed exile in Mexico.

They self-deported because Margo had a record—a permanent bar—and there was nothing his American wife could do about it.

* * *

Americans have always possessed a certain well-documented optimism when it comes to our futures, our abilities, our rights. It's right there in the founding documents: life, liberty and the pursuit of happiness. Any American child can grow up to be President of the United States. We don't, but we could. We can all be rich, but we're not. We can go wherever we want, whenever we want. Or at least we believe we can.

We travel freely across state lines and across most international borders because we are Americans and we are free. In January 2011 I walked into Ciudad Juárez, Mexico, from El Paso, Texas, over the concrete channel that is the Rio Grande. I was carrying a large green backpack and I passed a Mexican soldier who did not even look me over. It was an official international crossing point and no one checked my passport. No Mexican official asked me a single question.

Our optimism is infectious, intoxicating, addicting even, though it's also rife with bootstrapping myth and false hope. Mexican-American writer Richard Rodriguez, writing about the legacy of farmworker rights activist Cesar Chavez for *The Wilson Quarterly*, identified this uniquely American optimism as the catalyst for the rising tension along our border with Mexico:

> *"If you would understand the tension between Mexico and the United States that is playing out along our mutual border, you must understand the psychic tension between Mexican stoicism—if that is a rich enough word for it—and American optimism. On the one side, Mexican peasants are tantalized by the American possibility of change. On the other side, the tyranny of American optimism has driven Americans to neurosis and depression—when the dream is elusive or less meaningful than the myth promised. This constitutes the great irony of*

the Mexican-American border: American sadness has transformed the drug lords of Mexico into billionaires, even as the peasants of Mexico scramble through the darkness to find the American Dream."

Susie carried that homegrown optimism with her, thinking it would be easy to get papers for Roberto because she is an American citizen.

"It's unbelievable," Susie said. "He's an upstanding person, not a citizen *per se*, but there's no reason for this, no reason at all... The fact that we have kids too, it's obvious he wants to contribute to the community here."

Ben, who had heard all of the horror stories, remained an American optimist for a long time. He contacted his senator, he went to Washington to lobby for immigration reform, he screamed at then-President George W. Bush on his radio program, "Thanks for deporting my wife!" Then he ended up an expat.

"A lot of us are pretty damn pissed," Ben said on the phone from Mexico. "We don't want to go out and carry the American flag, some of us don't want to come back."

Beth was optimistic enough to trust the system and was rewarded for her optimism.

"I've always been the grassroots community organizer person," Beth said. "I never do anything easily, it always has to be an ordeal... I wasn't sure if I would be able to legalize him or not. The risk was more important than continuing to live like that."

Even into 2013, Veronica remained an American optimist. She believed that her birthright, her right to establish a family, her substantial stores of grit and determination would reunite her with Juan. She continued to believe that even after visiting Juan in 2009 and returning home to the United States without him. Even after the chances of a reunion in Canada looked bleak and the offer of a job and work permit for him in Los Angeles looked less and less realistic, she believed it.

"I need my husband now, like yesterday," she said.

Nicole Salgado was a constant American optimist, always trying to solve all the world's problems. She assumed that if it ever came to marriage with her partner, Margo, they would be fine because she's an American citizen.

She was wrong.

Susie was wrong. Ben almost gave up on the American Dream. Beth is still cleaning up the messes of an undocumented life and knows that they got lucky. Veronica is really trying to stay positive. Nicole is in an extended period of limbo, trying to balance her present reality with her undying optimism for her family's future.

All of them found out that in many confusing and maddening and highly subjective ways, that they and their partners and their parents and friends were wrong about America.

Chapter 2

Welcome to Exile

~

Nicole Salgado

CHAPTER 2

Arrival (2006-2007)

When we finally pulled up in front of *No.* 37, the house that Margo had grown up in and first left at age 25—seven years before—and the place we would call home for the next nine months, several of Margo's relatives were already outside waiting. Margo's mother, looking little and elderly, was wrapped in a navy blue *rebozo* with white stitching. I felt like we were on a cruise ship coming in to dock, parallel-parking the sixteen-foot monster of a truck while they watched us.

We got out and they greeted us, slapping hands and backs and asking polite questions about the drive. There was no major show of affection between Margo and his family. His brothers are not exactly reserved, but they are not the hugging type either, although a few of them have taken to hugging me. A family truck had recently been stolen from right in front of the house and so the twenty-four hour vigil on our hulking truck began until we could issue all our stuff into the two rooms upstairs left empty for our arrival. We remember that we went down the street to his eldest sister's house where she probably lectured us about the dangers of traveling and not being warmly wrapped in the cool night air because I was wearing a tank top.

From the moment we crossed the U.S./Mexico border four days prior, we felt that rush of freedom to walk confidently on soil that granted legal status to us both—Margo as a citizen and me with a Mexican immigration visa that I had proudly held out to the customs agent in the little booth on the Mexican side in Nogales. Margo was full of muted excitement to finally be back "home." Even so, he forgot where he was and spoke to the agent in English. We all laughed good-naturedly, and then we drove on, almost giddy in our sudden—if brief—respite from years of stress.

For me, it was the start of what felt like a big adventure, a journey I'd anticipated for so long. I was delighted by everything. All that my eyes fell on was cartoonishly cheery: the blooming yellow *ocotillos* outside Hermosillo, the yellow sulphur butterflies flocking to puddles on the roadsides, the colorful *puestos*, the figure-eight swimming pool in Topolobampo with the palm tree in the middle. Not even the marathon drive made my spirits flag.

We'd planned a road trip along the Pacific, turning inland after Mazatlán. The region had been hit hard after that year's hurricane season, and roads had sustained gaping wounds. Some sections had simply caved away into the grade below. Bridges were torn up and traffic was re-routed for dozens of miles along one-lane stretches of remote highway. But nothing fazed us those first days.

When we finally entered the small state of Querétaro—marked by the "Cradle of Independence" sign—around 10 p.m. on the fourth evening, we called his family from the Pemex on the city limits to let them know we were almost there. After we made our way through the maze of freeway exits and onto the city streets, my heart started racing and my palms got sweaty.

I recognized the area because I'd been there to meet his family by myself almost three years prior. I recalled the rise of the street, the order of the speed bumps and the signs painted on the fronts of the *locales*, the shops of the *barrio*. The OXXO convenience store, the *Farmacia* San Francisco, *Hospital* San José, the stand with the yellow awning selling *pollo rostizado*. We were approaching Margo's childhood neighborhood, *Colonia España*. The Unisex barber shop. The *Lucha Libre* arena, and then a left turn. Cars parked on either side of the narrow one-way street, *Calle Madrid*. Nervousness intruded on my mind and I tried to breathe steadily.

Then, bam! Just like that, we were *there*—my new home—Margo was "back home." The events of the first days in Querétaro have since faded into a haze in my memory but are clear from my journal.

September 25, 2006
Friday we hung out here [in the city] and went to my brother-in-law's. Saturday we hung out here and went to [Margo's family ranch in] San José (also bought a washing machine). Stayed overnight there, played with kids and hiked in the "cerro" [hillside]. Beautiful chaparral and wildflowers. Sunday went to see Margo's dad's new land [in Chichimequillas]—wide open expanse in a pastoral setting. Yesterday afternoon we did laundry and hung it to dry. There's a bit of a problem with the water usage, they want to use used water for the rinse water, but the machine goes ahead and keeps filling, so it overflows. We have to figure out a way to work it so it can meet both needs. Today was a bad day. I put my name and address in my FM3 and now I need to get a new one but I need to fill out all these extra papers that I didn't have to fill out before and take extra fancy pictures. We have

to certify our marriage with the Mexican government even though we have two copies of the marriage license. Oh and they don't accept payments at their office, they make you make a deposit at the bank instead. It's all very maddening, depressing and confusing. I almost had a nervous breakdown in the street—very close—I started to cry in the INM [Mexican immigration agency] and the girl wasn't particularly friendly [the agent at immigration had told me that altering an official document by hand was a crime]. Margo was very sweet with me up to a point—I'm sure he considered my blubbering somewhat excessive but I was just so defeated—something so small and simple causing me so much hassle. Getting along with his brothers and sisters: relations are a little difficult with [one of] his brothers because he has a very different style of parenting than I ever would and he can be an annoying drunk. Pues, otherwise, things to be thankful for are that [our] relationship is pretty much unchanged—a few stresses here and there but nothing unusual. And neither of us has gotten sick yet. Oh, and my cell service works here and the food has been yummy and there are two cool species of butterflies here on the property and I've lost four pounds, and there was a rainbow waiting for us in Guanajuato, and as loud as they can sometimes be, I love the kids here.

In those first weeks and months after arriving in Querétaro, I would walk around for hours with my camera pointed at every new sight: the colorful wares in the markets, the view from the roof, morning and night, our nieces and nephews. Out at my father-in-law Don Lupe's ranch and the hills above it, I took in all the farm animals, wildflowers in abundance after the summer rains, cacti, the rocks, the ground. I was easily entertained. I'm glad I didn't arrive here totally jaded. But I would be lying if I said that first year wasn't the hardest one of all.

The annoyances with Mexico began on our road trip down here when we arrived in Mazatlán and noticed raw sewage on the streets behind our beachfront hotel and craft peddlers sticking their heads in over our jumbo shrimp every other minute. I experienced my first taste of Mexico's dark side the next morning when Margo wanted to leave early so we could get to Querétaro by that evening. We checked out before 7 a.m. and packed ourselves back into the Ford F-250, tarp strapped over the box bolted onto the camper, all of our worldly possessions on the two-ton bed. Like any typical Mexican thoroughfare, the road posed unique navigational and bureaucratic challenges.

September 21, 2006
A bittersweet ending to our time in Mazatlán—a minor traffic mis-
take leads to a ten-minute struggle to avoid a fine or the taking of our
plates—fat, ugly traffic cop stopped us for turning the wrong way in
a traffic circle and then we went through all the motions saying sorry,
explaining our situation, asking for directions, pleading release, and
he, explaining the infraction, asking for our paperwork, complaining
that Margo's driving with an expired license, telling us how much the
ticket would cost, explaining that he would have to take our plate to
make sure we pay, telling us the right way to go and exhorting us to be
careful on the road to Tepic, that there are storms ahead. Weird thing
that once the subject of an offer was approached, he acted almost as if
it weren't his idea all along, but the 300 pesos were accepted and an
exit was found. I was burning inside because it was my first time. I still
feel angry. Like I've completely forgotten how beautiful our hotel was,
or our afternoon in Mazatlán. We're not doing as much sightseeing as I
envisioned but I am OK with it. Just being in Mexico is enough "sight"
for me, without needing to spend a lot of time in town doing tourist
type things. I also don't feel entirely safe traveling with so much stuff, so
it's probably better this way. Margo's seeing all the best stuff on the road
here. Yesterday, amidst the carnage of the storm below Culiacán, he
spotted a bald eagle and just now he saw a tortoise on the road. I better
start watching. Here in Nayarit it is very hilly and jungly, very beau-
tiful… New sights seen: a pesticide sprayer on a bike, an asphalt plant
spewing black smoke above the green carpet of trees… Here in Jalisco
I see dark jagged boulders and blue-green fields of agave plantations.

As time passed in Querétaro, novelties slowly morphed into irritations. A fifteen-minute errand back in the States was a several hour ordeal here. What were at first enjoyable day trips out to San José to help Margo's dad in the fields became a source of anxiety—neither of us had gone without a regular paycheck for the last several years. There were other, normal problems like clashes with any one of the eight in-laws with whom we lived over noisy music, differences in housekeeping habits, opinions about the children's discipline and the equitable payment of bills on time. Or questions that were innocent enough but also less than thoughtful, like "You're not from here, are you?" every time I spoke what I had thought was good Spanish. Or "Why didn't you guys bring a newer model truck, Nicole?" from my brother-in-law's teenage girlfriend, now his wife.

With my new large extended family household came unique challenges—the lack of personal space, bucketing water to the toilet for flushes, finding arthropods in the pots and pans, his mom hanging cow flesh to dry on the roof's clotheslines for *cecina*-style jerky, intestinal parasites, etc. I had thought that my previous travel experiences sleeping on dirt floors, in hammocks and in sleeping bags out in the open would have prepared me well for life here, but as Margo reminded me, "It is much different to live in Mexico than visit because when you are visiting, you can always leave." But I didn't want to go home, especially after all we'd done to get here. Especially in light of the fact that Margo couldn't come back with me.

In a short time, I began to pine sorely for California. Memories of good conversation, teaching biology and hiking in the redwoods tortured me. I missed my friends, my mobility, even my students. I would fantasize that I was back at the beach in San Gregorio or Half Moon Bay, inhaling the fresh, salty air. Lying in bed early in the morning, I would hear the long, low whistle of the pushcart selling roasted *camotes* from blocks away and think it was a foghorn on Princeton Harbor. That nostalgia burned brightly, like a candle amid my dark frustrations with my new residence. It caused me to forget that in the States I'd had my share of annoying former neighbors and housemates, and had resented flushing more than $900 in rent down the toilet every month.

I'd get excited to go out, even for a simple trip to the market where people clutched their coin purses and squeezed past one another in the aisles between fruit and vegetable stands laden with fresh meat and fried pork rinds, pig heads hanging high. I eagerly anticipated the occasional party that a cousin or a friend of Margo's would throw, where a Corona or two eased my anxiety about being the only güera and not being able to follow the conversations. But back home, it was as if the enormity of the move was too much for us to even discuss. Maybe my mood affected my appetite, but even the Mexican food I loved started to get old. I craved red wine, Pad Thai and frozen yogurt. Although he won't always admit it, even Margo still misses the Indian buffet on El Camino in Redwood City.

Our primary objective in Mexico had also stalled. After many luckless outings to look for land for a house, I began to realize we were never going to find the perfect spot. A rush of frustrations began to wedge between us. Margo returned to the guilty feelings he'd harbored for years in the States that he'd "ruin my life" by bringing me to Mexico. It clashed with a streak of *machismo* in him around his brothers that I'd never encountered with him in the States. It was a sort of "don't bother me woman" attitude when he was drinking with his brother.

In retrospect, he was just making up for lost time with his family, and our roles had simply flip-flopped from when he lived the foreigner's life in the U.S. I was the one who now lacked friends of her own in a strange neighborhood, dependent on him for my social life. To his credit, he was often sensitive to my difficulties, but unfortunately there was little he could really do for me. Our good intentions with one another all seemed to crumble. These creeping problems were temporarily masked by frequent consolation from friends back home, learning to cook new dishes from the Mexican mamas all around me and some good news from my *suegro*. Margo's dad offered us a third of an acre for the house we planned to build. We contemplated the pros and cons for days.

Since at the time the pros column contained more than the cons column, I finally gave the idea my blessing. If only I had known that the location was not ideal, aside from its size and the view, and that nothing is free—in fact, there would end up being several more unexpected drawbacks—I might have kept looking.

The site was flanked on the north, west and east sides by a low stone wall that Margo's father had put in years ago. Margo chose to build onto the existing north wall, to make use of the cemented foundation already in place. He quickly drafted plans, drawing on all those years building homes for other people in California, the vision he'd developed while North flooding onto his paper.

At first, Margo had gone al otro lado ("to the other side," as going to the States is often called down here) for curiosity's sake—curiosity fueled by a desire to master his trade and become a provider someday—but as he framed and finished those California estates, he imagined how he'd do his own in Mexico someday. We debated certain details, but since he's the boss in the construction realm, I let him be in charge. Things started to move quickly. Less than a week after accepting the parcel we broke ground. Margo rented a backhoe to dig to solid ground and chalked out the foundation lines.

Soon we were putting those American dollars we both had saved so hard for years to work. I began to master Querétaro's intimidating, chaotic and comparatively dangerous roads by hauling loads of cement and rebar across town in the Ford while Margo stayed on-site, working with the masons. The concrete and rebar system of construction was totally foreign to me, coming from the land of wood-frame houses.

I learned so much from building a house with my husband. We were working together for the first time, from 7 a.m. to 7 p.m. We would have coffee and *pan dulce* before leaving in the morning, and I'd make lunch at my brother-in-law's house nearby. I helped to make the *castillos* and *cadenas*. I learned to work with rebar, wire and concrete. When there was nothing for me to do, I'd clean, organize or just watch Margo and his crew of brothers and locals. By observing how Margo checked the bricklayers' work, I learned to tell a plumb line by eye. We were coming home exhausted and filthy each day for a few months. The project was progressing quickly toward pouring the concrete for the ceiling and second floor. It was exhilarating most days as well. Margo felt great to be in charge of a crew again, especially the crew that was helping build his own home.

But some mixed emotions got in the way too, especially upon going "home" at night. I tried to be appreciative that we were receiving rent-free lodging in Margo's childhood abode. But I couldn't help but miss my own apartment where I could clean as I wanted, control the noise level, pay only for my own utilities. When I attempted to share my feelings with Margo, he told me I was being ungrateful. But the sheer volume of the cash outflow gave me a fear of waking up bankrupt. These complaints made Margo uncomfortable, putting a new urgency on the whole project.

I also failed to balance the sensitive male ego with the brute force of the construction site. It was Margo's arena, a manly place where he could not accede to my wishes in front of the other guys. But having always been a leader myself in previous jobs, it was hard to be a peon, a mere crewmember, especially with my husband as the boss. Not understanding all aspects of the process when I really wanted to left me frustrated. The language gap was a real disadvantage for me as well. Margo was using far more Spanish than we ever had together in the States, and his fast pace on the job meant that even my innocent queries were met with brusque replies.

But we didn't have enough time or energy to properly discuss things at night, between making dinner in the cramped eight-foot-square kitchen, washing dishes in the concrete *pila* (basin) his mother washed her clothes in and showering with buckets. Eventually our irritations overflowed and we began petty fighting. Sometimes I would let him go to the site by himself just so we could have some space. But I knew no one, was having a hard time connecting with my in-laws and had little inspiration to go explore on my own. At most I would venture out to the corner store or up to the roof where we hung our clothes.

One morning while sitting on the whitewashed, sloping roof scattered with stray cat scat, similar roofs all about me, I noticed a peculiar sight in the air—like a dangling little toy. It was a Monarch butterfly fluttering overheard. A light breeze would push it upward or downward, but then the delicate creature would keep surging forward. Another, and another appeared, and looking farther around I realized that thousands of Monarchs were flying over the city in their annual migration from the Great Lakes, over the Continental Divide and into Central Mexico. They were headed to the Santuarios Mariposa Monarca, butterfly reserves in the mountains of Michoacán only a few hours from where I sat. I wished I could follow them. What I really wanted, rather idealistically, was perfect communication with Margo and for my culture shock and frustrations to disappear. That, unfortunately, was not destined to happen overnight, if ever.

December 20, 2006
Today began with somewhat of a morbid morning... yesterday having been my second [wedding] anniversary with Margo and the culmination of several days of emotional tension, I had made a good faith effort to remedy [things from] the night before by staying home yesterday and doing errands, researching activities for myself, hanging out with Alma and making a nice anniversary dinner. My best buddy Sara had counseled me to hang in there and understand that I am stepping on Margo's turf at the construction site, and even though he is mean to me it's not personal. So I was trying to take a step back and realize I need to get a life here... Dinner went swimmingly, but when we made a feeble stab at talking to each other, everything fell to pieces. I'm not really sure what the deal is, but I think it has something to do with us

not reaching each other's realities.

When we are unable to understand each other it exponentially grows until we are unable to even communicate. Needless to say he didn't want to continue talking or even open his gift and went straight to bed. In the morning, he opened his gift and seemed touched... but somehow we got on the subject of the previous night... his impatience level increased and my desperation for resolution as well... and he jumped up to leave, and I asked him if I should go, and he misunderstood me and was saying something like go ahead and go now, back to the States, it'd be better if I left so he wouldn't have to be worrying about hurting me or doing things wrong.

As he was leaving, I started into hysterics, not knowing if I could stand yet another day of fucking around aimlessly looking for ways to fill my time. As he was leaving, and I was breaking into sobs on the bed, visions of leaping out the window as he walked down the street started to fill my head. I put them away but they kept creeping back. And I thought how if you have suicidal thoughts you're supposed to tell someone... and I was thinking, everyone's at work in the U.S. and how am I going to go from zero to, "hello, I'm going to kill myself," so I made for the door throwing on a fleece, ran down the entire street in socks... just praying as I ran along that I wouldn't cut my feet on broken glass left by the drunkards the night before. He was approaching the gate of the parking lot. I had called out his name but he kept walking... until I got there and I told him what I was thinking.

He was, of course, appalled... about which I'm not sure... the socks or the suicidal thoughts... and of course it was embarrassing to be standing there like that when our friend Guadalupe who runs the parking lot opened the door... but I figured, well, she's been through a divorce so I'm sure she's been there before. As I got into the truck I heard Margo saying to her something about why I went out in socks... a bit of a clue about the extent to which I was distraught... but that didn't make me feel much better considering what a shithead I felt like for putting him through such antics.

I didn't see at the time that what I had were symptoms of depression as the realization of what I'd signed up for started to sink in deeply. When I tried to repress things, I started experiencing psychosomatic symptoms like those I'd had years before, when I had first moved in with Margo and experienced the fear that goes along with having an undocumented immigrant for a partner. But wasn't that precisely the reason why we had left? To have a better life in Mexico, free of persecution by the *migra*? Although he is generally uncomfortable with recalling such painful times, Margo remembers feeling frustrated that I couldn't be more patient (at least outwardly) with the process, and desperate to get me out of the family house and into our own space. I now have the calm of knowing we made it through a period that some friends in the States have referred to as the "Didn't You Know? If You Can Survive the Construction of a Home Without Getting Divorced, You Can Survive Anything" period. Well, I survived that phase, in Mexico to boot, though it sucked while it lasted, idyllic lunch breaks under the mesquites notwithstanding.

The only people in my new life in Mexico with whom I never got into a conflict were one sister-in-law, one brother-in-law and my mother-in-law. *Mi suegra*. I tried to emulate her endless optimism and endurance. I helped her water the cacti and geraniums she kept in old coffee cans and the chile pepper bushes in five-gallon paint buckets stacked precariously on the upstairs courtyard wall. I'd look at the picture of Jesus on the far wall of the drab front sitting room; the altars were the only places where she put vases of flowers. I'd listen to her chanting verses from the *Bíblia* after she'd argued with one of her drunk sons. I'd go in and sit next to her in her room while she complained of her high blood pressure and her knee pain.

Part of me wanted a closer relationship, but apart from the fact that she had thirteen children of her own, we also had many divergent views. I was more like my own parents—"recovering Catholics"—and wouldn't accompany her to her favorite activity, *misa*. Previous sermons I'd attended in Mexico were filled with messages about accepting poverty and women's submission. Margo had been even more rebellious as a kid, even if it meant being pulled around by his ears and whipped with wires.

But my *suegra* and I had much in common on the subjects of food, herbs and a love for the outdoors. It was harder for her to move around, but I could make *tamales* with her or pick things up from the market for her. Years later, after she had her stroke while I was away in New York, I came back to the sight of her lying on her bed, her entire left side paralyzed. She looked up at me, her face crumpled into tears and she said, "I don't want to be like this." So I put aside my rage about the failings of the Mexican government's medical system and made *Arnica* massage oil for her from the flowers in my back yard. With Margo at my side, himself paralyzed by his own inability to convince his father to attend to his mother's needs, I rubbed it into her dry, wrinkled arms and feet, covered with the sunspots of seventy decades in the hills, half wishing it was my own arthritic grandmother. Then she confessed to me: "I think I did this to myself, all those years of work." And I responded, "No, it was not your fault, but please just let others take care of you now." I remembered a story she'd told me about how her father hadn't let the sisters take her to the convent although she'd wanted them to when she was a little girl.

Her rigid Catholicism is now to me just a shared spirituality, just as we share our love for Margo. I think of her face when she saw Margo that first night after his five years of absence: "*Dios mío, ya estás aquí.*" And when things got bad enough, I let her best habit rub off on me. I started to do something my own mother long ago advised me to do, no matter the spirit I chose: I prayed.

Chapter 3

The
Binational Labyrinth

~

Nathaniel Hoffman

Nicole and Margo

It is hard to read Margo's expression in his grainy, black and white photocopied immigration mug shot. He is squinting slightly, his lips pursed—decisively not smiling but not angry either. He holds a white placard displaying his "A" number, the number assigned to his immigration record. His chin rests uncomfortably on the number. He is seventy inches tall and his hair is disheveled. He looks young.

The Border Patrol agents in San Ysidro, California, near Tijuana, found him at about 7:15 a.m. that March morning in 2001, stuffed in the trunk of a red Nissan Sentra with California plates. Margo remembers two other people in the trunk, but the incident report states that there had been only one other. Immigration officers stopped the car at the control point and made the driver open the trunk. When the officers saw people in it, Margo recalls, they closed it back up, detained the driver and took the car to an inspection area.

Margo had agreed to pay the coyote $2,000 once he had successfully crossed into the United States. The twenty-year-old mule told the Border Patrol he was to be paid $200 for driving them across. The driver, who claimed U.S. citizenship, was released, according to documents that Nicole obtained in a Freedom of Information Act request related to Margo's case.

Margo was not scared. He felt that entering the United States was both safe and rational. Also, it was not his first time crossing. The year before, when he crossed the border on foot, it had been a physically difficult trip and it took more than one try before he made it to Oakland. This time, Margo had not wanted to walk through the desert again. Since he could afford a higher priced coyote, he paid more and hitched a ride in that trunk. But the United States does not like when people cross her international borders as stowaways, stuffed in trunks of cars, so Margo was detained for three days this time, interviewed, fingerprinted, photographed and then booted back to Tijuana. Now he had a record stored on a government computer.

In San Ysidro he was held in a detention center with about seventy other men, fed the same boring sandwich, yogurt and drink for lunch and dinner every day. He was bored out of his mind. On the third day the deportations began. They called him to a room and asked what he wanted in the United States. He told them he wanted to work. They said there were no work permits available, that he'd have to return to Mexico, that he was going to be banned for five years and that if he tried to come back again he could be banned again.

Immigration to the United States, whether legal or illegal, is a waiting game. You wait to be eligible for a visa and then for your visa to be approved. Sometimes you wait five years or sixteen or twenty-three years for that visa.

You wait three days to get deported or you wait a year for the immigration courts to clear their backlog before you get your hearing. You wait for your brother or your father to fill out the paperwork for you, for a letter back from the National Visa Center. You press two for Spanish and wait, on hold. You wait for a pardon.

You wait and watch as Congress takes up immigration reform and drops it and takes it up again. You wait up at night for your loved ones to return home from work.

You wait for dark to fall, for the floodlights to pass and then you run across the line and wait for transport.

You wait for another mule with trunk space.

For Margo, back in Tijuana after the deportation—at the border it's called an "expedited removal"—waiting for another ride across was still a rational thing to do. First of all, a job was waiting for him in California. (Even American employers sometimes must wait in this game.) But as a legal question as well, it was rational for Margo to try again. The immigration officer had explained to him that he was going to be banned for five years and that if he got caught entering the country again, he could be jailed for a month and then banned for ten years. If he tried again after that, he could be jailed for a year and banned for twenty years. Margo knew that once he got past San Diego, he'd be relatively safe, so he went back to the house in Tijuana where he had stayed before. He waited three more days in the safe house with nothing to do, eating more boring snacks. He says the Mexican police were checking for border crossers, so he had to stay inside. After three days, another ride materialized, this time a lady driver, a U.S. citizen with kids in the back seat. There were four men waiting for that ride, but one decided he did not want to squeeze into the trunk, so Margo and two others loaded in and easily crossed into California. The woman dropped them at a house in San Ysidro, right near the border. Someone else took them to another house where they had to call their families in Mexico and tell them to pay the smuggler and then they were taken to San Diego. As Margo recalls, they hid in the back of a car again at night, and then at daybreak they got out at a McDonald's or some other restaurant and were allowed to sit in the front for the drive to Los Angeles. In L.A. they packed in a Voyager minivan and headed up to San Francisco where his cousin met them.

Margo was back and this time he had his tools and his truck waiting, he knew his way around, and he still had some cash in his pocket. But he had something new hanging around his neck as well, a designation that was easy to ignore for a while but not forever. It's what some lawyers call the "unwaivable permanent bar" and to many Americans, it comes as quite a shock.

Immigration to the U.S. is a waiting game and then it's an infuriating maze of categories and exceptions and vaguely enforced penalties. This unwaivable permanent bar, or lifetime bar, applied to Margo because he was deported and then he returned to the United States illegally. But it's not as clear-cut as it sounds because though it can be permanent, it does not necessarily last a lifetime. Margo's unwaivable lifetime bar can in fact be forgiven after ten years outside of the United States.

Nicole and Margo had to visit two attorneys in California before they kind of understood that. They had to see a third lawyer to reach an undeniable conclusion. The first lawyer, whom they paid for a consultation that included obtaining Margo's records, gave them false hopes. The second lawyer reviewed the FOIA and consulted with colleagues, telling Nicole and Margo about the permanent bar. The third lawyer agreed that Margo was headed for a lifetime ban from his wife's country and explained all of their options, earning Nicole's trust and finally convincing her that there was no way that Margo could obtain legal residency without returning to Mexico for at least ten years.

"After walking out of her office... I remember feeling like someone just punched me in the stomach," Nicole said. "I just felt so bad... I felt bad for us."

At that point Nicole and Margo were married and had been a couple for several years. That made no legal difference. Nicole had been to Mexico by herself to meet Margo's family over New Year's 2004. They were both excelling in their respective careers and moving up in the world. None of that would matter to the U.S. immigration authorities. The news finally confirmed what Margo had been suggesting and Nicole had been at first dismissing and then denying for years: that fixing that 2001 deportation was not going to be easy.

As of 2013, Nicole, now a Mexican citizen, was in Querétaro with Margo and their binational daughter. They had three years to go before they'd have a chance to possibly return to the United States together.

Susie & Roberto

Susie and Roberto are in limbo, waiting for something too, but they are not quite sure what. First of all, those are not their real names. This couple, the one that met salsa dancing, does live in Denver. And everything else about their story is real. But Susie, an American citizen born and raised in Denver, Colorado, and her two young American daughters cannot be identified because they live in that semi-underground world with their husband and father. They are part of that world within America that some twelve million people inhabit along with their extended families, friends and employers. It's a place where old friends and teachers and aunts and uncles quickly learn not to ask too many questions. It's an America where every road trip, any business with the government, any interaction with police is fraught with risk.

It's a parallel universe where jobs are doled out with a wink and a nod, where banks will open accounts for people with nonstandard forms of identification and happily charge hefty check cashing and money wiring fees, where commerce is conducted largely in Spanish with others who understand how to navigate that semi-underground space. It's a world where cell phone carriers and shopping clubs like Costco and websites like Facebook and Skype have thoroughly erased borders while politicians continually talk about fortifying borders. This is a semi-shrouded America with its own transportation networks, housing developments, and employment agencies, fully functional and even thriving most of the time.

It's an America with its own laws and cops and courts, controlled in turn by the State Department and the Justice Department and mostly the Department of Homeland Security, largely hidden from public view or even media scrutiny.

Millions of people live their lives in this alternate American space, waking every morning in violation of American immigration law and yet essentially American in many other ways— including their fully American families, fully immersed in the binational labyrinth. Millions more live in between worlds, having overcome the waiting game and gaining residency or citizenship themselves but with sisters and brothers, parents and cousins still living that life without papers.

And then there is Susie. Hundreds of thousands of Americans now find themselves in Susie's position: native-born, second, third and fourth generation Americans who first encounter undocumented America through a surprise relationship—a random meeting on the dance floor, a run-in at work or around the neighborhood, a conversation at a coffee shop or in line at the grocery store, an online courtship. It's impossible to know how many there are like Susie, but tens of thousands of Americans apply as sponsors on behalf of an undocumented spouse every year. And tens of thousands more, like Susie and her kids, wait quietly in the shadows, unsure how their country expects them to proceed, stuck in that limbo between love of family and respect for the nation's laws, torn between doing what's right and doing what's right.

Susie's ancestors came to the United States several generations ago. She's pretty sure her grandparents were born here. Her mother was from an Iowa farm family; her father is Jewish. She grew up in the sheltered atmosphere of Jewish Denver and became a teacher. She had a brief first marriage, bought a house and then divorced. And then she went dancing to celebrate a friend's birthday and fell head over heels into the underground. And it made her mad.

A few months into their relationship, Susie noticed that the name on Roberto's ID—a Mexican voter card—was not "Roberto." It was an old fashioned Mexican name that sounds rather effeminate in English. He explained that he didn't like his given name. Then he explained that he was younger than he had originally told her. And a short time later, Susie came to understand that he was undocumented, though she cannot remember exactly how he broke the news.

At first Susie was shocked. Then she was like, "how could you do this to me?" because she had already fallen for him. Then she was terrified that he would get deported and she'd never see him again.

Roberto doesn't think he's ever been deported, but he now faces the same lifetime ban as Margo, though for a different reason.

In the summer of 2002, eight or nine months after they had met, Roberto moved in with Susie. Susie started learning Spanish in earnest, taking two trips to Ecuador to study Roberto's mother tongue. It gave her a little taste of what it is like to be alone in a foreign land, not able to speak the native language.

Roberto bonded quickly with Susie's dad, helping him hang new siding on his house and talking shop with him. He started to really practice his English and take English as a Second Language courses. He got more and more of his own jobs working on houses for American bosses rather than Mexican labor contractors and started to earn more money. He took Taekwondo and Susie took him to yoga, inviting no shortage of teasing on the job sites. At parties, Susie's friends had lots of questions for Roberto and she thought he was happily socializing with everyone. But Roberto told me that he would just get a drink and try to avoid those conversations, moving through the party so he did not have to linger and explain.

Many conversations were tough for Susie too. Some white people judged her for dating a Mexican man—"He's your husband?!"—and Mexican guys looked down on her, she said.

By late 2003 Susie and Roberto were talking about marriage, but Roberto wanted Susie to meet his family first. He wanted to make sure that she liked them. He had not been home for four years and was also eager to see his parents and siblings. So in December 2003 Susie and Roberto got on a plane in Denver and flew to Mexico City. That flight was a small risk for Roberto, but it was the overall decision to leave the United States for that time-honored practice of introducing a potential intended to her in-laws that would come back to haunt them. Actually, it was the return trip to Denver that would hang over Roberto's head in later years.

The flight out was no problem compared to the trip back. Sometimes immigration officials check for documents in U.S. airports; sometimes they don't check. In recent years, more and more airports are hosting Border Patrol officials and checking travelers for valid residency, though there is still no national policy. Usually it's much easier to leave the United States than to enter, so in 2003, Roberto got lucky and made it to Mexico City with no problems. He took his gringa girlfriend home on a bus to meet his mother in the city of San Luis Potosi, in Central Mexico. Susie's Spanish was still terrible, but Roberto's mother spoke to her constantly anyway, as if she understood everything. His sisters did not like her name and just wanted to call her Elizabeth—they started calling her Ellie, for some misunderstood reason. She stayed a few weeks and forced herself to slow down. In Denver, Susie had plans all the time and was always prepping for the next thing. In Mexico, she kept asking, "When are we going to leave?" and "What time is lunch?" Her frustrations with time and the new family dynamics and her culture shock and inability to adequately communicate made Susie cry a few times, but she gradually learned to wait and relax. His family was pleasantly surprised that she was not a "typical American," the stereotyped image of a spoiled *americana* as viewed from the Mexican heartland. She liked their rural town and lifestyle and did not find it ugly in the least. She did not mind getting dirty and she had some agricultural heritage to fall back on. Later they would respect her for breastfeeding both of her daughters and using cloth diapers. But that was still a few years in the future. Susie's introduction to Roberto's hometown was coming to an end and she had to get back to work in Denver. She got on a plane and flew home.

This time she flew alone.

Roberto is the youngest kid in his family. He grew up with his mother and his sisters. His father and brothers were in the United States for most of his childhood. He never planned to go north. He had a job at the local candy factory, Productos Ultra, which makes red and white mints and lozenges for Halls. He worked there for four or five years, from the time he was sixteen or seventeen, making decent money for Mexico and getting a stipend toward a house. He learned to work the largest machines. Roberto never planned to go north, but he did not plan to work in the candy factory his entire life either.

One day, in 1999, one of Roberto's brothers, whom he barely knew, called and said someone would be coming by to bring him north. The next day a man showed up at his door and told him to be ready in a week's time. Roberto may have had no ambitions of going to the United States but a week later he was there.

Roberto crossed in the Arizona desert. His brother arranged it, but he said it cost $1,200 to $1,500. He was put in a big van with about thirty other people. They drove for twenty minutes and then the van stopped and they were supposed to run. But Roberto's legs were asleep from riding in the packed van and he'd lost a shoe, the same shoe he'd put two fifty dollar bills in. A man from Mexico City who was a runner had an extra pair of light running shoes with him and gave them to Roberto. They fit perfectly, inspiring cries of "Cinderella!" among the travelers.

The migrants jumped out of the van and everyone started to run, though Roberto did not see the point in running at that moment. Then he walked twenty hours through the desert, drinking from puddles like an animal, hiding like a mouse in the brush, thorns poking through his new shoes.

"It's really sad, all the things you've got to do," Roberto said. "You don't know who you are hiding from. Where is migra? What's a migra? You just do what they say: run, jump, lay down."

After twenty hours, another van came for the group. Their clothes were ripped; people were bleeding and injured. Roberto made it to Phoenix with the group and then was driven on to Denver and dropped off at a fast-food restaurant. He was told to call his family and release the money to the smugglers and then he was left there. He was embarrassed to go into a restaurant in his ripped, dirty clothes and he did not see his brother-in-law anywhere. Someone did come to pick him up, giving him a place to stay for the night and taking him to Taco Bell in the morning. His brother-in-law arrived and took him to Portland, Oregon. He worked in the Pacific Northwest for about a year, mostly baking cakes for a cousin's ill-fated Mexican restaurant business in Seattle. Then, when the restaurant went under, he met his brother back in Denver but had a hard time finding work. So he decided to practice his English in the meantime, started hanging out in gringo bars and wound up salsa dancing with Susie and then taking her home to meet his mother.

Back in San Luis Potosi after Susie had left, Roberto hung around for a few more weeks. This time he never intended to stay in Mexico. The problem was, he could not go home on the plane with his girlfriend because he didn't have a visa and did not think he could get one. He had not even considered a fiancé visa, though in retrospect, it might have been a possible option for him at the time. So after the New Year, Roberto walked through the desert into the United States for a second time. This time he hired a cheap coyote first and was caught two times near Nogales, Arizona, after spending hours and hours wandering in the scrub. Both times, the migra put him on a bus, waited for the bus to fill up and dropped him back in Nogales, Mexico. The third time he went with an expert smuggler who walked them right up to the border fence with a lovely morning view of Nogales and crossed them in ten minutes time. His brother and cousin drove to Phoenix to pick him up and drop off the $1,500 fee.

On the way home, Roberto drove and he was in such a rush to get home for Susie's birthday that he crashed the truck, pulling up a day late in a wrecked vehicle. Though he was caught twice on the way back there may be no official record of either of his crossings. He has not yet obtained his immigration records through a public information request to find out. But, then again, there may be some record; perhaps his one-way flight home was picked up in an immigration database that won't show up on the information request.

The couple was still blissfully ignorant of the immigration consequences of their trip and remained that way even after they started going to see the lawyers.

After his return, Roberto and Susie fell deeper in love and discovered more and more things they had in common. They both watched the 1980s TV hit "Dukes of Hazzard" as kids, for example. Their mothers had similar demeanors, almost like "Jewish mothers," even though Susie's mother converted to Judaism when she married and Roberto's mother was Catholic. Roberto worked with some Jewish guys and they would talk with him about taking off Yom Kippur. They called him "Rabbi" and the "Mexican Jew." He quickly learned to say "Shabbos" with just the right accent and that the best time to go to synagogue with Susie was when they were serving lunch or cookies after services.

And they both had a soft spot for animals, especially bunny rabbits.

A few months after they returned from Mexico, around Easter time, Susie found an abandoned bunny near the school where she taught. She brought it home and they named it Rosco P. Coltrane, after the bumbling sheriff in the "The Dukes of Hazzard." Both Susie and Roberto remember Rosco as the dog in the show (the dog was named Flash). They were also both familiar with "He-Man," though their shared 1980s pop culture reference points end there.

Pretty soon, the couple got a second rabbit, Bobo (after Beauregard "Bo" Duke), to keep Rosco company. That led to a class on raising rabbits with the Colorado House Rabbit Society, a group of serious rabbit aficionados, folks who keep rabbits as pets in their living rooms, not for meat and not in hutches in the back yard. It was called a "bunny tune-up class" and they learned to trim Rosco and Bobo's nails, to check their teeth and take their temperatures and clean their genital pockets. They also learned a bit about breeding. And so, as is want to happen when women in their thirties surround themselves with furry little bunnies and cooing bunny fanatics, with another Colorado winter coming on, Susie found herself pregnant.

That's how Susie and Roberto told the bunny rabbit story. They were a little embarrassed, but had obviously told it that way before. It's not too much of a stretch that taking care of rabbits together is enough to get the biological clock ticking. But they seemed a little nonchalant about Roberto's lack of papers up to that point. Neither of them had studied the issue very seriously, so when their first daughter was about a month old, late in the summer of 2005, Susie and Roberto finally sought legal advice. They went to an immigration attorney in Denver, on a friend's recommendation, and he gave them the impression that it would not be too difficult to get a visa and a green card for Roberto. He told them to get married and then come back and it would take about a year to arrange the papers.

The lawyer was suggesting that Roberto could apply for a waiver, essentially a pardon for entering the United States without officially checking in with anyone. He'd have to go back to Mexico for up to a year and prove that their separation would impose an "extreme hardship" on his U.S. citizen wife.

Susie and Roberto took his advice, though they waited almost two more years before officially tying the knot. They did it quietly, in their living room, not even telling Susie's family that they were getting married. They hoped to get Roberto a pardon and then, maybe, have a party. They even prepared for a year of separation with Susie taking full-time work at the school to supplement their income in Roberto's absence. But by the time they went back to the lawyer, in May 2007, his tune had changed, or perhaps they had misunderstood the first time around. First of all, Susie and Roberto did not want to be apart for even a year. But now the attorney was concerned about their 2003 trip to Mexico and was saying the process could take more than a year. It could even take a decade.

They left that second meeting distraught.

"He was using language that I didn't even know what he was talking about," Susie recalls. "I didn't write so much down. I think I was so upset that I didn't know who to talk to. He just took our money and our hearts and broke them."

Here's the problem: Deep in the U.S. law that regulates who is admitted and who is excluded from the country, one big Roman numeral away from the rule about re-entering the country after a deportation it states that if you leave the country voluntarily and then come back illegally and stay for another year you are also subject to a lifetime ban. That means you must wait a decade to apply for a pardon and marriage visa. Susie and Roberto knew there was some risk in Roberto going home to visit, but they had no idea it would become a potential lifetime ban.

There is a chance that the government does not know about the 2003 trip and Roberto's return to Denver. But no immigration attorney of any repute will recommend lying to an immigration officer because if caught in a lie, the immigration penalties increase even more. So they would have to disclose the second illegal border crossing and Roberto would get a lifetime ban and have to wait ten years to ask for a pardon, just like Margo.

But unlike Nicole and Margo, Susie and Roberto already had a house and a young daughter together in the United States. They were not prepared to pack up their lives and move to Mexico for an indefinite period of exile. Susie was shocked that it was turning out this way. Roberto tuned out all of the new information. He did not want to hear about it, much less obtain a record of his paper trail from the feds. Their attorney suggested that they wait to see what Congress was going to do that year. In 2006, the U.S. Senate had approved a new immigration law that would have given many people like Roberto a new chance to become legal residents and then citizens but the bill died in the House. In 2007, immigration reform advocates were still pushing for a legalization program, but the prospects were not good. Still, Susie and Roberto did not have much to lose by doing what they'd been doing for six years, staying just below the radar as long as they could.

Now, six years and another beautiful daughter later, Susie and Roberto have not taken any more action on their immigration situation. Beth Corona, a friend of theirs, encourages them to apply for a visa and see what happens. It's only ten years of your life, Beth says. But Susie is thinking of her kids too. It's the most important ten years of their lives—their entire childhood.

"I know theirs isn't going to be the same as mine anyway, but you have your idea of how you want your kids to grow up," Susie said.

Roberto would like to take his family to Mexico for a few years, but he and Susie agree that they need a way back to the United States before they commit to that.

Susie's mom, the former Iowa farm girl, says she'd be crushed if her daughter and son-in-law ended up in Mexico.

"I'd be very, very upset, sad," she said. "I am crazy about those grand-daughters."

Beth & Carlos

Beth Corona, who introduced me to Susie and Roberto, is speaking from experience when she urges Susie to go for a waiver. But she also knows that every case is different. Beth did not think she and Carlos had a very good case themselves when they went for it in 2008.

Beth started out with a little more information than most. Her father is an attorney and she had aided undocumented workers through a volunteer stint at a day labor center and through her teaching, even dating an undocumented man briefly. So Beth went into her relationship with Carlos somewhat aware of his situation. But she had a lot to learn as well. She experienced the problems he had cashing checks and obtaining a driver's license, the shame of having his tax records intermingled with those of another José Torres—perhaps the real one, perhaps not—in Georgia, and especially the constant fear of getting caught. It was that fear that really drove them to seek papers.

Beth and Carlos reasoned that in an ideal America, they were the type of couple that immigration officials would welcome with open arms. They were relatively young, though not too young. They did not have very much debt. They were healthy and professionally stable. And by 2008, they had a baby boy together.

So Beth and Carlos hired a reputable immigration attorney in Denver and prepared a meticulous package, arguing that Carlos should be re-admitted to the United States for the sake of his American wife's mental and financial health. And then Carlos set off for the border. They took a large risk in applying for a pardon. This was never a sure thing for Beth and Carlos.

"That was a very brave thing for him to do," Beth's father, Terry, told me when we met in Denver. Terry drove down to Ciudad Juárez with Carlos so that he could present himself at the U.S. Consulate there. That was in 2008, when the violence in Juárez had just begun to rise dramatically; there were about 1,600 murders in Juárez that year. But driving into what was quickly becoming the murder capital of the world was not even the most courageous aspect of Carlos' act, Terry said. It was his willingness to appeal to the U.S. government for papers with the full knowledge that he could be banned for a decade or more. It was his willingness to do that with his baby son and wife waiting back home in Denver, without a backup plan.

Carlos had become pretty comfortable in Denver. He made decent money as a plumber—$20 to $25 an hour. He'd been in Denver almost a decade without any run-ins with the law and he was very disciplined about staying under the radar, Terry recalled. Beth's mom, Alice, said that self-deporting in order to apply for a spousal immigration visa required Carlos to put all of his hopes and dreams on hold: "The spirit has left the spouse who is going back," she said.

But it also comes down to risk. Carlos was subject to a ten-year ban as well, because he had been in the United States without permission for more than a year. But his ban was waivable. If Beth could make that hardship case, he could apply for a visa and pardon as soon as he returned to Mexico. Though Beth did not think their case was that strong, at least they'd have a chance to plead the case before the U.S. government immigration services in a timely fashion. Both Margo and Roberto lost their chances to apply for an immediate waiver when they entered the United States for a second time. Margo and Nicole are waiting out the decade in Mexico before they will have a chance to argue their case. Roberto is waiting for the right moment to start waiting.

Ben & Deyanira

Benjamin Reed waited for a year and eight months after his fiancée was denied entry at LAX and deported back to Mexico. Remember Deyanira on her way back to Idaho in February 2007 with a suitcase full of wedding paraphernalia? Well, she arrived in Los Angeles and presented her Mexican passport with a valid U.S. visitor visa stamped in it. It's called a

Laser visa and lasts for ten years. She got her Laser visa in 2001 when she had planned to visit an aunt in New York City, but the trip was canceled after the September 11 attacks. That visa was still good though, so Deyanira handed it to the Border Patrol officer at the desk in Los Angeles. She cradled a box of artificial flowers in her hands as he flipped open her passport.

The officer asked her the purpose of her trip and she declared, "I came to get married."

When going through customs and immigration, speed and disinterest are what you want from your inspector. At airports like LAX, U.S. Customs and Border Patrol officers look at tens of thousands of passports a day. Usually it's a smooth process. Most foreign travelers who go to the trouble to fly to Los Angeles—like Deyanira—have ensured that they'll be admitted to the United States. So when a border patrolman asks you to wait and walks off with your passport, it's usually not a good sign.

The officer came back and escorted Deyanira to a room where another male officer asked her again for the reason of her visit. She told him she was engaged to an American but was told that she did not need a fiancée visa to enter the country. The agent told her it would be fine, but another Mexican woman, also a detained traveler waiting in the office, was not as optimistic for her. Deyanira sat and waited and then a policewoman brought her luggage. They opened it in front of her, finding the wedding invitations and other evidence that she was telling the truth. The officer took out her journal and read it, noting that she was Mormon. Mormons tell the truth, the officer declared, in a tone that Deyanira could interpret as neither positive nor negative. She waited for hours in the airport without any information, unable to call Ben or Beverly, her future mother-in-law. Then another uniformed official took her and the other Mexican woman away in a paddywagon, like criminals. Deyanira still did not understand what she had done wrong.

"I was just telling the truth and I never imagined that this would happen," she said.

Still, the officers kept telling her that she would be fine. They gave her *"una esperanza,"* she said, a hope. They patted her down, took her fingerprints (she calls them footprints, because in Spanish, fingers and toes are pretty much the same) and stuck her in a room for more hours.

Deyanira was supposed to arrive in Salt Lake City at 4 p.m. that day and take a bus to Idaho. Instead she spent the night in detention. The immigration officials interviewed her, had her swear something on a Bible, took her picture and told her to smile. They gave her one phone call, again, like a criminal in the movies. Beverly was going to be waiting for her, but she could not bear to call her, so she called Ben instead so that she could speak Spanish and cry. At two or three in the morning another official told her that they were taking her back to Mexico.

"I just felt that my life was broken because we were supposed to get married in a month," Deyanira said, tearing up again after recounting her detention. "All your castles are tumbling down."

Deyanira fell into a serious depression back at home in Mexico City. All of her friends and family in Mexico expected her to be married, but all of a sudden she was back, alone. She did not have a job and all of her life plans were shattered. After a few months, her family picked up and moved to the colonial city of Querétaro, a tranquil escape for many middle and upper class families from Mexico City, hoping to lift her spirits.

Ben was furious. He thought that they'd be able to change her immigration status in the United States once they got married and he had advised her to return with the Laser visa. He had sponsored a partner once before, obtaining papers for his ex-wife in 1995 in Argentina. At that time, he called his congressman, Idaho Rep. Mike Crapo, now a senator, and asked for advice and a letter of support. He walked into the U.S. Embassy in Buenos Aires and left with an immigrant visa in less than an hour. But then that marriage did not last.

He knew the process, but Ben also knew that immigration policy is constantly shifting, so he had checked with an attorney again before setting a plan with Deyanira and was reassured that they could apply for a new visa category once they were married. And that is usually true. But they forgot to tell Deyanira to keep the wedding plans on the downlow as she went through passport control because you can't say you are going to get married if you are presenting a temporary tourist visa to a U.S. official, even if you are telling the truth and your intentions are good.

Ben knew a lot about immigration from a previous life, albeit from a different angle. His knowledge of U.S. immigration politics began in college at Brigham Young University, where he was chapter leader of the John Birch Society, a virulently anti-immigrant, arch-conservative group that was founded during the McCarthy era to supposedly fight the domestic spread of communism. In many ways "illegal immigrants" supplanted "communists" and African-Americans as the Birchers' archenemy sometime in the 1990s. Ben quit the group in 1995, after he realized that he had been in bed with a largely racist organization. But he kept his conservative line, even while beginning his career in Spanish radio. He started at *La Super Caliente* in Idaho Falls, spinning Latin music and starting to develop his on-air Spanish persona. But he also did conservative talk radio in English with a man named Zeb Bell in southern Idaho. He now describes Bell as a massive bigot. At the tail end of the Clinton administration the two shock jocks tried to outdo one another on the air, though Ben says he was never into the racist stuff.

Around the year 2000, things started to change for Ben.

"I gotta give Mr. Bell a lot of credit because I started to open up my brain cells a little bit," Ben said. He asked himself: "What the hell does he believe in?" And then: "What the hell do I believe in?" And Ben started to move to the left.

Around this time Ben also got very sick and checked into the hospital several times, keeping him off the air for weeks at a time. He realized that the only people who came to visit him in the hospital—his only fans and his only friends—were Mexicans. When he was on his back, members of the immigrant community in southern Idaho cooked for him, did his laundry and cleaned his house. They did it because his radio voice was already a huge part of their community. He realized he could not continue to speak to the Latino community on the radio in the afternoon and then stab them in the back on his English slot the next morning. So in 2000, Benjamin Reed made a mad dash to the left, as he puts it. He started reading more, especially Latin American politics, and he took up the cause of immigration reform, becoming a champion for the Mexican farm laborers and the larger Latino community in Idaho.

But his transition into a leftist was still in process when his own government deported his Mexican fiancée. Still wielding the bully pulpit of Spanish radio, Ben ripped into then-President George Bush for not getting immigration reform through Congress. He interviewed Deyanira on the air about what happened to her. He joined a pro-immigrant activist group on a lobbying trip to Washington, D.C., to push for reforms. His story appeared in the *L.A. Times*. And he interviewed his old friend Sen. Crapo on his show, asking questions in English and translating for his Spanish-speaking listeners. He might have pushed the senator a bit too hard. He might have lost some allies in fixing his case.

None of his efforts were helping anyway.

After Deyanira was deported, Ben filed an official complaint and then he filed the forms for a fiancée visa. They were told the visa would take nine months to come through so they put their wedding plans on hold, canceling the mariachi band that had volunteered to play, putting the rings and the dress aside, notifying guests of what happened. Ben traveled to Querétaro to visit and picked up all of his fiancée's documentation. They video chatted on Skype every day. And they waited nine and then eleven months and heard nothing.

A year went by, and Deyanira's family moved again, this time to the beautiful town of San Miguel de Allende, a destination for American bohemians and artists since the 1950s. Ben had visited San Miguel on one of his trips to Mexico and he started to think it would not be a bad place to live. In August 2008 he decided to join Deyanira there, so he convinced his boss to allow him to telecommute from Mexico in exchange for a large cut in pay and benefits. He sold all of his stuff. His one hundred and fifty antique radios went to a friend for $500. His DJ sound system with subwoofer and colored lights went to a pawnshop for $200. He packed up his green 1992 Toyota Corolla and drove to Mexico. It was October 2008.

Two months later, Ben and Deyanira wed in San Miguel. Ben's parents viewed the ceremony from Idaho Falls via a Skype video call. They had a festive party, complete with balloons, funny hats, *lucha libre* masks and a guy on stilts dancing the cumbia. Ben and Deyanira danced more than any of the other guests. The DJ screwed up their song (it was supposed to be "I Wanna Know What Love Is" by Foreigner, but he played something by Atlantic Starr instead). After the wedding they lived in San Miguel and then Querétaro and then moved to the coast when Deya got a teaching job.

I visited Ben and Deyanira in January 2011 and they had just gotten a letter back from the U.S. Embassy in Mexico City. They had long ago given up on the fiancée option and applied for a spousal visa instead in the fall of 2009, sending a personal check and copies of all of their original documents, including two passports and Social Security numbers, to the embassy. More than a year later they finally heard back from the feds: the packet had been returned because they needed a cashier's check or money order in U.S. dollars—two methods of payment that are very difficult to secure in Mexico—instead of a personal check. They had returned the packet to an old address and it was lost in the Mexican postal system—complete with all of their identifying information—probably forever.

Ben and Deyanira's immigration case was on hold for a long time. They had not decided what to do. She wanted to save up a little more money and buy a suburban house in Playa del Carmen, the booming beach town where they now live. But she also wanted to live in the United States. He wanted to keep living in their gritty Mexican neighborhood, living in Spanish and beaming his radio show into Southern Idaho for as long as possible. He was not sure he could forgive his native country for the way it treated Deyanira. Their impasse would not last forever. One day they would be able to return to the States.

$$* \quad * \quad *$$

Beth and Carlos have largely untangled themselves from the mess of a once-undocumented life. Carlos is finally straight with the IRS and up to date on his taxes. He had to start over as a plumber, earning his license from scratch despite thousands of hours of experience, because the state would not recognize his experience from before he got papers. He actually had a hard time finding a job even though he finally had a green card. Beth worries there is a bias or fear of hiring any Mexican workers these days in Denver. They had a baby girl in March 2011 and Carlos is trying to convince his mother to visit her grandkids in Denver.

Susie and Roberto remain in their own personal limbo, hoping to wait out this particular period of xenophobia, hoping that their girls at least get through school before they have to follow their father into exile or that an act of Congress might change their fate. They live fairly normal lives—Susie teaches, Roberto gets odd jobs—mostly through word of mouth—enough to make ends meet. They don't go dancing much anymore, consumed by raising their two kids.

Nicole and Margo are trying to make it down in Mexico. They built a beautiful home, Margo has fairly steady work, though at Mexican wages, and Nicole has adapted in many remarkable ways. They have major worries like reuniting with Nicole's family and scraping together enough cash to pay their bills, and buying a truck to fit the growing family. They also have regular problems like agreeing on a spot out of the wind to change the baby's diaper, dealing with an abundance of in-laws and figuring out what to cook for dinner. Still, the exile is always there. It's in the back of their minds and right in front of their faces, stretching 2,000 miles from California to Texas, a bright red line in their life plans. For Margo, the guilt of bringing Nicole along in his self-deportation weighs on him like a ton of bricks. For Nicole, it's not easy being the only *güera* in the family, a binational partner, a *gringa* in a strange land.

Chapter 4

Fourth Winter in Mexico

~

Nicole Salgado

Early 2011

I woke up to the sound of our baby making gurgling noises in her crib. The winter sky was just beginning to highlight the curtains' edge. Stars appeared on the ceiling when I sat up and switched on the papier-mâché cutout lamp I had made for her while I was pregnant. I peeked into the crib and Bea smiled up at me, sucking her thumb. I lifted her out and we settled on the bed where she ate hungrily while Margo snored. When he heard her finish, he rolled over, took her to burp her and groaned that the *pinche perro* hadn't let him sleep.

A dog had awakened us at about 4 a.m. with sharp barking just outside the house. Margo staggered outside to throw a rock at it, muttering "*pinche perro*." It's normal to hear dogs barking at night in this neighborhood—animal control is not big around here. I usually just put in my earplugs and sigh, as I do when the neighborhood band practices late, or as I did the time a circus came into town and parked itself, loudspeakers blaring, a quarter mile away. But now whenever we hear a dog barking close by, I think of the worst encounter we've had with a *pinche perro*.

I was on a trip to the States by myself when it happened. It was pouring rain. Margo, who was home alone, woke to an ungodly screaming in the middle of the night and ran outside. It was our rabbits screaming. Somehow a dog had clawed open the wire mesh on the bottom of their cage and climbed all the way in where it proceeded to kill the majority of them, including babies and a pregnant mother. Margo pounded the fiercely growling dog with a stick until it threw itself from the cage and ran away. Soaked from the rain, Margo set the dead rabbits aside and repaired the hutch where the survivors huddled.

The next morning, when the sun came up, he went out to check on the survivors. He found a baby bunny in the water container, miraculously still alive. He brought it inside, warmed it with the hairdryer, and returned it to its mother's belly. The tiny creature rooted its sightless face through its mother's brown and white fur and found her pink nipple. For days, Margo warmed the baby bunny and returned it to its mother.

This time it had been a less dramatic affair. "Where was it?" I asked sleepily when Margo returned from shooing the dog. "It was behind the rabbits," he replied, groggily sinking back into bed for some needed rest—it had been a long day at the *Seguro*, the vaccination clinic, and Margo had to leave early to go to work. Apparently Margo, worried about the rabbits, never fell back asleep. But that was just like him.

A few years ago, before we arrived here, I harbored a fear that Margo would change once he left California. He didn't. The man I fell in love with in California is still here with me in the flesh in Querétaro, Mexico.

After nine years together spanning two countries and cultures, Margo and I had finally arrived at a place that was new for both of us: parenthood. In coming to grips with raising our daughter in exile in Mexico, my challenge is in finding the place where exile ends and life begins.

Our home is in the city where my husband was born and raised, capital of the small state of Querétaro. It is in the central Mexican highlands, a.k.a., the *Bajío*—perched over a mile high, just west of the Continental Divide. Even the most tired eyes can't fail to appreciate our high desert sunrises. When that magenta-rimmed, brick red carpet rolls out, lighting the entire horizon on fire, I see the benefits of a treeless landscape—an unobstructed view of a ridiculous palette of colors spread across an entirely open sky. Waves of crimson, tangerine, and gold slowly run into the deep beryline ocean, scattered with rafts of cotton and poofy grey whales until all that is left is a classic blue sky rimmed with a brilliant lemony rind. The caramel clouds light up and send streaks of shine in all directions as a searing blaze appears from a spot on the mountains toward Hidalgo.

At that very moment of sunrise during the winter, a trickle of birds begins to flutter in and grows into a veritable river of black pepper flowing northward, undulating like a slinky. They are headed to the *milpas*—fields in the valleys on the other side of the urban basin—from their overnight roosts in the enormous ficus trees of the city center. But that morning, by the time Bea and I awakened again, we'd missed the show, and our daily routine began with sun already streaming in the windows.

I carried her into the upstairs bathroom, and secured her on the changing table Margo made and I painted white and fuchsia. I contemplated Margo's tilework: cream colored ceramic on the walls above the tub, with three rows of iridescent purply red as a decorative border. Below, chocolate colored tiles wrap around the tub and then intersect with copper-colored tiles of the floor. The money we'd saved from our years working in the U.S. was disappearing fast, but he had sold his last piece of gold jewelry—aside from his wedding ring—to finish this one last room. At the little window where you pay for the tiles at *Azupiso,* he'd handed me a wad of cash and then looked the other way.

I pulled the curtain and gazed outside to the corrugated metal roof on the storage building next to our house. Beyond that lay a barren neighboring property where several *mesquite* trees once stood with lush branches that almost reached over our rear property wall. The trees were cut down and burnt for charcoal leaving the land empty. I could see the highway above, the same one we live along, where the *Transmetro Linea* 4 chugs daily up the grade, a few kilometers away from its last stop over the hilltop at the state penitentiary.

If you keep going uphill, over the north rim of the valley of Querétaro, you encounter another large valley filled with cornfields as far as the eye can see. In the opposite direction far below, you reach our city's historic downtown. Both directions lead to the *autopista* connecting Mexico City with the U.S. border. But we wouldn't be heading up that freeway any-time soon. It would be 2016 before that even became a possibility. My typical day "in exile" blurs the lines between an extended vacation, early retirement, a prison sentence and an identity crisis, so I take things one day at a time.

On the property adjacent to ours, bricklayers had almost finished a wall. The single *mesquite* tree that remained had impossibly green leaves in the semidesert dryness and a trunk twisted almost into an "S" shape. I could still remember the first time I spotted a Vermilion Flycatcher hunting from the branches, its red breast brilliant against the drab background.

Through the window, I heard the neighbor's goats bleating and then the *atole* and *tamales* guy calling out his wares. Bea grinned at me, kicking her chubby legs back and forth in the air.

I had at first been intimidated by the idea of having a child in a foreign country, but I quickly relaxed into the overwhelming sense of joy and privilege of raising her. I dressed her in one of the secondhand onesies an old friend from college had sent down in a large box.

Tears welled up in my eyes as I gazed at my daughter. Her café-au-lait complexion is a perfect mix of her father's coffee and my milky skin, which gets me called *güera*—light-skinned—here. How was I doing this alone, without my old circle nearby for support? I wished I could show her to all my friends, to be together with my family. Having a baby was something I waited so long to do, and then, like the home and life we'd built, we were unable to share Bea with my loved ones whenever we wanted.

My parents had come to see us several times, but my brother hadn't seen Margo since we left the States, and my frail grandmother saw him last at our wedding eight years prior. Some families don't mind being separated—in fact, they prefer it, but that's not the case with ours. To try and travel together, we applied for Margo's tourist visa to Canada where the whole family could meet us, but it was denied.

For my Grandma and brother to meet the baby, I had to travel home to Syracuse alone. It was a trip that I used to make twice a year without blinking an eye during the time I'd lived in California. But this time I had to scrape together what was left of my U.S. savings, odd jobs in Mexico and help from my parents to make the trip. Even when I can afford it—which isn't often—I dread making the journey without Margo. For me, it's not just the stress of taking care of Bea by myself, although that is a big factor given how involved a father Margo is. What always fuels my angst is that I have no choice but to leave Margo behind in Mexico. How do I explain why Daddy can't come with us?

I fantasize about how to get my family together more but there's no guarantee of anything. Seeing the rest of my family and old friends in person regularly seems equally unlikely. Ultimately, I dream of the possibility of the U.S. visa that Margo can't yet apply for. All of these options are long shots.

Wanting to stay upbeat for Bea, I wiped my eyes, held her in front of my face and kissed her cheeks. Later that afternoon, Margo came home early to watch Bea because I had a dentist's appointment. When he came in, his hair was covered with cement dust and his brow was shiny with sweat. He'd obviously had a day filled with lots of hard labor.

When people first meet Margo or work for him, they might think he's too serious. He is brusque and has a good B.S. detector, but he is also a selfless caretaker, especially with innocent beings like the animals under his watch, or children. Especially with Bea. Which is why, unlike many moms, both Mexican and expats, I didn't have a single qualm about leaving her with him when I looked at the clock and realized I had to run.

Even though it's a national pastime to be unfashionably late, many institutions don't tolerate "Latin time." Once, two hours after the stated start time, forty people showed up to a party to which I had invited only fifteen. On the other hand, Margo recalls some previous employers who would fire workers on the spot if they were five minutes late, and I once missed an interview after showing up ten minutes late. When my parents visited for the first time, the power was cut off for four days even though my brother-in-law had paid the electricity bill the day it was due. Medical appointments also require punctuality here. This inconsistency is only one of the maddening aspects of Mexico for me, but as they say, *ni modo.* Oh well. I filled a bottle of water, grabbed my keys, wallet, cell phone and sunglasses, kissed Margo and the baby goodbye, jumped in the old Toyota and tore onto the southbound lane of *Carretera a Chichimequillas,* dust billowing in my wake.

The drive between my house and the glitzy *Plaza Boulevares* mall, where I had my dental appointment, is not unlike the drive I once used to take to town when I lived in rural Northern California. It's a twenty minute or so journey that descends through hills and crosses a few different worlds. But that's about where the similarities end. I'm forever fixated on the contrasts.

First the drive passes through our *pueblo*—San José el Alto, then the gritty *barrio* of Menchaca, then the commercial district flanking the *Plaza del Parque* mall, not quite reaching the colonial eye-candy of the *Centro.* On that dry, late winter day in the pueblo, the few existing trees were caked with pinkish-tan dust. Mangy dogs that had been out all night trotted by girls in tight jeans and boy-men in black vests waiting for the bus. The only thing that slowed me down was the first of fourteen speed bumps over the next four miles. At one particular *tope,* ample women clutched their children's wrists and hurried across traffic to the one kindergarten serving a town of 30,000. I passed the streetfront *locales,* concrete blocks of various sizes stuck together with rebar and decorated with handmade signs or tarps describing the family trade.

I popped in a *cumbia* CD. Tears welled up in my eyes for the second time that day. Maybe the music recalled the dance lessons we took when we first got here. They were fun, but my mood those days was often dark from the endless dead dogs in the road, the rank odor of *carnitas* in the air and drainage ditches filled with murky brown water. Or maybe it was just that every time I rounded the large, steep curve in the road at the edge of our town, instead of seeing a vast ocean framed by sandy bluffs as I once did on my drive out of San Gregorio, I saw a sea of grey and pastel pink brick covered in graffiti—the older unfinished *barrios* interspersed with the newer townhouses.

Seven *topes* later, at the intersection of *Corregidora* and *Bernardo Quin-*

tana, I'd started to pull myself together. Two grimy kids were eating sections of an orange on the corner. Three men, window washers, stood nearby. One of the men wore a red Coney Island Hot Dog 5K t-shirt with white bubble letters; a grey flannel wipe rag hung from his pant waist. A young woman walked by with a box of *chicle*, a colorful striped *rebozo* hanging heavily from her small shoulders, two tiny stockinged feet peeking out from under her elbow.

At my appointment, the dentist replaced some fillings. When she was done, she hugged me goodbye and wished me well with Bea. Everyone loves babies here. I tried to smile and nodded, my tongue numb in my mouth.

On my way back home, I tried to sort through the feelings I'd had on my way down. I've read that a difference between the United States and Mexico is that in Mexico you are judged by *who you are*, whereas in the U.S. it's *what you do* that's important. In reality, it's *what you have* that people really care about, both here and there. But, since my life has been split between the two countries, how I choose to define myself has become even more challenging.

From what I can gather, I'm still the same person I was in the States. Well, maybe I'm more patient now. Perhaps I've changed a lot—it's tough to observe my own growth. But what I do here—what I'm *able to do* here—has clearly changed the trajectory I had in the States.

So I try to focus on what I've achieved here that I never could have done back home, and in that light, it's a lot. Even just *being* here, in itself, is an accomplishment.

I often wish that we could be back in the States, that we'd had more luck with the immigration system, but I can't continually lament over something outside of my control. Trying to assign blame for our predicament is like trying to track the butterfly effect. To the extent that I define my life by a situation in which I had little choice, I will continue to feel disappointed. And yet, I vacillate between hating my adopted home and feeling indebted to it for my roots, for giving me Margo, for putting up with me. I fixate on the physical shortcomings and the endless contradictions here, like when you can be late or when you must be punctual. Or how so much apathy and gumption, bureaucracy and improvisation, opulence and oppression can coexist on the same block. Or how some Mexicans prefer to just shake hands, while others love hugs. No tourist guide can even come close to characterizing the uniqueness of this land.

I passed a newly built pedestrian bridge that people were just starting to use, rather than darting across four lanes of speeding highway traffic. Below me was a *tortillería*, next door, a *papelería* with internet, like the kind I used to go to catch up on world news for four years before I finally got broadband the week before Bea was born. To my right, an old man walked slowly by, a *petaca,* or bag of woven agave fibers, slung over his shoulder. These continual paradoxes sometimes make me feel like I'm in a dream from which I'll simply wake up someday.

I noticed the odor of smoke—at first I thought it was a trash fire, the kind that permeates the air every so often with the smell of toxic fumes and sends me running inside the house to shut all the windows and hide out for an hour. But it was a grassfire smoldering on the hillside.

Then I noticed something strange—although the creeping flames had blackened a stretch of hillside about the size of a basketball court, the bougainvillea shrubs remained untouched. The ground was charred entirely, right up to the base of their slender trunks. Their sprawling pink, red and orange blossom-filled branches swayed gently and reached tentatively toward the sky like supplicating arms in prayer.

Farther up the highway, just beyond the endless sea of grey buildings, lay a vast expanse of mountainous slopes and cliffs covered with dry forest and cacti. Despite some local conservationists' efforts to protect the zone, in another five years it would probably be paved over, and there wouldn't be a thing I could do to stop it.

As I approached the family compound, I pulled off the highway and a little *remolino*, a dust devil, spun over the cows' corral. In the hundred or so yards uphill to my house, I passed the homes of four of Margo's brothers, all in differing states of construction. Along the way, cacti and fruit trees I'd planted thirsted for more water than the skies can provide. Where I parked the truck, *mesquite* trees were just starting to get their leaves and fluffy yellow racemes dangled from thorny branches. The two cats were curled up in front of the house and the aloe plants were flowering, sending up dozens of towering spikes of yellow tubes for the hummingbirds.

Pictures of California and New York, and Querétaro's wildflowers, greeted me just inside the door, framed reminders of our past and the things that make us happy here. Margo was on the couch with the baby on his lap. He looked tired but content to spend his last moments of the day with his daughter.

Margo gladly takes care of almost every possible baby detail, and for that I am grateful. I took Bea upstairs and put her to bed. As she fell asleep, I stared at the stars pouring out from the holes in the lamp onto the opposite wall and ceiling and nearly forgot everything about my trip to town and back.

Downstairs, Margo was watching "CSI: New York" in Spanish. I set out to prepare some food atop the yellow counters grouted with brick red. I was careful not to let the cupboard doors slam, first not to wake the baby, and secondly, to avoid Margo reminding me, "You aren't the one who will fix them." Although I'm often still careless, in Mexico, I've developed greater appreciation for the things we've built with our own hands. That's allowed me to relate better to Margo. Just the other day, vacuuming the baseboards made me think of the days it took for him to install the tile floor on his knees and the hours I spent alongside him scouring the grout lines. Struggling together here has allowed us to grow closer in ways that might have been impossible in the U.S.

I made a simple dinner of *nopales en vinagre* and *quesadillas,* which we ate mostly in silence while I checked my e-mail. Our conversations have almost always consisted of either an ESP-like harmony, or a dissonance of misinterpretation. It's true that Margo is a man of few words and I am a woman of many. We still struggle at times to overcome our language and cultural gap. But we share a bond that transcends cultural boundaries and has carried us through the years.

Margo once said, "You do not choose *la vida loca,* it chooses you." *La vida loca.* Some of us call that fate, chaos, karma. Not *la vida loca* in the scandalous way that Ricky Martin sings about it. It's a lack of autonomy, how our lives are subject to the whims of the U.S. immigration system that feels like *locura*—craziness. No matter how well things are going here, the state of exile often has a way of bringing us some new ugliness.

And yet, for the past ten years I'd kept loving Margarito, my *moreno,* with his furrowed brow that never wilts, that endures the heat like the bougainvilleas in a way that I envy. I'd refused to let a set of laws tear us apart.

Later that evening, after we'd turned in, I rolled over and faced him. He draped an arm around my waist and his toes curled around the soles of my feet. At that moment, there was nowhere else I wanted to be than in those strong arms, and I was reminded of why I chose this path. Fortunately, I've always preferred paths to highways—the kind of paths that wind uphill to incredible views and return you to the trailhead with aching knees. That bitter, disorienting "what am I doing here?" culture shock feeling might hit me out on the highway, but I never ask myself those questions within these four walls, my sanctuary. At least for now, our little nest is my version of the American Dream—our dream.

"What made you happy today?" I whispered. "Let me think," he said. I saw the outline of his jaw in the dark. "I was happy I left early... I was happy to get home and find the baby sleeping on the couch—she looked up at me and smiled..." I grinned in the dark. "I'm happy you're here with me..." he said sweetly.

*   *   *

On our fourth New Year's Eve here together, Margo and I were invited to a friend's home downtown, for a great view of the fireworks from his living room window. Barry, a real estate agent, is one of several English speaking expats I know who lives here in the *Centro Historico* of Querétaro. I was eager to go, but we had to consider our three-month-old. We decided to take a risk—cannons, fireworks, flowing liquor, New Year's bedtime—and go for it. So at 8:30 p.m., we strapped the baby, full of milk and asleep, into her car seat and pressed ourselves into the bench seat of the Toyota. I noticed almost all of the shops were closed for the holiday—even the *carnitas* stands, their roll-down metal doors shut tight.

Once downtown, we decided to take a chance on the normally packed, bumpy roads and see if we could find a parking spot. For a late winter evening it was a delightfully balmy 60 degrees. Even so, we saw wind-wary local folks bundled up in scarves. Luckily, a car pulled out less than a block from Barry's house. I stepped out onto the empty street. An older American couple passed me and headed south on the cobblestone, alongside the stately houses with chipped stucco, built centuries ago in the colonial style. Excited the baby was still sleeping, we took her from the truck and walked up the block to the party.

I did not meet other foreigners in Mexico immediately. I went two years without hearing a single English word outside of my house in Mexico (except at the airport, immigration office, and when giving English classes). Then one day, while waiting in line at the state DMV, I spied an organic grocery across the street. The woman who owned the shop had lived in Monterey, California, for a few years. Through her email list I met Grace, a Feldenkrais instructor in town. The size of my network snowballed from there and has not stopped growing since. Although in retrospect it seems unfortunate it took so long to meet some fellow expats, at least my Spanish got pretty good in the meantime.

The New Year's Eve at Barry's was my second visit to his house. When we entered, I immediately felt a mixture of warm welcome and an awkward factor settle over me. The room was filled with genuinely smiling faces, but we were the only couple under fifty—as can often happen at retired expat parties—and Margo was the only *Mexicano* in the room. It can be strange when going from the only *gringo* around to being surrounded by English speakers. We stationed ourselves on the living room couch, adjacent to the buzzing kitchen.

As soon as we sat down, I got up again and got drinks for Margo and I—white wine and a *Negra Modelo*. Holding off on the spread of Mexican/gringo-themed snacks for the moment, we sat together on either side of Bea. Soon friends began arriving and we were socializing. An older woman was telling Margo how she was volunteering to teach English at the local public university. One longtime resident's house was newly up on Barry's realty website.

I eventually began chatting with a younger couple visiting from Washington, D.C.—the woman's parents were the couple that had passed us on the street. Then a Mexican friend I hadn't seen in a while distracted me from the conversation.

Feeling that I'd been rude, I later found the D.C. couple in the kitchen. We'd been chatting about their former D.C. superintendent of schools over cups of chili with chips when the familiar line of questioning began.

"So, how long have you lived here?" she asked.

"Oh, four years, three months, a week and..." I wasn't sure how many days.

"Really! That bad?"

I had blurted out my response with a little too much wine behind it.

"Nah, not that bad, just that well, my husband and I had to come down here under unusual circumstances." *Yeah—unusual.*

"Oh really? What happened?"

Now that I had dug my hole, I was stuck. I sized them up. They looked like nice people. And besides, how much contact would I likely have with them in the future? Barry, who already knew our story, stood beside us.

"Oh, my husband wasn't able to get papers in the U.S. so we decided to move down here." There, it was out. I've gotten so used to saying this I hardly ever tear up anymore.

"Oh," was the collective response and the group fell quiet. I'd delivered a buzzkill. I saw Barry out of the corner of my eye. He wore a grim smile as he gripped his glass.

But then, as nearly everyone does at the tail end of this exact conversation, they suddenly become bubbly again and exclaim: *"But you're married?!"*

I answer, as I have hundreds of times, *"Yeah, but it doesn't matter."* The smiles return to frowns. My brief explanation that "laws have changed" and a forcibly cheery comment sufficed to turn the conversation in another direction, much to my relief. I had come to the party to enjoy myself in our fourth social outing since the baby had been born, not to get into a depressing discussion about U.S. immigration policy.

These conversations are always uncomfortable, whether here in Mexico or in the States: Why we're here, why he couldn't stay there, whether I like it or not. Sometimes I feel embarrassment for what people might think of either Margo or me, even though deep down I have no shame of the fundamental choices we've both made.

Sometimes I feel like an outcast, not quite Mexican, not quite fitting the typical American expat profile—more than half a million of them live within a five-hour radius of Querétaro. I try to resist my urge to compare our situation to theirs, first because living in a foreign country isn't always easy for anyone, and second, because considering how much I used to like visiting Mexico, I could easily have been someone who moved here by choice. Years ago, I used to travel to Mexico with gusto, as a tourist—to Tijuana on the heels of a San Diego trip, Mexicali via Joshua Tree, grey whale watching in Laguna Ojo de Liebre, or leading high school volunteer service trips in Baja. But my experience of Mexico has since diverged from the purely temporary and the purely pleasurable.

Although the majority of fellow expats are here for business, language learning, the relatively cheap property and cost of living, decent weather or retirement, I can't know everyone's reasons for being here. Also, we have a kinship as expats trying to embrace the host culture. At least these *gringos*—or foreigners from anywhere else in the world—try to reject the blanket media stereotypes about Mexico. As one friend put it on her Facebook page, "Why does the U.S. media keep reporting that Mexico is a dangerous country to travel? Brazil has three times the rate of violence and murder. But there is not a warning about Brazil."

These folks contrast with some of my other compatriots, the million or so Americans who are just here for the party. They also throw official travel warnings to the wind and flock here for Spring Break, a rite of passage in which I also once partook.

Where we live now, more than a mile high astride the Continental Divide, the sun burns hot and dry with dusty winds blowing tumbleweed between the organ cacti and trash strewn ditches. If there is anything worse than not being able to pick up and go for a weekend trip or a night on the town in one of our old haunts in the U.S., it's knowing that most of our old friends probably won't make it down here to visit either. I know the American media doesn't do much for Mexico's reputation, but it's more than that. There are no natural bodies of water, much less white-sand beaches, for miles around. It doesn't matter that there's plenty of entertainment nearby in all directions.

Friends who associate Mexico with the *playa* ask, "How far is the beach from you?" And I respond, "Oh, about eight by car." A disturbing silence usually follows. Diehard friends and family say they will come on their next vacation. Some have to save up enough money or vacation time to venture a visit... others will think about it when the narco-focused Mexico media craze dies down... or maybe we'll just meet up next time I go back North.

Let me give you some advice: If you have a friend who lives somewhere off the beaten track, do them a favor and don't pretend you're going to go see them if you never really plan on going. It just makes them feel like losers waiting to be discharged from a hospital. Or even better, you could actually go and visit them, forsaking the beach and the tourist traps for once. People talk about Mexican hospitality, but most vacationers only experience that in hotels and restaurants. It can be a treat to experience Latin time in a Mexican home, to really relax away from the rat race. Folks staying with us are not only treated to homemade tamales, a stroll around our beautiful historic downtown and hot springs, but also all the whipping wind, urban grit, and authenticity that Central Mexico has to offer.

Which, to be fair, is not always that bad. When I can forget I'm in exile, life feels fairly "normal," especially when I'm employed. It can even feel like a blessing of sorts given the climate and cost of living—a refuge from things on the decline in the U.S.

On good days, when the neighbors aren't burning trash, I can go outside, sit on my porch with a glass of wine in my hand and enjoy the vista of the mountains toward Michoacán across the valley and the abundant flora and fauna of our yard. The once scrubby trees are now flourishing since our arrival, as are the birds that flock to take a dip in the dishes of water I've set out for them. Behind me is the house my husband and I built with our own hands, the mosaic murals we made with all our leftover ceramic tile scraps—something I never would have had the idea, much less the time, to do up in the States. At these peaceful junctures I think: This is the life.

I am not the only one who suffers this double vision in my adopted land. I have several friends my age, or close enough to it, who sought adventure, whether professional or recreational, and ended up relocating permanently to Mexico. They now live here, many with their partners and families they've raised here. They, as I, vacillate between letting go and allowing themselves to adapt to long-term life with a foreign lover in another country, and holding on to the sensibilities they forged in another time and place, or the desire to return someday. We all exist as if on an island accessible only by ferry. For the most part, we are content in our daily lives knowing that our lifeline is just a boat-ride away.

Yet some of us, those of us exiled with partners who are unable to return with us, would have to make that ride alone. Because Margo and I choose to honor our marriage in making our home together here—not with an international border between us—and because we honor the law by awaiting the day that he can attempt to immigrate legally to his wife's and baby daughter's nation—island life can be pretty damn isolating.

Chapter 5

A History of Love, Marriage and Immigration

~

Nathaniel Hoffman

Uncle Jim & Aunt Fern

Uncle Jim always brought us knives whenever he came home from Bolivia—decorative wooden knives or clay-handled knives molded in the form of indigenous masks, with cheap Chinese blades. Uncle Jim, my Tío Jaime, offered us this early model of *machismo* with the knives and the Playboy calendar on his office wall and his VHS footage of my cousins and I playing on the beach, interspersed with random cuts to bikini-clad Atlantic Coast bathing beauties whom he also called his "*primas.*"

I think *prima* was my first Spanish word.

When I was young, Uncle Jim confounded me in many ways. He smoked constantly, yet could also hold his breath under water longer than anyone I had ever met, presumably a result of the high altitude of his birthplace. His obsession with Coca-Cola and television seemed so utterly American—much more patriotic than my own parents who never gave us Coke and got rid of the TV for several years. As a kid, I figured he had always been on my grandparents' sofa, sipping a Coke or a *tequila* and smoking a Marlboro.

Also, he was a Reagan Republican, which, as a kid, never made sense to me.

Tío Jaime was born and grew up in La Paz, Bolivia. His mother was Polish and moved to Buenos Aires, Argentina, when she was three years old. His father's family was Russian and Romanian. Jaime's great-uncle lived in France after the Russian Revolution and exported goods to South America. He then moved to Bolivia, where the rest of the family joined him in the 1930s. Jaime's father eventually built hardware businesses in La Paz and Buenos Aires. Jaime grew up in a white, European merchant family in an impoverished, majority indigenous South American country. He went to a Methodist American college prep school through high school where he learned book English. After high school his father refused to send him to college in Argentina, or even in Miami, for fear that he would party too much.

Instead, he sent Jaime to Baltimore, where a close family friend—a U.S. Agency for International Development official who had worked in Bolivia—would keep an eye on him.

Uncle Jim came to the United States in 1967 on a student visa, first to bone up on his English with a semester of high school and then to study engineering at Johns Hopkins University in Baltimore. He completed one semester at City College, a prestigious public high school in Baltimore and also took an Americanization course that covered the basics of living in the United States, including civics and how to get around. In the fall he entered Hopkins as a freshman engineering student.

A few weeks into his first semester, Jaime went to a mixer on campus and had a few drinks. Coincidentally, my Aunt Fern—my dad's baby sister—was at the same party, standing around while her girlfriends danced. Fern, who was still in high school, had meant to go to a party at a Jewish fraternity house but ended up at the campus mixer instead. Toward the end of the evening, Jaime went up to her to talk and she wrote her number down in his little black book.

They struck up a phone relationship for about six weeks, mostly because Jaime did not have a car or driver's license. Fern dutifully reported that she had met a Bolivian guy but couldn't understand his name, and my late grandmother's first question was, "Is he white?" Soon after, Fern's older sister, my Aunt Wendy, answered the phone and pumped Jaime for his last name. When he let on that it was Jim Schwartzberg, Wendy dropped the phone—the Bolivian was a white, Jewish guy, which, to my grandparents at that time, made him an eligible enough bachelor for their youngest daughter.

Early in the relationship, Jim took the bus out to the suburbs to visit Fern on the weekends and my grandfather drove him back to college on Sundays. Then Fern drove him around for two years. On Fern's eighteenth birthday, Jim—who had finally gotten a driver's license—picked her up in a red Ford Maverick and took her out for a nice dinner at Haussner's, a now-shuttered upscale restaurant in Baltimore. She was nervous riding in the passenger seat, unsure of his driving ability.

Fern and Jim had a volatile dating life for many years. He spent a lot of time at the house—the house that they would later buy from my grandparents and raise my cousins in. Fern recalls that her parents got along well with Jim from the start, though my grandmother was always a bit suspicious that he would pressure Fern into marriage.

When Fern went off to college at the University of Maryland and Jim transferred to George Washington University to complete his degree, the relationship got more serious but remained unstable. They broke up and got back together many times, spending weekends at each other's campuses.

In 1973, after Jim graduated, he got a job at an engineering firm and a six-month work permit, renewable up to four times. He hated the job, but it taught him the discipline of structural design, designing retaining walls, bridges and roadways in what amounted to a civil and structural engineering sweatshop. The bosses sat at a table in front of the rows of drafting tables to keep an eye on the young engineers.

After his third renewal, the Immigration and Naturalization Services—the agency that handled immigration matters for decades before the Department of Homeland Security was established—gave him a summer deadline to leave the United States. The agency's rationale was that there were already too many German civil engineers in Philadelphia, an argument that still makes no sense, since he was not German and he lived in Baltimore. Fern and Jim were not seeing one another at the time, but he called her up and took her out for another fancy dinner, this time at Tío Pepe's, an expensive Spanish restaurant in downtown Baltimore where Jim still takes the family when he feels like treating.

"Very politely, I said to her, 'If you don't marry me they are going to kick me out of the country,'" Jim recalls. Fern's response was one of skepticism and anger. Her older sister, my Aunt Wendy, had married to keep a guy from going off to Vietnam. It was a marriage that did not last, and Fern thought her parents would frown upon another marriage of convenience in the family. But she also thought it was ridiculous that there was no other way for him to renew his visa and she vowed to do something about it.

Fern, a young elementary school teacher, became something of an activist, for a short time. They started going down to the INS offices together and doing research. But every conversation ended with the same conclusion: They had to get married or Jim had to leave.

"We were young and neither one of us were sure that we were ready to get married," Fern recalls. "We had dated for a while and probably could have gotten married. I didn't want that to be the reason that we got married."

So my grandmother was right again—Fern was pressured into marrying Jim. But it was more complicated than that. The pressure was not only coming from him—she also felt frustrated with the government. She wanted him to stay and he clearly wanted to stay in the U.S. But after four or five visits to the immigration office, they were convinced of two things: marriage was his only option and overstaying his visa was a scary proposition.

"We were both kind of afraid to go against the department of immigration," Fern said. "As much as we thought we were children of the '60s and we were these rebels, we really were scared of authority."

Fern and Jim went through that stage of their relationship totally alone. Aunt Fern did not know anyone else dating a foreigner and could not talk to her parents about it. At first they split when the pressure got to be too much, but one night Jim came over and proposed and they planned a wedding. Well, they planned two weddings actually, because they were running out of time. In August 1974, they took Fern's roommate, Beth, as a witness, and secretly went to see a Justice of the Peace in Washington, D.C. Jim returned to La Paz briefly to pick up his new visa.

Meanwhile, my grandmother planned a big wedding for December. My grandmother passed away years ago without knowing that Fern had two wedding licenses in a box in her basement. In fact, no one except Fern, Jim, Beth and maybe Aunt Wendy—though she may have forgotten—knew about the first wedding. When I recently interviewed Fern and Jim about their past together, they both took a deep breath and said it was time to come clean about the two weddings, almost forty years later.

$$* \quad * \quad *$$

Aunt Fern and Uncle Jim became an American couple during the brief period in American history when immigration was tied to an expansion of civil rights. From 1965 until 1996, the American government took a generally more open view of immigration. Congress finally dropped racial quotas for entry, which opened up immigrant visas for Asians and Africans and Southern Europeans. New laws allowed more foreigners to reunite with their American relatives, heralding a renaissance of immigrant communities that continues today. And in 1986, President Ronald Reagan provided amnesty to some 2.7 million undocumented immigrants, recognizing that the government—and American employers—bore some responsibility for the growing numbers of unauthorized workers in the country.

But by the time that Nicole and Margo, Beth and Carlos, and Susie and Roberto met—in the years following the September 11 attacks—all of that had changed. Politics and politicians had changed the laws, although most of the public—and many immigrants themselves—were not aware of the major changes. The federal government and the media and the public viewed immigrants in a different light, the realms of immigration, criminality and terrorism had become muddled, and the era of amor and exile began in earnest.

Fern and Jim grew up in the era of Desi Arnaz and Lucille Ball, the first Hispanic-Anglo couple to gain prominence on national TV with their show, "I Love Lucy." The show taped throughout the 1950s, but reruns played in the background at my grandparents' house through the 1990s. Arnaz and his father fled the Batista regime in Cuba in 1934, landing in Miami and seeking political asylum, which they easily won, as most Cubans did. In the show, Arnaz played a character named Ricky Ricardo, based on his real life marriage to Lucille Ball and his career as a Latin bandleader in 1950s New York. "I Love Lucy" made light of the cultural differences between Lucy and Ricky, romanticizing Hispanic culture as Lucy played the fool. But Arnaz and Ball insisted on the normalization of their relationship in the face of skeptical television executives, nervous to promote a mixed couple—not even mixed race, but mixed ethnicity to be sure. The show was the most watched show in the United States for most of its run.

In accent, complexion, sense of humor and culture, Ricky somewhat resembled my uncle. Arnaz/Ricardo came to the United States from Cuba to seek asylum and Jim came with a visa to be educated. They were drawn to the promise of prosperity, just as Margo and Deyanira and Roberto and Carlos and the others were. But by coincidence of time, geography, economics and race, immigrants like Desi Arnaz and my Uncle Jim found paths to the American Dream where many others do not today.

Those paths were gradually walled off by the turn of the millennium. Now the dominant television stereotype of "the immigrant" is an out-of-context video loop showing anonymous Mexican men with small backpacks and ball caps climbing over fences—the light humor of CBS's "I Love Lucy" supplanted by the ideological imagery of Fox News.

$$* \quad * \quad *$$

This tale could go back even farther to the early reaches of human history, when direct human ancestors first encountered one another in the most intimate of terms. The history of early human migrations is still unsettled, but recent evidence from Australia and Asia points to at least three human ancestor subspecies that intermingled in the millennia after early humans traveled out of Africa. Sixty to eighty thousand years ago, according to some scientists, modern humans (*Homo sapiens sapiens*) first paired with Neanderthals, a separate human subspecies, in Western Europe and East Asia and later on with the recently discovered Denisovans, another archaic human group, throughout southern and eastern Asia and Oceana.

It is still not clear how or when the offspring of these early human migrants arrived in the Western Hemisphere. Estimates range as widely as 40,000 to 12,000 years ago. But when European explorers "discovered" the New World in the 15th Century, their arrival heralded a whole new era of immigration love stories.

Even before the establishment of the union, the Atlantic Coast was well known for its mélange of cultures and nationalities and races. Conquerors and the conquered, travelers and settlers, slavers and the enslaved, Protestants and Catholics and Muslims and Jews and animists and Yorubas all met in the early colonies and explored all of the possibilities that came with seeking their fortunes, building a nation, defending territories and falling in love. This, of course, is a generous reading of American history—the conquest of America's indigenous people was brutal and the young nation was clearly built on the back of African slave labor. But there is no doubt that amidst that brutality, there were also instances of humanity and love between members of different ethnic groups.

These relationships—both the loving ones and the many abusive ones—are what the early 20th Century black scholar W.E.B. DuBois called the "stark, ugly, painful, beautiful" fact of American life.

A history of cross-cultural relations in the West could begin with Pocahontas, the heroine in the continent's first well-known binational love affair. Pocahontas' interactions with the European settlers at Jamestown demonstrate the first and most basic principle of the American immigration story, as the late Harvard historian, Oscar Handlin, wrote in his 1951 book *The Uprooted*: "Once I thought to write the history of American immigrants. Then I discovered that the immigrants were American history."

Disney, which took up the Pocahontas story in 2005, gets the principle a bit backward. The Disney treatment of Pocahontas leaves children with the impression that the Johns—John Smith and John Rolfe (who does not even appear in the original film)—are the civilized hosts while the Indians are wild savages, "strangers in their own lands," as Native American educator Cornel Pewewardy put it. But Smith and Rolfe were the strangers on the Virginian shore, and only through the forceful passage of time did Pocahontas become "ethnic" or foreign in her own land.

"In comparison to the Europeans, the Jamestown Indians were the more 'American' in that they had 'immigrated' far earlier, at a point too distant to pinpoint..." writes Mary V. Dearborn in her book, *Pocahontas's Daughters*. "When John Smith—an immigrant, after all—arrived in Jonestown, Pocahontas began to be ethnic."

And so we have a second principle of American immigration history: White, Christian aristocrats—immigrants all—wrote that history, including Pocahontas' own story. Her name was not even Pocahontas. Matoaka, as her father named her, and her Powhatan people, had a more open immigration policy than the colonists they met, whose descendants would eventually write the first anti-miscegenation laws, and later, grant full citizenship and voting rights to a very limited set of propertied white men.

Pocahontas' father, Wahunsonacock, or Powhatan, viewed marriage with English colonists as a culturally acceptable practice as well as a means to form new political alliances.

"Powhatan's offer of tribal women to cement an Anglo-Indian concord was apparently sincere as well as shrewdly self-serving. His subsequent prompt approval of the marriage of his beloved daughter Pocahontas to Rolfe was the memorable case in point," writes David Smits, in a study of colonial English attitudes toward intermarriage. "[Early 18th Century Virginia historian Robert] Beverley probably had Powhatan's offer, among other things, in mind when he wrote that, 'intermarriage had been indeed the Method proposed very often by the Indians in the Beginning, urging it frequently as a certain Rule, that the *English* were not their Friends, if they refused it [*sic*].'"

Smits recounts several Jamestown colonists who sought refuge among the Powhatans, including some who married and lived with Indian women. But he and many other historians argue that overall, the English settlers harbored religious, elitist and racial biases against intermarriage, preventing widespread mingling. This was not true of French and Spanish colonists, who beat the English to North America by almost a century in 1492 and depended more on the native population for survival as they pushed west. Spanish conquistadors, and later, the French, harbored fewer sexual taboos than the English, embodied by the now mythical character of La Malinche, a Nahua woman said to have birthed the first *mestizo* child with Hernán Cortés in 16th Century Mexico.

John Rolfe—the man who first commercialized tobacco in colonial Virginia—married Pocahontas in 1614. The settlers took their union as a great ego boost, imagining that the English might indeed be successful in assimilating the native population into their Christian worldview. But just a few years later, in 1622, after Pocahontas had died in England, the Powhatans rose up against the colonial encroachment, killing several hundred English men and women. The English fought back, decimating the native population and driving them from their land.

Despite this dread history, Pocahontas and Rolfe's descendants, prominent Virginia gentry, would play a continued role in the future of interracial relationships in the United States. The "Pocahontas Exception" was written into early Virginia law, allowing Caucasians with some small amount of "the blood of the American Indian" to be considered white, for purposes of marriage. This small chink in the consistency of state anti-miscegenation laws would garner a footnote in *Loving v. Virginia*, the 1967 Supreme Court case that finally ended state bans on interracial marriage in the United States.

Relationships between Africans and Europeans were generally condemned in the early settlement years as well, though also tolerated and rather common. While white men raped and kept African women as concubines, starting on the coast of Africa, on slave ships across the Atlantic and through the violent crucible of the slave economy, there were also examples of black-white family relationships. White indentured servants and enslaved Africans formed couples frequently enough that the white slaveholder class began to legislate against such relationships, condemning their multiracial children to lives in slavery.

In the 1660s, the first anti-miscegenation laws appeared. Some of these early state bans on intermarriage made outcasts of white people who had relationships with black people, condemning them to servitude with their African-American partners or banishing them, according to UCLA Law School Dean Rachel F. Moran's 2001 book *Interracial Intimacy: The Regulation of Race and Romance*.

"These laws stripped whites of racial privileges based on their intimacy with blacks," Moran wrote.

Those racial privileges merged with citizenship privileges after the United States became a nation, assuring immigration policy would be an early and continued stain on the young democracy, conceived from the start for racial control and exclusion. This forms a third principle of American immigration policy: Citizenship has always been tied to the dominant racial ideology of the times.

In 1790, Congress codified that only free white people could be citizens. It was only after the Civil War that "aliens of African nativity" and "persons of African decent" could apply for citizenship. After Reconstruction, as the regime of Southern segregation set in, many of the privileges of citizenship were again revoked for African-Americans, including voting rights.

During the nation's first hundred years, enslaved Africans and their children were not eligible for citizenship. White control over the black population also extended to marriage, as Henry Box Brown, who escaped from slavery, relates in his 1849 narrative:

"Marriage, as is well known, is the voluntary and perfect union of one man with one woman, without depending upon the will of a third party. This never can take place under slavery, for the moment a slave is allowed to form such a connection as he chooses, the spell of slavery is dissolved. The slave's wife is his, only at the will of her master, who may violate her chastity with impunity: It is my candid opinion that one of the strongest motives which operate upon the slaveholders, and induce them to retain their iron grasp upon the unfortunate slave, is because it gives them such unlimited control in this respect over the female slaves. The greater part of slaveholders are licentious men, and the most respectable and the kindest of masters, keep some of their slaves as mistresses."

Still, even in the face of the extreme sexual and moral abuses of slavery, there were examples of people who broke through the color line. Harriet Jacobs, a remarkable woman who escaped slavery and went on to become a prominent anti-slavery activist and writer, took a white lover in her efforts to gain her freedom.

The criminally insane power dynamics of the slave trade made a couple like Jacobs and Sam Sawyer nearly impossible. But Jacobs, who never accepted her enslavement and endured seven years hiding in an attic and many years on the run to attain her freedom, appears to have had genuine feelings for Sawyer. The possibility that he respected and loved her as well, despite his upbringing in the racist antebellum South, must be considered.

We can trace these three principles of immigration in America—that we are a nation of immigrants, that white immigrant men wrote the first draft of U.S. immigration policy and that citizenship has always been tied heavily to race, through the five centuries since Europeans arrived. The U.S. immigration system maintains other defining features: It is haphazard, without clear national priorities. It constantly shifts with the winds of public opinion. And, as is commonly recognized today by partisans on both sides of the aisle, it's broken. The period between the end of slavery and the Civil Rights era demonstrates many of these features.

For several years after the Civil War, African-Americans were still denied citizenship. While that was somewhat rectified in the 1870s, other racial groups were denied access to lawful immigration and citizenship for decades to come. In 1882, after a wave of anti-Chinese sentiment originating in California, Congress passed the Chinese Exclusion Act, which banned most Chinese immigration and set a precedent for both racial and national quotas on immigration that lasted until 1965.

The Chinese Exclusion Act, combined with new state laws and court rulings throughout the early 20th Century, set up a complicated system of racial controls on immigration and marriage. Chinese women were denied permission to immigrate, unable to join their husbands on the West Coast. Japanese agricultural workers who started to arrive in Hawaii and then on the West Coast were at first granted but then denied citizenship in a 1906 Attorney General's ruling. People from India were declared ineligible for citizenship in a 1923 Supreme Court Case.

The citizenship controls merged with marriage controls during the same era. In 1879, California voters banned intermarriage with "negroes, mulattoes and Mongolians," and after a wave of immigration from the Philippines in the 1920s, added "Malays" to the list. Filipino men often defied this ban, going to other states to marry both white and Mexican women, according to Moran's thorough history of intermarriage and U.S. law.

The late 19th and early 20th centuries saw large waves of immigration from Europe including Irish, Italian and Jewish immigrants settling on the East Coast. Immigrant numbers reached more than a million per year in the first decade of the 20th Century, and Congress soon reacted, setting quotas and stemming the immigrant tide. In 1923, Congress set national immigration quotas based on the demographic profile of the United States in 1890, before Southern and Eastern Europeans began to settle in earnest, and immigrant numbers dropped precipitously throughout the 1930s and 1940s.

Throughout the early 20th Century, Mexican and other Western Hemisphere immigrants held a privileged position, exempt from national origin quotas. The southern border of the United States remained fluid and largely unguarded. The United States had acquired Texas, Arizona, Southern California and much of the Southwest just a half-century prior, in 1848, after the Mexican-American War. Still, there was no large-scale out-migration from Mexico during this time.

The U.S. Border Patrol was not established until 1924, and even then, it was a small agency manning the sprawling southern and northern borders. According to Douglas S. Massey, a Princeton University demographer and custodian of the Mexican Migration Project, only 13,000 Mexicans immigrated to the United States between 1850 and 1900. Some 728,000 came between 1900 and 1930 as industries like the railroad and agriculture looked south of the border to replace banned Asian workers, however the numbers remained low and most workers returned home after a period of employment—often returning with fewer earnings than expected because of suspect recruitment practices.

During the Depression era, public opinion turned on Mexican workers as jobs grew scarce. Hundreds of thousands of Mexicans were rounded up and deported. But during World War II and the years that followed, a severe labor shortage drew millions of Mexicans back to the U.S., many under the auspices of the bracero program. Braceros were contract laborers from Mexico, tied to specific farm employers, who came to the U.S. on a seasonal basis starting in 1942.

The bracero program established new migratory pathways for Mexican workers into the interior of the country where many began to form local ties. It also set up a low-cost workforce that U.S. farmers quickly took advantage of, skimping on wages, housing and worker safety. But the jobs drew more Mexican workers than could get work permits, establishing the first significant unauthorized workforce. U.S. employers—exempt from punishment for hiring undocumented workers—actively recruited well beyond the number of permits that Congress had approved. At the same time, industrialization, mechanization and urbanization in Mexico left many rural Mexicans needing work and cash. Nearly five million Mexicans came to the United States during the bracero era.

Starting in the 1960s, Mexican migration north, particularly activity along the borderlands, became the major feature of the U.S. immigrant landscape and has continued to shape U.S. policy since. The bracero program ended in shambles in 1964, as awareness grew about working conditions and the rampant abuse of migrant workers, including failure to pay promised wages. Despite the official end of the bracero program, farmworkers continued coming to the U.S., as they do today—in some cases, for the same jobs.

* * *

Whenever Americans travel, whether in peacetime or wartime, they meet foreigners and fall in love. Elizabeth Gilbert's *Eat, Pray, Love*, the 2006 runaway bestseller in which Gilbert falls in love with a Brazilian man while traveling in Bali is testament to this well-worn trope. Though at times frustrating and bureaucratic, a relatively simple method has always existed to bring home a foreign spouse or fiancé: The American files a petition on behalf of the noncitizen partner. The petition is granted if the relationship checks out. Then the foreign partner picks up his or her visa at the nearest U.S. Consulate and books passage to the United States.

Gilbert did not follow this procedure, not wanting to marry her lover, and faced the consequences in a sequel to her book, as her boyfriend was denied entry at the Dallas/Fort Worth International Airport. As a result, they eventually married. Gilbert's experience raises questions about the way the U.S. government views relationships—there is no immigration mechanism for domestic partnerships.

Even more significantly, committed gay and lesbian couples are also denied the immigration benefits of marriage. U.S immigration law has historically held a bias against gay immigrants, in times past equating them with psychopaths, subversives and Communists as unfit to join the nation. The 1996 Defense of Marriage Act, which bars same-sex couples from accessing more than a thousand federal benefits according to a 2004 U.S. General Accounting Office report, forces married gay couples to scramble for other types of visas—mostly tourist and temporary work permits—in order to stay together in the United States. Many live together underground and many more relocate to one of the growing number of nations that recognize same-sex couples in immigration law, countries like Brazil, the Netherlands, Canada and England.

But what happens when a foreign visitor in the United States—a student, tourist or temporary worker—meets an American and falls in love? In many ways it is the same process for Americans who meet their spouses abroad. For many years the foreign partner was required to leave the country and re-enter with a fiancé or spousal visa. Starting in the 1930s, some of these partners of Americans could visit a U.S. consulate in Canada rather than fly across the world to change their visa status.

Then, in 1952, Congress consolidated one hundred and fifty years of piecemeal federal immigration laws into the first Immigration and Nationality Act. It allowed foreigners to adjust their immigration status without leaving the country. At first, adjustment of status applied only to people who were legally present in the country—on a temporary student or tourist visa, for example—and wanted to become permanent residents. In 1958, Congress expanded the adjustment of status regulations to include those who had overstayed their visas as well.

My Uncle Jim was careful not to overstay his temporary work visa. He did go home to pick up a new, permanent visa after marrying my aunt, perhaps because it was quicker that way or perhaps because he didn't know about adjustment of status. But even if Jim had let his temporary work visa expire in 1974, he most likely would have been able to get a green card by marrying Fern, without ever going home to Bolivia.

This system worked for many couples, but by the 1990s, a large percentage of immigrant spouses could not adjust their status because they had no visa at all. They had entered the U.S. illegally and later fallen in love with an American. These couples were eligible for marriage visas, but the immigrant partner had to return home first and visit a U.S. Consulate abroad to obtain the visa.

In order to understand the hurdles that mixed immigration status couples face today, we have to understand the intricate mechanics of U.S. visa allocation.

Congress finally ended racial and national origin quotas in 1965, in favor of a relatively more egalitarian formula to distribute immigrant visa spots around the globe and to provide for an orderly preference system for prospective immigrants with relatives or jobs in the United States. The new system set annual immigration caps for certain relatives of Americans—adult children and siblings of citizens, for example, or the spouses and children of legal permanent residents. They were called "family preference" visas. Immediate relatives of U.S. citizens—spouses, minor children and parents—were exempted from the new immigration limits.

In addition to a worldwide quota for family preference immigrants— today it's 226,000 each year—the annual number of visas from any one country was capped at seven percent of the total available worldwide visas for the year. It was the first time that immigrant visa numbers from Latin America were limited.

These two new features of the nation's modern immigration system— family preference within global limits—quickly butted up against one another, leading to lengthy waits for many. The new visa system was more democratic and spurred consistent annual growth in the immigrant population, especially immigrants from Asia and Africa. But the new per-country limits meant severe backlogs for certain countries, particularly Mexico, with its proximity and long history of cross-border family and work relationships. It was a similar case with the Philippines, which became a key source for U.S. immigration after the Spanish-American War in 1898 and again after World War II, when many U.S. soldiers married Filipina women.

These backlogs continue today. In the 2012 fiscal year, a maximum of about 25,900 spots per country were available to siblings and adult children of U.S. citizens and certain relatives of permanent residents. For some countries like Togo or Sweden, that yearly total is almost never met, though they are still subject to the global ceiling and subject to delays of up to a decade. But for countries like India, where 343,401 people await a visa, or the Philippines, where 503,266 people wait in the family preference immigration line, the quota fills quickly.

For Mexicans in that "line"—those who have U.S. citizen siblings or whose parents are permanent residents, for example—the wait is even longer: 1.37 million people are on that list with only those 25,900 spots open. Mexicans who are married to U.S. permanent residents and want to immigrate had to wait three and a half years for a visa, as of early 2012.

Some waits are even longer: Filipino siblings of U.S. citizens who applied for a visa in 1988 were finally being processed in February 2012. Some of them had passed away while waiting in the family preference immigration line.

Prospective immigrants can apply for employment based visas as well, but there are even fewer available than family preference visas—only 144,000 for 2012—and most of the work visa categories also suffer from backlogs of several years.

The visa backlog—the line that pundits often speak of—dates to the 1970s, and is a significant factor in the growth of the undocumented population in recent decades. By the mid-1970s, there was already a three-year wait for Mexicans and other Latin Americans in some visa categories. By the 1980s, the United States had a growing class of several million unauthorized workers, mostly from Mexico. Some of them were the original braceros or their children, families that continued to migrate even after the temporary worker program ended. Many had settled in the United States by that time, raising American kids and only going home to visit family in Mexico once a year.

In 1984, the popular Mexican band Los Tigres del Norte released the song *Jaula de Oro*, (the golden cage), describing the United States as a cultural prison for Mexican migrants: "*Tengo mi esposa y mis hijos / que me los traje muy chicos / y se han olvidado ya / de mi México querido /del que yo nunca me olvido / y no puedo regresar* (I have my wife and my children / that I brought very young / and they have already forgotten / my dear Mexico / that I will never forget / and to where I cannot return).

In 1986, government demographers estimated that there were 3.2 million undocumented immigrants in the United Sates. For several years, political debate had wavered between penalizing migrants with stepped up deportations and border patrols, and sanctioning employers who used illegal labor. Politicians reached a grand compromise in 1986, providing permanent resident status to immigrants who had been in the country illegally for at least five years, in addition to a large group of farmworkers.

The overall intent of the Immigration Reform and Control Act of 1986 was to discourage illegal immigration and appear tough on immigration for political reasons. But the undocumented population—people from all over the world but especially from Latin America—continued to grow through the 1990s until the mid-2000s.

In Mexico's case, as the U.S. government increased penalties on undocumented immigrants and their employers and militarized the border, it also signed the North American Free Trade Agreement in 1994, ostensibly increasing cross-border trade and cooperation. While there is wide disagreement on the overall impacts of NAFTA, it's very clear that free trade has negatively affected the rural Mexican economy, flooding the market with cheap, subsidized U.S. corn, displacing millions of traditional Mexican *campesinos* and driving agriculture toward mechanization and consolidation. Millions more rural Mexicans sought wage labor north of the border in the wake of NAFTA. Coupled with the Mexican economic crisis in 1994, in which the peso lost almost half of its value, Mexican emigration northward—particularly unauthorized border crossings —continued to rise steadily.

Along with the soaring undocumented population came a rise in mixed immigration status marriages. In 1994, Congress recognized that thirty percent of the people applying for visas at foreign consulates—mostly spousal visas—had already been living in the United States without proper documentation. This was seen as expensive and wasteful, compounding the already significant delays for other visa applicants. And so Congress authorized a new program called 245i that allowed undocumented immigrants who qualified for a visa to apply for that visa in the U.S., paying a $650 fine, rather than returning home to apply. It was essentially an expansion of adjustment of status.

Approximately 345,000 people applied for 245i in 1995 and 1996, reducing consular processing by twenty-five percent and saving the Department of State $5 million, according to the Congressional Research Service. In fiscal year 1996—the second year of the program, almost 81,000 spouses of U.S. citizens qualified to adjust under 245i and another 76,000 spouses and children of permanent residents qualified.

But 1996 was also the year that the "Republican Revolution" Congress, led by then-Speaker of the House Newt Gingrich with support from Democratic President Bill Clinton, gave new meaning to the phrase *Jaula de Oro* by throwing away the lock and key. The Illegal Immigration Reform and Immigrant Responsibility Act of 1996, known as IIRIRA, built on the anti-immigrant sentiments that had been embedded in the 1986 reforms without granting any new legalization or amnesty.

The new law effectively sealed millions of people inside the United States.

The law established a series of new penalties for being in the country illegally. People who entered the United States without being inspected by U.S. Customs and Border Protection, or CBP, and were later caught would be subject to bans before they could apply to re-enter legally. Congress established three-year bans for people who had entered illegally and stayed for six months to a year. Those who stayed more than a year would get ten-year bans. And a host of other violations, from two illegal entries to anything considered an act of terrorism, brought permanent bans.

These bans, or bars, as they are also known, dramatically changed the options for unauthorized migrants, but not necessarily in the way that Congress or the president intended. Congress wanted the new bans to discourage illegal immigration. But several different estimates of the unauthorized immigrant population demonstrate that it continued to grow for a decade after the 1996 legislation, doubling to 11 million by 2005. Families that had migrated back and forth for generations were unable to return home for fear that they would be banned for a decade or more.

Overnight, 245i went from a bureaucratic convenience to a humanitarian necessity. Without it, hundreds of thousands of people who qualified for spousal or other family and work visas, would have had to leave the country and face three- and ten-year bans. But 245i was meant to be temporary and was set to expire in 1997. Congress and President Clinton extended the measure three times, but it finally did expire in January 1998.

In 2000, Clinton signed the Legal Immigration Family Equity, or LIFE, Act, which extended 245i for another year. About 245,000 new 245i applications were filed. In April 2001, Congress allowed 245i to expire again. In May 2001, President George W. Bush wrote to Congress asking for another 245i extension:

> *Dear Mr. Speaker: I am a strong proponent of government policies that recognize the importance of families and that help to strengthen them. To the extent possible, I believe that our immigration policies should reflect that philosophy. That is why I support legislation to extend the window created under section 245(i) of the Immigration and Nationality Act during which qualified immigrants may obtain legal residence in the United States without being forced to first leave the country and their families for several years.*

Bush estimated in his letter that there were, "more than 500,000 undocumented immigrants in the country who are eligible to become legal permanent residents, primarily because of their family relationship with a citizen or legal permanent resident." Two bills were introduced in Congress that year and one of them, House Resolution 1885 passed both the House and Senate. There were a few differences in the House and Senate versions of the bill and the House scheduled a date to debate the Senate version of the bill. That date was September 11, 2001.

On September 11, nineteen legal visitors to the United States crashed passenger planes into the World Trade Center in New York and the Pentagon, turning U.S. foreign, domestic and immigration policy on its head. In the ensuing decade, lawmakers made several attempts at comprehensive immigration reform, including efforts to reinstate 245i, but nothing significant made it through a bitterly divided Congress.

$$* \quad * \quad *$$

Since the 2001 expiration of 245i, another option for Americans with undocumented spouses has been an extreme hardship waiver. This is what drove Beth and Carlos to Ciudad Juárez in 2008, but it was never an option for Nicole and Margo. Susie and Roberto are still not sure if they could get a waiver and are hesitant to try.

It's difficult to know how many couples are stuck in this 21st Century immigration limbo, half-American but without access to spousal visas for their partners. It's likely in the hundreds of thousands, as the Bush administration estimated. Based on my analysis of data from the Mexican Migration Project, a thirty-year Princeton University longitudinal study of Mexican migrants, some 4.6 percent of unauthorized migrants to the United States have a permanent resident or citizen spouse. If extrapolated to the entire undocumented population of the U.S., currently estimated to be 11.2 million, that's more than half a million couples. Only some of these couples might have access to visa waivers, and only after a complicated and risky process.

In addition, according to a 2011 University of California Los Angeles study, there are at least 28,500 binational same-sex couples in the United States who cannot access spousal waivers or 245i or any type of family-based visas. Many more reside abroad.

In the face of this policy stagnation, Americans continue to meet visitors to this country and fall in love. A 2012 study on interracial marriages showed large increases in the numbers of mixed couples—more than 15 percent of new marriages crossed racial and ethnic lines. The Pew Research Center study includes mixed immigration status couples—14 percent of foreign-born Hispanics and 24 percent of foreign-born Asians married an American of a different ethnicity. Some are couples like Nicole and Margo who, in bringing together families from disparate racial and ethnic backgrounds, manage to overcome cultural and language differences only to run up against a maddeningly complex and unfair immigration bureaucracy.

Despite new spending on border patrols and fences, the undocumented population continued to grow in the early 21st Century, peaking at more than 12 million in 2007, according to several estimates. Immigrant workers and their increasingly mixed immigration status families continue to spread to new parts of the country, creating new incarnations of the American Dream, that elusive notion of life, liberty and the pursuit of happiness.

Though much has changed in the United States, the three principles of U.S. immigration remain. We are still a country of immigrants, with more than a million visas granted every year. Immigration law and the national debate about immigration is still largely controlled by white lawmakers and pundits, despite an increasingly diverse media and an African-American president with immigrant parentage.

And most of all, racial attitudes continue to drive the stalemate over immigration reform, with lingering fears of diversity and disagreement over what it means to be American. If one group has been left out of this equation, it is those Americans who embrace the immigrant population with their hearts only to find out that the nation has taken their most sacred relationships off the books.

Chapter 6

Pebbles and Bam Bam

~

Nicole Salgado

Margarito looked over his shoulder at the young woman in a midriff-baring camouflage halter top following closely after him. His black hair was hanging loose over his bare shoulders and starting to frizz up. He and his companion were below a maze of freeway interchanges and the wheels over the asphalt forty feet above them made a rhythmic ca-thunk, ca-thunk. His feet hurt because he was wearing a pair of borrowed flip-flops two sizes too small, and he was also half naked. But he kept his complaints to himself because it wasn't worth it at this point.

They were headed to an elusive destination and they didn't have a map. If they hadn't been moving so quickly, the late October wind would have felt chilly. When they arrived at a chain link fence, they scrambled up and over it like lumbering spiders. Margo went first, and his zebra striped garment got snagged. On the other side he turned and offered his hand to help her down. As she landed feet first next to him, she looked up and smiled. How had he let her talk him into this, he thought.

After a few more corners and down some side streets, they arrived at a warehouse-like building in an industrial district of the city. Margo stepped forward and opened the heavy metal door for her. A bald guy in a suit waved them in. Their hearts began to pound as a wave of heat and noise hit them in the face. Margo instinctively stepped closer to his companion, dressed in skin-tight brown camouflage, when a strange woman approached them, gesturing to a table where they could get something to drink.

The stranger was wearing a fire engine red tutu, a crown of devil horns and a pointy tail. Near the drinks table, a tall man stood bent over a larger table, impervious to the chaos around him. He wore only full body paint, a headband with a few feathers and a skimpy loincloth. He held a pair of impossibly fat headphones to one ear while he fumbled for a disc with the other. World beats blasted from enormous speakers by the wall. Margo turned to his partner and grinned. Not only had they finally made it, but their Halloween costumes were perfect: She was Pebbles and he was Bam Bam.

Fate Night (October 2001)

October 7, 2001, was like any other afternoon: I came home and worked in the garden. It was special because it was my mom's birthday, and the day Margo and I got together. I was working on an herb spiral in the front yard of the house where I lived. It was a garden in the form of a snail's shell where I was planting rosemary, basil and sage.

That afternoon, I had been scheduled to attend an NAACP dinner with the San Mateo County Green Party, but a friend stopped by to chat, so I left late, got stuck in traffic, decided I'd never make it, and turned around. Back home, I put on work clothes and got absorbed in digging and moving rocks until I heard some voices and soft guitar music coming from the field in the back. After a few minutes I ducked under the fig tree and peeked behind the overgrown privet bush to see who it was.

Margo, his cousin Beto and his friend Vlas were standing by the fire pit. Beto's wife, Nina, was playing her guitar. It had been a while since I'd last talked with Margo—since a Cinco de Mayo party I'd thrown five months earlier. He was a lot cuter than I remembered. He wore orange cords and a powder blue polo, and his hair was pulled back into a ponytail, his cell phone at the waist. I wanted to go out and say hi, but for some reason I felt shy and retreated to where I was working.

After a few minutes, I went to find my housemate Rudi and asked him to join me in saying hello. Rudi had been on a job with Margo recently and said he was a sensitive, hardworking and intelligent guy. Overhearing him, Rudi's wife Sue chimed in that Margo was different than the rest of his buddies in that he disdained some of their *machismo*. I'm not sure if they were purposely trying to set us up, but their comments didn't hurt.

Out in the field, where the sun was starting to dip toward the horizon, we made small talk. Nina and Beto were living in a trailer on the property and she had made some food but apparently the guys weren't into it. They asked if I wanted to go up to Tres Amigos in Half Moon Bay to grab something to eat. I asked them to wait for me while I changed yet again. It was unlike me to bother dressing up for tacos, but I'd remembered my father poking fun at me during college about skipping showers and makeup, so I rushed off to change before they all left for the *taquería*.

When I got back, the sun was setting. Rudi took off, leaving me with Nina and the three guys. But they weren't in a hurry. They were sitting around the fire and before long it was dark. Nina asked me for some incense and after I brought some back, I found myself sitting on the same bench as Margo. When he saw me rubbing my back, which hurt from lifting rocks, he thought I was trying to scratch it and offered to do it for me. Beto laughed and said Margo gave a good massage.

Before I knew it, Margo was massaging my shoulders, commenting that

I was pretty strong, and I was saying it was from work and yoga. Then we switched and I was commenting how tight his muscles were (besides noticing how buff he was). When we finally got up to leave, someone had Santana playing on the truck stereo, and I moved to the rhythm as we walked toward the cars. In Spanish, Margo asked if I liked to dance, and I nodded. We should go together sometime, he suggested, and I agreed.

Margo had a bronze-orange Nissan pickup with the word *Professional* in white lettering on the side of the bed. Vlas had a gold Volkswagen Golf, and Beto and Nina had a blue Nissan truck. Somehow even though Beto and Nina would be coming back down to San Gregorio while the others would go on to their houses in Half Moon Bay, I ended up in the *Professional* Nissan with an eight-ball handle on the stick shift. It was just a ten-mile drive to Half Moon Bay and back along the Pacific Coast Highway that fateful night. I couldn't imagine the thousands of miles I'd journey with him years later, the borders we'd cross together, the fights we'd have, the millions of laughs and tears of pain and joy we'd share. Or our little daughter who would one day also ride shotgun with us. Now, many years later, it fills me with amazement and contentment that I'm still Margo's *pistolera*.

San Gregorio (1999-2001)

After early graduation from college in December 1998, I moved from Upstate New York to San Gregorio, a small town on the California coast. I was twenty years old. I'd been drawn to the redwood forests and ocean bluffs of the "Coastside" since backpacking in the area with my college boyfriend my junior year. He was the director of a local nonprofit, the San Gregorio Environmental Resource Center (SGERC), and I was on the board. Sue Henkin and Rudi Haas, my good friends, had begun to restore a several-acre historical property in town with gardens and artists' spaces. We rented a dilapidated cottage and helped fix it up. When my ex and I went our separate ways in 2000, I moved into the big crimson house where Rudi and Sue lived, a late 1800s hotel under renovation.

The breakup threw the basis for my West Coast residence into question. During one homesick call, my father reminded me I was welcome back anytime and that gorgeous landscapes weren't everything. But I wasn't in a hurry to abandon the Coastside. The area's inherent beauty and my work snagged me. I'd found jobs that were perfect for my ecologist and environmental activist background, as well as kindred spirits who shared a love for nature, good food, open minds, and music.

One of Rudi and Sue's partners in the property owned a residential construction company and had a crew on which Margo worked. The crew would occasionally stop by to store leftover building materials in the barn. Once in a while they would stick around to barbeque some steaks, and this was how I got to know some of them and started speaking more Spanish.

While hanging with the guys on the crew, I aired out my rusty Spanish with phrases like *carne asada*, *yo soy vegetariana* and *sólo esta vez*, when finally giving in to Margo's cousin Beto's offer for me to try something off their grill. I only learned a few things about Margo at first: He was from Querétaro (which I'd never heard of before), he used to have a red Honda CRX and his latest ride was a late '80s model Nissan pickup. Beto was engaged to Nina, also from the East Coast like me. In early May, they got married in the field between the old hotel and the cottage I used to live in. At their party afterward, I met several more Mexican immigrants, some of whom would become friends over the next few years.

I have a few photos of the wedding, which Margo now claims to have taken. People are gathered on a lawn in front of a century-old barn and stables built of broad redwood planks. Hills are visible in the distance, willows in the creek below, and a stand of eucalyptus sits on the opposite bank. It is a simple affair: an apple tree's pink blossoms and papery white irises are perfectly appropriate as the only decorations. A woman is smiling wide and another is biting her lip. Three Mexican men wearing collared shirts and shiny shoes are joking with each other. A little girl is running across the field. Behind her, the Universal Life wedding ministrant (my Jewish landlord Sue) is looking on as the bride's left hand comes down past her leg. Three women's arms are stretched up to the sky. One woman's fingers overlap those of the woman to her right. Her back is to the camera, and a bunch of daisies is falling straight into her hands. The woman who caught the bouquet was me.

But at the time, my mind wasn't on marriage. I was enjoying my independence, the single life. That week, I was hosting a Cinco de Mayo gathering. When I ran into Margo and his brother in the driveway, he was wearing a bright yellow North Face fleece. "*Vienen a mi fiesta de*

Cinco de Mayo," I told them. They smiled, nodded, and told me they'd be there. I even sprang for a party-sized jug of Jose Cuervo and margarita mix. I envisioned civilized portions for all the guests, with some leftover for the next bash. I don't know what I was thinking.

The evening started out pleasantly enough—folks had brought some food to share, and some friends had brought their instruments. Even Margo was playing one of the drums for a little while. I joined him in some laughs over our lack of rhythmic talent. In his halting English, he asked me where I was living and if I was still with my old boyfriend. In my shaky Spanish, I told him I was living alone and asked him if he also was. He confirmed, and acknowledged he was sometimes lonely. But then he added that we were lucky to have friends and work even though we were far from home, and I agreed. I took a picture of him and a friend, and then I was off playing hostess again, distracted enough to forget my conversation with Margarito. Or so I thought. In actuality, our encounter had left an impact on me—one that I recorded in my journal that night. But strangely, I didn't recall it until many months later.

That summer I had my hands full at work, managing an organic horticulture program and native plant greenhouse at the Log Cabin Ranch for incarcerated San Francisco youth in nearby La Honda. I was also coordinating a study of coastal migratory birds, still on the SGERC board, and putting in work-trade hours at the hotel. Aside from all that, I was enjoying living less than a mile from the ocean.

When I got lonely, I would find solace in the surrounding valley. The vegetation, inhaling the fresh salty air and the sound of birdsong and the crashing waves refreshed my spirit. On the way home from long walks, I always stopped in the middle of the bridge over San Gregorio Creek.

The psychedelic melody of the Swainson's Thrush often spiraled out from the overhanging branches, although it was rare to actually see one. The birds had a grueling annual journey and dwindling habitat on both ends, but this didn't stop them from warbling away under the bridge in the dark.

Having traveled far from home myself, I had a soft spot for my feathered neighbors—and I was passionate about working with them. What I didn't notice at the time was studying them gave me a greater appreciation for the life of a migrant.

Courtship (Fall 2001)

That trip to the *taquería* with Margo was technically our first date. When we said goodbye, Margo asked me for my phone number so we could go dancing the next weekend.

Back in my room, I journaled happily about hanging out with him. But two days later, I hadn't heard anything. Beto told me Margo had lost my number, and then he was having troubling dialing the number so he'd told Beto to give me his number and suggested I call him myself.

October 13, 2001
On [Friday] at 5 pm I called him. He was washing his truck. He said, are we going dancing? I said, I hope so! He came by at 8 after an hour of car trouble. Sara joined us… but of course, as fate would have it, we were not to dance last night. M was very gentlemanly, opening doors, holding jackets, allowing me to go first, touching my back. He was patient when we couldn't find anything… I think he may have been disappointed but if he was he got over it. We came back to my porch and talked til 3 am over coffee and two cigarettes. I learned a bit about his family, his work, him… he is such a hard worker—maybe too hard. Anyways, I find myself so comfortable around him… we talk easily. [When] he needed to go, we stood there awkwardly until he moved closer and in one swift move wrapped my shoulder and neck in the crook of his elbow, essentially catching me in a really nice hug. I hugged him tight. He held me close, down low, near the small of my back, his fingers curling beneath my jacket, to the edge of my tank top. It was nice, warm, strong. I melted right there. It's amazing how much a hug can do. Anyways, we decided we would try again, for the dancing, that is…

The next time we hung out turned into an all-day affair, but the hours flew by in his company. He impressed me with how gentlemanly he was, with the small exception of when he pointed out my split ends while laying with me on the blanket at the beach.

October 15, 2001
Since then, I invited him to the beach [on Sunday]… he came with his housemate… wearing tight shorts and shirt… it felt less personal be-

cause so many other people were there and there was more conversation in Spanish, but he held my bag, threw the Frisbee to me a majority of times, asked me to run on the beach (duh! why didn't I?), sitting by me at sunset, taking me out to dinner… I have to say I find him attractive…

After the beach outing, we made plans to see each other the following weekend, but then he called me on Thursday asking to stop by after work. I agreed, and we hung out on my veranda until late. Since he had a long drive home, I offered for him to crash at my place. I gave him the futon and then climbed into my bed and switched off the lights. As I lay there, I couldn't help but feel so silly—this nice, hot guy was laying on my floor less than twenty feet away while I was pretending to sleep. So nervously, I got out of my bed and went down and lay next to him. We didn't do anything together that night, but I remember the electricity between us was literally tangible, from my nervous fingertips down to the heat radiating off his fuzzy shirt.

Margo and I planned to hang out again on a Saturday night. Before he arrived though, I'd gotten pensive. Despite how attracted I was to him, I felt hesitant about how quickly things were moving. So I asked Rudi, who spoke better Spanish than me, if he knew how to say "dating" in Spanish. I wanted to clarify my idea of dating vs. being in a relationship to Margo. "I don't know, *hasta la fecha*?" he ventured. I tried it out, and then used it when we had a conversation that night in the hotel library:

October 21, 2001
It's nice dating Margarito… I'm glad I was able to convey to him some limits on my willingness to be in a relationship. I think if he's smart, he'll continue to not put any pressure on me. But of course the affection is there. I had him here for dinner and dessert… later, we sat in the library for a while. Talked about some cosas, como dating vs. amigos vs. novios vs. casados. I am trying to reinforce to Margo that I want to see him "hasta la fecha."… I love the time I spend with him, but it's gotta be on my terms. I think he understood, he said I have the reins… So we decided he'd spend the night.

We still laugh about that night today. Margo had told me he thought he could "help" me. I'd cockily responded, "How can you help me?" I'm still eating my words, as was made clear one night not too long ago, after we'd bathed the baby and put her to bed, we toppled exhausted into our own. "Do you ever think about why we're together?" I asked him, settling my head on his shoulder. He paused thoughtfully. "To help each other, I think," he responded. I smiled in the dark, amused by the irony of my reaction ten years earlier.

The other funny thing about that evening was that we'd agreed to just date, but then we spent the night and almost the entire following day together. He'd given me a CD of cumbia music, Los Askis, and told me to listen to "Tú." It's a very romantic song, and although I didn't get all the lyrics, I understood that the protagonist says a girl's name over and over—leaving me touched but mystified why he shared the song with me. Although the CD got lost over the years, I downloaded it recently and asked him if he remembered. "Of course," he smiled. "When we were first together, I would think about you so much that I'd accidentally call other people Nicole."

Dating status aside, by late fall Margo and I were total sidekicks. It was ironic because I never pictured myself in such an inseparable relationship. But then I found myself quite attached to Margo and enjoying his regular company. We spent moonlit nights at the beach and attended concerts together. We dressed up as Pebbles and Bam Bam and went out to a Halloween party in San Francisco together. We took a ferry to Angel Island for a friend's birthday celebration and went for a weekend to Reno together. I sewed curtains for his new place. When he dropped by after work unannounced and walked into our communal kitchen, the whole room would smile. "He settles yet inspires me," I wrote.

Besides our physical chemistry, I thought Margo to be gentlemanly, smart, and a man's man—strong and handy from years of industrial work but also earthy from working on his father's farm since childhood. He even liked to shop, dance, clean and cook. But perhaps his most refreshing characteristic was how affectionate he was. Not like over-the-top PDA, but a tender, self-confident manner. Part of it was cultural, and I loved it, but that level of TLC was new to me coming from a guy. *Time spent with Margarito is like a… vacation in the middle of… life,* I penned after Thanksgiving Day, which we'd spent in the company of friends at a potluck dinner held at the hotel.

A luxurious couple of months passed with no worries, just wonderful feelings propelling us forward as a couple. I spent very little time in my head as I was falling for Margo. But the moment did arrive when my mind started to check in with my heart. As the holidays neared, we were in closer communication with home and the social crush of holiday parties. It was impossible for us to exclude our "significant others" from our conversations with our friends and families. While explaining to his family that he wouldn't be coming home for Christmas that year, Margo told them about his new girlfriend. I would be traveling home to New York, and it caused me to reflect on Margo's background in a way I hadn't yet.

Although most of our circle was happy to hear "our news," there were a few exceptions that caught me off guard. For one, Margo's name was error-prone. Marco or Marcos were understandable. One friend even thought Margo was a female and that I was lesbian until she met him. But one "friend" who referred to Margo as *Mango* went a little too far. If name blunders were innocent enough, prejudiced opinions about Mexicans were blatant.

One time, while out for drinks with the former executive director of the organization I worked for in San Francisco, I found out she'd spent time doing graduate studies in Mexico. She basically told me to be careful of "those Mexican guys," sharing her opinion that most of them were drinkers, adulterous or had some sort of damning character flaw. I found the generalization insulting, but laughed it off to save face with her.

Unfortunately, her opinions planted a seed of doubt. I wondered why Margo was still a bachelor at 27, when the majority of his kin were married with kids by that age—why was he single? I'd observed some unsavory behavior in some of his relatives who were living far from their wives, and it worried me. Maybe he was a male chauvinist after all.

Concerned that he might pull some *machismo* on me and wanting to be upfront with him, I told him "he might get annoyed with my tendencies to always be speaking my mind," to which he replied, "I love your mind, you are better than me." Then I asked him point-blank if there was something else he'd like to tell me about his family back home, i.e., a wife or kids? He found that quite amusing, and told me I was crazy. But nervous jokes about his "other wife back home" still came up until they just weren't funny anymore.

Then he brought up the idea of me moving in with him. Things were great, but I forced myself to apply the brakes. I could picture it happening someday… but I also knew how moving in together could affect a couple's dynamic and wanted the "honeymoon" to last. So I told him I'd like to wait.

I only had a basic understanding of Margo's immigration status at that point, but it was enough to cast a shadow. A week before I was to leave for Christmas at home in New York, I had a nightmare about being chased by wild pigs. A group of immigrants who saw me up in the trees convinced me to come down, and I saw that they were not scared. Before we even began to investigate his case as a couple, the political atmosphere struck me as daunting. Margo's cousin got picked up by the INS on a trip home, which, according to my journal from the time, filled me with fright that Margo too could be apprehended at any time. "Scary shit," I wrote. This was the first time I began to realize what could happen as a result of his undocumented presence in the States. A few days later, ecstatic feelings were again interrupted. "My man is amazing," I wrote. "He does not stop when it comes to making me happy… I am only still worried about his status…"

I took the train home to New York that year. Spending several days riding the rails gave me plenty of time to reflect on all that had happened that year. Life felt full of possibility, and I felt grateful for the work I was doing and that I had a wonderful boyfriend.

When my family and I discussed my relationship with Margo, I didn't react well to my father's initial concern about Margo's legal status. I also had my first experience of missing Margo. We had a few long conversations on the phone, but I realized how alone he was. I felt bad that he was away from his family at Christmas while I was with mine.

In those days I still didn't have many clear opinions about immigration, but the connection between Margo's inability to travel home and our country's policies was beginning to crystallize. I was still trying to figure out how I felt about undocumented immigration. My ancestors were from Mexico and Germany, but it appeared as if things were a lot different now. It was enough to get me wondering why the rules of the game had changed so drastically since then, why some people were so easily welcomed while others weren't.

Although at first I questioned the wisdom of how Margo arrived in the U.S., I knew he was a good person. If he had risked so much to come, he must have had his reasons. I never judged Margo as a law-breaker, mainly because, although I have great respect for rule of law, my understanding of civil disobedience taught me that not all rules are created equal. I never thought there was something wrong with him because of his immigration status. I eventually came to see how he was caught up in a system that many people assume is fair and just, but that in reality is often far from it.

Before I was scheduled to fly home, Margo called me to let me know he'd pick me up at the Oakland airport. The day before, his cousin had run out of gas and stalled on the San Mateo Bridge and instead of calling his U.S. citizen wife, he'd called Margo to go and help him out of his bind. As Margo explained how he'd pushed Beto's truck to safety with his own until someone stopped and offered them extra gasoline, I couldn't help but think of the risk he was putting himself at out on the road.

His story made me anxious about him driving out of his way to pick me up in Oakland, an area he was unfamiliar with… I didn't want him to get in trouble because of driving without a California license (he was licensed at home in Mexico). I told him I'd take a taxi home, but Margo wouldn't hear of it. I asked him naively if he wasn't scared. He responded that of course he was nervous about the police, but that he felt like that every day. "This is what his life is like," I wrote in my journal. "A clear and ever present danger… he will expose himself to these dangers for me—I have no say in the matter—because he wants to see me—and my heart warms, sings, involuntarily, to this folly. I love him."

When I arrived in the Bay Area, he picked me up in Oakland with his friend, who snapped pictures of me grinning. We got a flat tire and spent the night at another friend's house. The next morning, I woke up with a sore throat, so when we got back to Margo's place in La Honda, Margo made me a *remedio casero,* a home remedy with *tomatillos* to alleviate the pain. He was renting a cozy little cabin in the redwoods from his boss, with a woodstove. It was cold and rainy, so we holed up over the long weekend, reveling in each other's company on our last days off from work. We exchanged Christmas presents, and I was embarrassed to discover how many more gifts he had for me than I had for him. It wouldn't be the only time his degree of selfless generosity would put me to shame.

Margo and I planned a night on the town in Santa Cruz for New Year's Eve. That afternoon, he asked me what I thought about his place. It was cute, but I was still cagey about moving in together, so I responded that the bigger, adjoining apartment with more light was nicer. Then I regretted being so blunt. To make up for it, I suggested we give each other a spa treatment before we went out.

As our hour to head out approached, we were squeaky clean and glowing from the salt scrub, and the smell of lavender was going to my head. There was something I wanted to talk to him about that I meant to save for the fireworks. My heart in my throat, I blurted out my question: If he was deported to Mexico, would he marry me so he could come back and be with me? "No," he replied and my spirits dropped… "Because that's not happening—but I still want you to marry me." My heart soared. I never felt so much happiness and nervousness at the same time in my life.

Commitment (Early 2002)

After our breathless New Year's proposal to each other, I spent a few months trying to wrap my mind around marrying someone with such complex legal issues. I was trying to balance a genuine respect for him and a desire to let our love unfold naturally, with concern and hope about adjusting his undocumented status. Margo cared for me intensely, but had no illusions about his case. He foresaw that it was going to be difficult, due to his last encounter at the border. Regardless, I was confident that getting married was the solution; it was just a matter of when.

On one hand, I didn't want to rush into marriage just on account of his immigration issues. On the other hand, I didn't want to unnecessarily drag my feet when I could have been helping his case. We decided we needed more information. Margo had a contact at the Coastside Opportunity Center, an organization that helps immigrants file their taxes every year. During one of our heart-to-hearts, we talked about getting in touch with her.

January 10, 2002
When I asked him what we would ask of Violeta, he said: how he can get his papers, if I am in danger driving him around, other legal type questions, what's the best way to proceed for safety's sake. I was going to ask him something but stopped—he read my mind and said, she will ask us if we will be married—and I thought, shit, I don't know what

*to say yet—he only smiled, and waited—I thought, what should I say
(because although I'm not ready to say yes, it's definitely not no)—he
got very happy and said, "it's possible, no?" And I beamed and said
yes...*

That conversation was one of many we would have leading up to our
decision to move in together and get married. I became protective of
him, and thought about it day and night. In a dream, Margo and I were
boating down a river only to go over the spillway of a huge dam, plunge
into a deep pool, and get stuck against electrified grates at the bottom,
where I finally leaped onto a platform and dragged Margo to safety.

January 29, 2002
*Well we've been worrying about where to live, when to marry, will M
have to leave, can I possibly go with him, what work would we do,
can he be safe here, will he be able to stay. It is all so very scary. I love
him so. I want to build a life with him... It's overwhelming to think
that the laws of my country block me in this way. On the weekends, we
cling to each other in delicious appreciation of being able to be in each
others' arms... but there's so much anxiety I feel about the future...
Margarito tells me sad stories from Mexico, the pollution of the rivers
and air, the poverty...*

In spite of the stresses that so quickly peppered the landscape of our
relationship, our bond kept growing. Even though we had very different
upbringings, Margo and I shared an appreciation for many things, such
as nature and social justice. Where language failed us, music filled in the
gaps. I picked up more Spanish by memorizing the passionate lyrics from
the many CDs he gave me: Chayanne and Eros Ramazotti and Maná.

In late February 2002 we finally moved in together, after considering
for weeks whether he would move in with me at the hotel or I would join
him where he lived in La Honda. I finally opted to move in with him up-
stream. One day we explored the towering forest above our cabin. Even
though Margo didn't like going for walks much, saying that as a kid he
had to walk miles daily to school and to pasture his father's milk cows, he
wanted to make me happy. And since he knew I liked to hike, sometimes
he'd surprise me.

Several hundred yards away was a clearing where you could see the open valley downstream for miles. The view must have brought back memories for Margo: "We didn't have much time to play because we were always working with my father." I sensed it was a painful subject for him. Not too long after that outing, he came to help me with water quality monitoring in the creeks. And when I volunteered at a Coastal Cleanup Day, he was right there picking up and carrying heavy bags of garbage. It touched me deeply that he was willing to step even further outside his comfort zone for me.

In March, we got officially engaged, exchanging rings. I was overjoyed in that girlish sort of way, but part of me was also a little nervous about telling others the news, mostly because I felt like everyone in my generation dates for years before getting married, but also because I didn't know how people who knew of his immigration status would react. But if I was tentative about others, I was clear about my own path: "It's a fear I've been having, for sure, not being able to answer these questions. While I don't want to be naïve about what's going on, I am going to embrace the beauty of my life… [and] I am sure I am following my heart," I wrote.

Lucky for us, we had nothing to worry about with our parents—both his and mine were overjoyed. Granted, they were surprised about the news, but my Dad graciously welcomed his son-in-law-to-be with a warm, "*mi casa, su casa.*" My mom confided that even her parents, my grandparents, had been harsh about my father when they first started dating. She was a white girl from Central New York with a Chicano boyfriend from San Diego in the early 1970s, but her parents later accepted him like a son. I was happy that my parents made the effort to embrace all the good qualities their future son-in-law had to offer.

I brimmed over with love and possibility at our engagement. Our cultures began to permeate each other—as evidenced by my exploding second language and new eye for the Mexican culture. Almost overnight, I began to see signs of their community everywhere. At work, I was able to reach out more to my Latino students with my improving Spanish. One student was an undocumented young man from the Yucatán, and as we traded English and Mayan words, I wondered what his fate would be after he got out. In Half Moon Bay, we visited little shops I never noticed before I met Margo.

While my attitude toward the Spanish-speaking community was one of curiosity, I encountered some neighbors who were not as open-minded.

CHAPTER 6

One afternoon while visiting with friends in San Gregorio, we stopped by the General Store for a beer. Margo was inside with our friend Shauna, and I was outside conversing with the locals. From where we stood, you could see clear up to the top of the mountain ridge, where the green hills set off the deep blue sky. It was good to be hanging out again in the place I'd called home for a few years.

Then a friend who'd had plenty to drink, started mouthing off. He was a proud fellow of Irish ancestry who lived nearby and whose wedding I'd just attended the year before. His face showed the signs of sun and booze. Puffing his chest out with a look of defiance, he growled that everyone should speak English in the U.S., "especially all those Mexicans." I could feel my ears get hot, and I glanced to see if Margo was still inside. I reminded him that California was once territory of Mexico. "Yeah, don't forget she's dating one now," one of the other guys, who also lived in the valley, added.

I stared across the street at a cattle ranch, where bulls were circling a large expanse of dirt. Then I looked witheringly at the two and scoffed angrily, "You guys don't get out much, do you?" and took off. Another friend of ours shook his head as I walked by. After collecting Shauna and Margo and complaining bitterly about what had just happened, they told me not to think twice about it. But thanks to my redneck friends, I couldn't stop asking myself, how *dare* they? And just *who* has native bragging rights, anyways?

On our way up the coast to do our weekly grocery shopping, cattle were scattered over the bright green hills, the ones that, come summer, would be toasted golden. In Precolumbian times, the hills were green year-round, thanks to native, cool-season grasses, but European grasses distributed by the hooves of livestock overtook the native grasses. They weren't well-adapted to summer droughts, and died back in the dry months until everyone thought golden hills were a hallmark of native California.

In late April, my coworkers and I loaded a few hundred containers of native plants into a U-haul truck and drove up to the top of San Bruno Mountain for an Earth Day plant sale. The sale was sponsored by the California Native Plant Society and several of its members were there.

After we'd unloaded the plants and arranged them on tables under tents, we sat down to wait for clients to arrive and discussed the latest news. I decided to tell the others about a bill I'd learned of in Congress that was refreshingly favorable to immigrants. I wanted to do something positive for Margo.

"Have you heard about this bill?" I gushed. "We should encourage our elected officials to vote for it." Someone shifted in their seat and replied that it sounded like a good idea, especially after all the post-9-11 xenophobia. But then one respected member of the group forcefully disagreed. "I would never support a bill like that," he growled, "when immigrants are the number one threat to the environment in this country."

My mind raced for a comeback but nothing came. I was caught off-guard by how he'd framed his opinion. The environment being my specialty, I knew that pollution, habitat destruction and invasive species were the top offenders. But I genuinely couldn't figure out why he'd chosen to pin the blame on immigrants as opposed to the rest of us.

Everyone in the group was a product of immigrants—none of us were Native Americans. So he must have meant recent immigrants, but the majority of them are native to North America. There must have been some kind of disconnect if his organization was committed to protecting natives. Was it a plants over people thing? I suspected a hypocritical—or worse, racist—element to this viewpoint, and that angered me. But he was one of our most important clients. Feeling naïve and inarticulate, I swallowed hard and turned away, leaving the others to continue debating.

I had been hit very close to home, and I needed to take a break. I walked a few dozen yards away from the parking lot, out into the grass. In that moment I could have cared less whether it was native or exotic. The cold spring wind blew up strong to where we were on the saddle of the mountain, and I felt my back seize up. I instinctively went under a pine tree, and began to stretch in an effort to relax. My supervisor, Amanda, my good friend, came out to ask if something was wrong. Struck by temporary amnesia, I replied that I was a little achy, probably from the loading of plants that morning. "Mmm," she responded, rubbing my back for me and suggesting I wrap up in something warmer. She may have intuited what was wrong, but neither of us realized the full impact of what had just happened.

The next day, Margo, Vlas and I had plans to go to the San Francisco Zoo, but my back was still hurting. When we got there, I could barely walk, and Margo was concerned that I was off-kilter—*chueca*, he called it. It was a severe spasm. They took me home and I lay down in the bed.

A few hours later I could not sit up, let alone stand up. When there was no improvement by the next day, Margo took me into my doctor's office, where she diagnosed me with muscle strain and I was put on painkillers, ice and bed rest.

The amount of pain was frightening. I couldn't roll over or push myself up to sit without paralyzing spasms. Luckily, I had Margo to help me to the bathroom, although I shed hot tears of shame as he lifted me on and off the toilet. He wasn't embarrassed like I was, but he was troubled, and massaged me when I could stand it and encouraged me to relax so I could get better. After ten days, I was finally back on my feet and tentatively back at work. I thought I had beaten the beast.

> *May 1, 2002*
> *My job has overtaxed me. I have hurt my back. I have been working hard... and got injured... I will be on partial leave from work and attending physical therapy with acupuncture... it makes me look at my work and if it's worthwhile... and I am forced to transcend the stresses and difficulty at work and learn to ask for help. At home, it means managing my fear better... to sublimate my feelings about Margo's immigration difficulties... my injury was acute and frightening, but in a week's time I am back on my feet and bouncing to get on with my therapy and life...*

Though I didn't know it then, my struggle had just begun. It would take me five years, numerous and varied pain treatments, a change of jobs, vocational rehabilitation (getting my master's), and reading up on a novel theory of back pain before I started to get a handle on my pain. Even though I correctly intuited at the time that it was more than just a muscle strain from lifting plants, it took years before I saw how my emotions contributed to my chronic back pain. Then it dawned on me that I'd experienced what my therapist refers to as trauma.

The event on the mountain wasn't the first time I was traumatized by society's reaction to my partner or people like him. It wouldn't be the only time that I'd encounter prejudice, xenophobia or hypocrisy on the subject of immigration. But it was the first time I'd been left speechless by someone's rancorous opinion, and it hurt all the more for the weight it carried. It exposed a potential divide between two of my deepest ideals—love and compassion for my fiancée and love for my planet, embodied by environmentalism.

My logical mind knew—and my heart felt—that immigrants *per se* weren't an inherent environmental problem. If that were true, the problem would have started with the first humans in Africa over a million years ago. But the truth is much more grey than that. As our ancestors populated the Earth in a thousand shades of color, they left mixed legacies of sacred respect and irreparable damage. The immigrant/native label, when applied arbitrarily to people with dates, laws, papers and DNA strands, is a dangerous distinction, especially when applied for the purpose of conveying stigma or privilege. As a conservationist working for sustainability, I understood that cultivating knowledge and responsible action were the true tools for environmental protection. But for me to see people, the kind I once admired, disguise prejudice as enlightened or informed opinion and use it to breed discrimination and hate was the deepest injury I sustained that day.

Realizations (2002-2003)

Although we'd exchanged rings and begun fantasizing about our first home and child, it would be some time before Margo and I were ready to foray into the typical anticipations of soon-to-be-married couples such as planning our wedding and honeymoon. Instead, we started seeking out legal advice.

Our first consultation was with an immigration lawyer whom Beto and Nina had visited. The assistant obtained Margo's clean FBI record and his immigration record through a Freedom of Information Act request. I was overwhelmed to see Margo summarily damned on the neat package of white paper. Tears filled my eyes when I saw the file photo of him that the Border Patrol took after picking him up during his last border crossing. To picture him stuffed in a trunk with other men gave me the chills. For someone who's always complaining he's hot or about bad odors, how did he stand the heat—how could he *breathe*? Although Margo was ordered out of the country, the *coyote* who was making money by crossing people was simply released. Where was the justice in that? After reviewing the FOIA, the lawyer's assistant told us it would be difficult, but they could get legal papers for Margo, to the tune of about $5,000.

We were still contemplating going with this lawyer when we got word that Margo's cousin had been milked for cash and then deported at his interview. Needless to say, we didn't hire the lawyer. Even though it would take time to get up the courage again, I continued searching for reputable counsel. Anxious and low on cash, I looked into the California Rural Legal Assistance and La Raza Legal Center in San Francisco. But I didn't get any responses to my phone messages, and I didn't persist.

Not being able to get answers to our legal questions left us confused and scared when we should have been excited about starting a life together. Margo was working on a job site near Santa Cruz where there was no cell phone reception, over an hour's drive away. During the summer, since they'd usually work until dark, he sometimes wouldn't get home until quite late. He didn't like driving at night because it was inherently more dangerous, but he had no choice. Although I told myself he was just fine, I was often worried sick, picturing him getting pulled over, arrested and deported. Even though he didn't enjoy taking the risk, it was impossible for him to obtain a driver's license. He arrived home to find me upset on more than one occasion. Some nights I cried while waiting for him to get home.

Despite the clear memories, I recorded little about these feelings in my journal. When I asked Margo about it recently, he recalled that I asked him to get a ride with someone else, which he said would be too inconvenient. Then I begged him to let me drive him to work, and I got upset when he refused, saying it would be impossible with my schedule. "But I was right to be so worried, right? You really were taking a risk," I reminded him. He replied, "We take risks every day. I really think it was more dangerous that you rode with your cat in the car... that cat got under the pedals one time." I used to bring my cat, Honeybee, to work with me without a carrier.

But as we continued reminiscing, he waxed serious: "Before we got together, I never went out at night, only to work. The police were often behind me. But every morning I would check my truck, to make sure all my signals were working. I got lucky." Having gotten used to Margo always driving when we ride together in Mexico, I'd almost forgotten that in the U.S., I drove everywhere when we were together, especially at night. It must have felt humiliating to Margo that his wife wanted to drive him everywhere, but it was something we just got used to. The preoccupation never went away for either of us, but for me at least, the fear eventually numbed somewhat.

Our legal situation depressed me, and problems at work didn't help. SLUG was in debt and falling apart from mismanagement, and so I needed to look for another job. I still hadn't made the connection between my back and the stress, and the pain would sometimes take me out of commission.

When Margo and I were approaching a year together, we began to have our first major relationship difficulties. He tried to understand my unhappiness. But he had his own worries, and encountered discriminatory treatment on a regular basis. One night he came home in a funk after a clerk at Big Creek Lumber refused to take his lumber order, pretending that he couldn't understand him. Although another clerk helped him, these kinds of situations drove Margo to keep working on his English. They would also make his nostalgia for Mexico resurface.

> *August 19, 2002*
> *We've been talking about saving up to go to Mexico… I was and still am thinking it would be OK… but then last night I got paranoid. I started thinking about how they would laugh at me like they laugh at Margo. And he would try to protect me, but it's the same on the other side—no shortage of prejudice. He thinks we could save $ to buy a house, not have to pay rent, possibly return here [someday]. More thinking required, since we can hardly save a dime…*

The initial idea of having to move to Mexico together was an uncomfortable possibility. When I was low, he would say he didn't want to cause problems for me, i.e., obligate me to come back with him. He'd also lived alone for a long time, and had gotten used to his independence, and sometimes thought I was trying to micromanage his lifestyle out of fear. So sometimes he'd put up a cold front of not needing anyone, including me. Instead of seeing that he didn't want to get hurt if I decided to end the relationship, I assumed that he was being his typical honest self and didn't want to be with me. This worsened our dynamic.

Our relationship strife was usually episodic—and between stressful moments, we remained the staunchest of allies. But it was a wake-up call that I needed more outlets. I enrolled myself in a six-week yoga workshop. I wanted to regain my carefree side. I didn't want my troubles to make me closed-off. I wanted to confront the questions before me with strength and resolve. Luckily, I made the right choice—by taking better care of myself, my spirits lifted. We continued to have our good times with pot-luck parties and afternoons on the beach watching pods of dolphins, peppered with bad times like anniversary miscommunications and problems on the job. But with every challenge, we just found a new equilibrium.

Legal concerns took a back seat as life loomed large. I was paying off school loans and a car, and Margo wanted to save up for the house he envisioned having before getting married. My job in La Honda came to an unceremonious end the summer of 2003. I landed a position as a biology teacher at an all-girls Catholic school in Belmont, which would start in the fall. I loved our little spot in the redwoods, but wasn't ready to endure a two-hour round trip commute each day. We would have liked to cut down on Margo's daily driving as well, but since his construction job sites were constantly changing, it was hard to take them into consideration. We thought about moving again.

We finally settled on Half Moon Bay—an ocean side town that was closer to my new job, but still on the Coastside. To offset the higher rents, we downsized, renting one room in a Oaxacan family's house, along with eight other people. For Margo, it wasn't a big deal—he'd lived in much tighter quarters while growing up and when he first arrived from Mexico. But for me it was my first taste of culture shock—in my own country—and it added a new layer of tension.

Half Moon Bay is one of the places on the Coastside where the Latino population is concentrated. The house was part of a suburban development built along the state beach. The owner was a forty-something-year-old guy from Oaxaca who lived there with his wife, three kids, brother, sister-in-law and two other renters. The kids were sweet, and I became friends with one of the renters, but the owner and his wife were a bit tyrannical. We couldn't use their washer or dryer, or phone, and at first, we weren't given a key—we could only come in when the husband was home—although that changed fast.

The day I got my own phone service installed, the wife, who up until then had been quite aloof with us, knocked on my door to ask me if she could use the phone. "I thought you had your own?" I asked, dumbfounded. "Yes, but my husband has the long-distance blocked," she responded, "and I haven't talked to my mother in over a year." She cradled her infant son in her arms. "Sure, whatever," I responded in Spanish, rolling my eyes as I turned away. Her standoffishness had initially rubbed me the wrong way, but this was my first glimpse that maybe this twenty-something Oaxacan woman wasn't so happy with her *jaula de oro*.

May 20, 2003
This new challenge Margo and I have undertaken, to consolidate into a different space, is difficult! Not so much the actual smallness and cramping of space and possessions (yet), but rather, the social environment. I don't even so far mind the suburbanness of the place! Still, the issue is our status in the house and the lack of amicability of the "headmastress" [sic] of the house and the rest of us renters.
Transitioning to the life here has been hard so far. I miss the peace of the redwoods and the rural San Gregorio Valley where I have lived for four years. But I also embrace this change as a new experience.

It was in that house where Margo and I went through perhaps the most difficult trial of our relationship in the States.

May 22, 2003
My lover's situation [is] a continued awareness of fear of deportation, of knowing he cannot be a legal, legitimate member of our society. Of knowing you are always on the run. Of knowing you can hardly ever trust. It's in your face, way more than normal situations.

May 29, 2003
You have come to my life as a gift—the time I spend with you makes me feel great—no matter how often I see you, each occasion is special to me. Although sometimes I am sad, you know how to lift me up, and then I am happy. I appreciate the time you dedicate to me, with all the love I feel for you.

June 5, 2003
My whole body hurts… I do my stretches almost daily, but perhaps I need to add in a walk or a bike ride? This morning it was hurting so much I could hardly even turn/breathe. Is it me? Is it society? The environment? Is it unreleased pain? It's almost driving me crazy to not know why I'm hurting so much…

CHAPTER 6

July 8, 2003
I left for vacation [home to NY] 2 days before the summer solstice.
Now I feel totally rested and ready to get to work! I had a wonderful
time, very good to see family and friends. Later, a beautiful reunion
with Margo will be cherished forever... my dear Margo, my soulmate,
sweetheart, extra strength—my spirit enriched, supported, loved.

And then one day, one of my worst fears came true, something beneath
even my lowest expectations. Up until that point, I was still convinced
that I could obtain legal status for Margo through marriage. But that
illusion was shattered the day we finally obtained reliable legal counsel
from a lawyer who gave us a free consultation in San José. Together we
encountered, for the first time, the impossible wall of frustration that
every couple faces when informed that their legal situation is nearly in-
surmountable. And it brought us down hard.

August 1, 2003
I said, I never imagined it would be this hard. I asked, what were you
thinking? He said, I didn't know anything. If I had known any of this,
I would never have come and bothered you. I said, Baby, don't say that!
He said, why? I said, why? He said, I don't like to cause problems for
anybody. I cried. I stroked his cheek. I contemplated the truthfulness of
Nolo Press, the straight-faced lawyer, the bad feeling Margo got from
the slippery looking lawyer... the injustice I felt seeping into my bones.
Not even fully comprehending how this has, is, will rattle my world.
My friends, family, colleagues, don't have much comprehension...
Nolo says the TIME BARS are a "new phenomenon." You got that damn
straight. How we so easily conform, comply, accept these bullshit laws
without even reacting. I am deep in Thoreau's Walden, and it sounds
like encounters with songbirds were just as special in the 1800s as they
are now. He speaks of migratory songbirds. Maybe that's why they're so
exceptional. A life of migration, a lifestyle where you never quite fit in,
where you share homes across geopolitical borders, and no one else who's
a "rooted" or "native" can really intuit or understand your different
rhythm, keeps you on your toes—you imagine the worst. You prepare
yourself for the negative reality—you are, in the words of Tupac Shak-
ur, "ready for whatever."

[Two days later…]

Today I did one of the most dramatic things I'll probably ever do in my life, and I pray[ed] to God. I don't regret it; there's a chance I may. Today I gave Margo back my engagement ring. He had just finished telling me that I don't accept that he doesn't know if he wants to marry me… I just got so frustrated, and felt so on the spot, so compromised and sick of feeling liked I'm being played (even though the chances are so slim, I don't even want to feel anything close!) that my anger, my sense of pride, got the better of me. Off came the ring and I gave it back to Margo, after holding up my hand and asking what my ring and his proposal of marriage signified and his response was, "I don't know." This overall, has been a very hard week. It was my first week unemployed. Margo was recovering from a really poor appetite after his grandma passed and his family's missing him… It's true that it's probably better to bring this to a head, but the pain that this situation produces is almost unbearable! Only time will tell… will the love endure… and I can't stop thinking about loving him…

The night that I gave him back my ring, Margo went out and didn't return for hours. When he finally came back, he had cut off all his hair—practically a buzz cut. I was shocked but said nothing. We didn't speak to each other for three days, which was quite a feat considering we were sharing a room. In those seventy-two hours, I walked to the beach and back, sitting for hours on the sand contemplating how much I cared for him. I wrote poetry about what he meant to my life. I called friends, family, and sat staring at the surf in thought or sat at home poring over my journals, wanting to will myself back to a time when things felt so much less complicated, when our dynamic was solely based on mutual attraction and love. I wanted that dynamic back.

I found the entry in my journal from the night of my Cinco de Mayo party, more than two years earlier. That evening, in my room alone, after everyone had gone home, I'd foreseen that I would spend my life with Margo. Though he had been long gone, I could have sworn he was there with me—not standing there, but just *present*. I heard the crickets chirping and the water in the creek rushing softly over the stones.

Seis de Mayo, 2001 [midnight]
So I think the man I may marry is Marguerito [sic]. I mean, he's the
sweetest, most serious, sober, cutest, best hair by far, of the guys here in
San G… He's always respectful… eyes of dark onyx, the cutest laugh.
He's just NORMAL. Intelligent and sensitive. Yet such a man. Integ-
rity, honor, sensitivity. A sense of humor. Cautious. Loyal. Communi-
cation could be difficult… but I think with time it could develop…
should I go for it? It would be great to have a companion and body-
guard on trips around Latin America… a compassionate, strong part-
ner. Only question would be, green card, culture difference, and would
he expect me to be a stay at home mom? Would I? If I could pursue my
degree and career at the same time, who cares? But no responsibility
for meals, ay! … By the fire… Mago [sic] and I shared a few genuine
laughs. They were so inspired it felt good. I hadn't seen him laugh like
that before… I asked him if he thought we'd have sueños malos [bad
dreams] after the [incident with the drunk guy], and he said we can't
always avoid them. Well, perhaps I will be blessed enough to create a
dream with Marguerito [sic] in it tonight…

[hours later]

I haven't even slept but I feel him. He could actually be my soulmate.
I see the moonlight, and I shed tears that I cannot be with him to
express my love, too fearful to express… scared, why? Because he is
[so] amazing… it doesn't seem possible for him to be single. Would he
accept me…? I am filled with crazy questions. And the waves crash
outside my window.

Since that night, we'd come so far together—a vision had become reality. We had the passion and the devotion to stay together, but I was asking
for more than that. On the day we were told we could not stay legally in
my country together, I realized we were in for a much more challenging
journey than I could have ever imagined. And because of that, upon
experiencing the pain that news brought us as a couple, I wouldn't accept
anything less than absolute commitment. I was prepared to make—had
already made—that sacrifice, but I needed to know that Margo really
wanted to—consciously. That no matter how hard it got, we were both
in it for better or for worse.

I prayed for a way for our relationship to be healed. I knew we had it in us. The month before, I'd written about our ability to surmount obstacles together.

July 17, 2003
Patience and love. They heal all wounds… We both grieve for separation from our families. For the difficulties encountered by our cultural and language differences. We talk things over together. Secure and stable, taking steps toward a deeper commitment. We raise issues together in front of other people, testing responses, reality, and our sense of humor. We seek refuge in solitude… It is a tenuous calm, his stay in the States. It is a difficult choice, actually, not really, because if I were ever to have a child, biologically, it would be with this man—if he wants to have one, we will—if not, we won't, if he wants to stay together, I want to, and if we don't, I can adopt. Now that feels pretty soothing. Choices. Even with my back against the wall from our government's aggression toward certain humans, I can still react with Amazing Grace.

This time, Margo's fear that I'd be better off without him was the only thing standing between us.

Chapter 7

The Waiver Scene

~

Nathaniel Hoffman

Betty Campbell has a mischievous, sardonic grin for a 77-year-old nun. My first night in Ciudad Juárez, she offered me her cluttered bedroom, insisting that she preferred sleeping on a mat on the living room floor so she could hear sounds from the street—the sounds of gun shots, peeling tires, and screams, maybe not every night, but frequently enough.

I threw my bag down in the quiet, cold back bedroom at Casa Tabor, Sister Betty's house in one of Juárez's northwestern *colonias*—the unpoliced and forgotten dirt and cobble street neighborhoods that house tens of thousands of underpaid factory workers and urban poor and now drug dealers and gangsters as well. It's a neighborhood of concrete block houses of mixed quality—some with iron gates and red roof tiles, others run down and abandoned with tin roofs, boarded up windows and holes in the walls. The modest Casa Tabor stood out with its neat yard and pink hued adobe façade.

Later that first evening, with a warm smile and slightly manic glint in her eye, Betty handed me the May 2009 issue of *Harper's Magazine* folded back to Charles Bowden's "The Sicario," an intense interview with a Juárez hit man that Bowden later turned into a book. At first I thought that Betty was trying to haze me into the fraternity of fear that has gripped this town since about 2008, when murders began to skyrocket. But the gleam in her eyes also served to inoculate me from that fear with her absolute faith in the resiliency and creativity of poor people in Latin America.

I wrote "*sicario*" in my little notebook, knowing it would come in handy over the next couple of days. Mexican *sicarios* have gotten the upper hand on reporters in recent years, enforcing a regime of censorship through fear at Mexico's still spunky and highly competitive newspapers. Ten journalists were killed in Mexico in 2010, according to the Committee to Protect Journalists, which ranked Mexico among the top ten deadliest countries for reporters every year between 2004 and 2011.

At least 29 people were murdered in Juárez during my five days there in January 2011. That statistic comes from the "Frontera List," an archive that New Mexico State University librarian Molly Molloy maintains, dutifully recording Mexican media crime reports and relevant commentary on the drug wars, mainly from Juárez. I read Molloy's dispatches every day for a few months, but then had to stop reading every single report because they were becoming too easy to dismiss, as in: There were only three murders in Juárez today.

For the *Harper's* story, Bowden, an American writer who has followed drugs and crime along the border for decades, tracked down a former Mexican police officer who had worked for years as a hit man for narcos, kidnapping and executing and burying people across the country. The man was in the U.S., hiding from the drug cartels. Bowden sat with him at an anonymous motel, recording his life story in gruesome detail: the stranglings—his expertise—the chemicals he used to literally disappear bodies, the anonymous holes in the ground where mass graves still lie, undiscovered by authorities. The cocaine and whiskey and paranoia and the eventual salvation that came with being hunted himself.

Betty warned me before I read the piece that it's a searing account, essentially damning to the Mexican authorities in passages like this one:

> *"They hardly ever do police work; they are working full-time for narcos. This is his real home for almost twenty years, a second Mexico that does not exist officially and that coexists seamlessly with the government. In his many transports of human beings for bondage, torture, and death, he is never interfered with by the authorities. He is part of the government, the state policeman with eight men under his command. But his key employer is the organization, which he assumes is the Juárez cartel, but he never asks since questions can be fatal."*

I had walked across the border from El Paso early that morning, over the Santa Fe Bridge, which is also called the *Paso del Norte*—the passage north—only I was headed south. The bridge, which connects two important border towns between the states of Texas in the north and Chihuahua in the south, crosses high over a disappointing cement channel that is supposed to be the Rio Grande and then gradually descends into Mexico. The toll for pedestrians heading south is fifty cents.

Very little foot traffic heads to Juárez in the morning hours, but a steady line approached Texas along most of the east side of the bridge. A hundred or so cars idled in the middle, awaiting inspections by the U.S. Border Patrol.

When I got to Mexico, no one asked to see my documents. The lone soldier standing at attention, his mouth obscured by a half ski mask, did not even acknowledge my presence. No signs directed me to customs. Americans are free to travel some twenty miles into Mexico and stay for a few days without registering.

I was a bit early, which was really a shame because I had no knowledge of the security situation near the bridge. The nearby military checkpoint was both reassuring and disturbing. The Mexican Army had been patrolling the streets of Juárez in open pickup trucks since 2008 as part of a major federal counter-narcotics operation in the state of Chihuahua. They rolled through town in small caravans, four heavily armed soldiers standing up in the beds.

There are many cities under siege across the world. But Ciudad Juárez in 2011 was a city in its own league. The stories coming out of Juárez at the time read like a Hollywood blockbuster account of a pre-apocalyptic second world city torn apart at the seams.

There were an average of seven murders a day in Juárez in January 2011, the month I visited, according to the newspaper *El Diario de Juárez*. In 2010, at least 3,111 people were killed in Ciudad Juárez—a city of 1.3 million people. That's ten times the number of murders in Baltimore, where I grew up, at the height of its drug war in the early 1990s. In 2011 the number of murders in Juárez dropped but still approached 2,000. Conventional wisdom and the government storyline in Mexico is that only people involved in the drug trade are targets of the mounting violence. It's written off in the newspaper headlines as *delincuencia*—delinquency, a problem of misguided youth. But the statistics and the testimony of hundreds of Mexican citizens belie this myth: fourteen high school and college students slaughtered at a party in January 2010, gun battles on soccer fields and extortion and robbery rampant in working class neighborhoods.

This social disintegration is writ large on the faces of *juarences* as they ride the bus or lay low at work or cry openly on the evening news. People in this town routinely cover their faces with scarves pulled up over their mouths and noses, both to stave off the morning chill and to maintain their anonymity. *Juarences* speak in muffled voices, eyes downcast, a sadness for their suffering city palpable.

In the minds of many Americans, the level of violence in Juárez is generalized to the whole of Mexico. But drug war violence remains localized, generally along smuggling corridors into the United States, and many regions of Mexico remain safe. After leaving Juárez I visited Querétaro,

Michoacán, Mexico City and the Yucatán and was not confronted with any of the fear that I felt in Juárez.

My plan was to meet a priest on the Juárez side of the Santa Fe Bridge. I knew he was an older priest, but I'd never met him and was not sure what he looked like. I fantasized he'd show up in a big black Cadillac looking like Cheech Marin in *Machete*, a large gold cross around his neck and maybe a bodyguard. That's what I was hoping as I stood on the Mexican side of the bridge trying to relax and interpret the street scene laid out before me. I asked the Mexican soldier in the black ski mask if I could stand next to him while I waited, but then that seemed stupid so I moved some distance away and leaned nervously against a wall.

In this instance, I did not like being early. And Father Peter Hinde, Sister Betty's partner in liberation theology for the last half-century, was also concerned that I'd been standing there for fifteen minutes when he strolled up in civilian clothes and a dorky baseball cap. Where was the guy's collar? I couldn't even make out a cross, and almost all the Mexicans I know wear crosses.

We wasted no time, walking up a side street, in case anyone had spotted me and was, perhaps, laying in wait. Father Peter had not anticipated that I'd have a big, old backpack and he seemed slightly stressed about that fact but hid his concern well. Here we were, backpacking around Ciudad Juárez, the city with the highest raw number of murders in the world, and my 88-year-old guide—whom I'd assured my wife and kids would take care of me—did not even look like a priest. A few prostitutes cat-called to us and Father Peter remarked that this used to be the Red Light District when Americans still came over to Juárez to party. He tried to give me a little tour, pointing out an area where entire city blocks had been razed in order to make way for urban redevelopment that never happened.

We walked quickly, snaking through the streets up to one of the main east-west roads in Juárez to meet a friend of his who runs a small hardware shop, the old fashioned kind that you still see in Mexico where the goods are kept behind the counter. The corner shop is below the house and five sons eke out a living there.

Like most legitimate small businesses in Juárez, it's not going well. The father of the family said that they are too small to get the attention of drug gangs, which charge protection money to many small businesses in

Juárez. But they don't dare get bigger or stay open during certain hours of the day for fear of drawing extortionists.

From the hardware store, we got on a city bus and headed up to Peter and Betty's place. I was not even sure where I was on the map or how I was going to get around the next day.

After dropping off my bags, we ate some freshly made *gorditas* from a roadside stand—lightly fried corn *masa* pockets stuffed with spicy, pulled pork—and walked around the neighborhood. We peered down on the local soccer field, and Father Peter indicated the house where a beloved coach had been shot and killed a few weeks prior—just a block away from Tabor House.

Peter showed me the house where the son of a doctor was stoned to death for allegedly snitching on drug dealers. We walked by rows of abandoned houses, curtains drawn, their inhabitants fled to safer parts of Mexico or over the border to El Paso. We looked north into the hilly neighborhoods of El Paso, just across the border, and into the New Mexican wilderness. Peter pointed out the new highway that skirts all of the western *colonias*, depriving the poorer residents of Juárez access to transportation infrastructure. I did not know it yet, but this common and discriminatory failure of modern urban development would loom large for me the next day.

On nearly every block, Father Peter knew a murder story. Fourteen people have been killed in their immediate neighborhood in recent years. He described all of these murders dispassionately, delivering the details in his earnest, matter of fact tone, informed by decades of living at the nexus of U.S. foreign policy and poor people in Latin America. Peter and Betty have lived and worked in Latin America for most of their lives. They encountered early practitioners of liberation theology, including Father Gustavo Gutierrez, while working in Peru in the 1960s. They traveled together through the 1970s and 1980s witnessing civil wars in El Salvador and Guatemala and Nicaragua and documenting human rights abuses and U.S. involvement in arming and propping up authoritarian regimes up and down Latin America. They now live on the border in the new murder capital of the world in what will likely be their final home.

Tabor House was founded by Tadeo "Spike" Zywicki, a lay Catholic worker and peace activist who died in 2003. Father Peter Hinde and Sister Betty Campbell serve the poor of Latin America in the finest tradition of the Catholic Church: liberation theology. It joins a radical, fresh reading of the gospels with the radical politics that swept peasant movements across Latin America in the 1960s. A generation of priests was moved to question the power structures in the Western Hemisphere that enforced extreme dependence on the United States and created highly stratified societies. They challenged U.S. backed dictatorships—and U.S. hegemony—throughout Latin America by living and working among the poorest people and taking sides in national conflicts. It was a deeply religious and deeply political movement.

Though Peter and Betty live in Juárez, their mission actually lies north of the border, in the well-appointed, staid churches of the United States. It's called "reverse mission." They serve the church as witnesses in Latin America—living amidst the despair that U.S. dominated free trade and demand for narcotics has wrought on Latin America—and try to inform Catholics and others in the North of their *de facto* culpability and responsibility. For many years they hosted dozens of groups a year, introducing them to their neighbors and to the hard reality of border life. But now that tide of visitors has almost completely dried up. Even I would only last one night at Tabor House, my fear—rational or not—driving me to a gated hotel near the U.S. Consulate.

On my second day in Juárez, I got up at dawn and took a creaky, old bus from Peter and Betty's neighborhood in the hills above Juárez through many run-down *colonias*, swerving around burnt tires, wondering at every seemingly unplanned stop. People did not make eye contact on the bus. We bus riders all had our collars turned up and stared straight ahead. I worked up the nerve to ask a lady next to me if the U.S. Consulate was getting close and she briefly explained it was close and then promptly got off the bus.

All this death, all this nervousness, made me nervous, so I checked into a hotel near the consulate. I had survived twenty-four hours in Juárez. But I still had to go back and get my stuff. I wanted Peter and Betty to know that I really appreciated their hospitality and deeply respect their choice to live there, but that I needed to move to a more secure location.

Juárez was not my first time navigating dangerous urban spaces. Baltimore had one of the highest murder rates in the United States in the 1990s, averaging more than three hundred killings a year. Although I lived in the suburbs, I spent many Saturday mornings on 28th Street, handing out canned goods in a drug-addled neighborhood. The food pantry where I worked was named after a black student at my high school who had been shot in the back and killed. The man who ran the pantry was murdered and his apartment set on fire a few years after I went off to college. After graduating, I traveled and worked in Gaza and Beirut and across southern and eastern Africa. In 1999, I was mugged in Johannesburg, while taking the scenic route back to my lodging.

The mugging is a small example and proves nothing, but I did not want a repeat in Juárez. I was about to retrace my steps to Tabor House and wanted to exercise caution and not take the scenic route. In my previous travels I had been young, single and naively courageous. Now I had two little girls at home and was not willing to take the same risks. Luckily, while doing interviews that morning, I had met a man who worked for a local health clinic. He offered to take me in his van to get my stuff and bring it back to the hotel. I told him the neighborhood and he said it was not a problem, though in retrospect, he did not know where it was and had no idea what he was in for. This man was in his fifties and had grown up in Juárez. He was trained as an attorney, had adult children and held a decent job. But I had to navigate for him and as we climbed into the barrio, his agitation became very obvious. We were driving a pretty nice, new passenger van and I noticed him checking the mirror, his face turning red, his gaze getting more serious with every bump or turn in the road.

We pulled up to Tabor House and he said sternly, "five minutes." I rushed in and told Sister Betty, my hostess, that I was moving closer to the consulate, because that's where my story was unfolding and because it would be safer for me. She was very gracious but wanted to show my friend her little garden and two beautiful chickens. I scanned the block for approaching vehicles while he got a quick tour of the yard and the house. This was most likely all irrational fear, but we were ratcheting up one another's irrational fears. I didn't like that he was so nervous, assuming he knew the area. He maybe didn't like that he was driving a gringo journalist around in a fancy car in the *colonias*.

Then he decided to take the scenic route back, trying to head for the beltway that Peter had shown me the night before—the one that speeds past the ghetto. We were now experiencing the classism of infrastructure improvements as we could clearly see the highway on the horizon but were still speeding along dirt roads, imagining gangsters chasing us, until we finally came out to the asphalt. We both breathed huge sighs of relief.

I know that it was all in our heads. But it was also a symptom of living in a town where the daily paper features a murder count and the police do very little to intervene.

We dropped my bags at the hotel and went out for double shots of Don Julio and some deep fried intestines with guacamole. I'm not the kind of person who regularly needs a drink. But I needed a drink after that drive.

In my first twenty-four hours in Juárez, I felt that I had experienced the siege that the U.S. and Mexican drug war had wrought on that border town. But I was not there to produce another surface account of "violence gripping the border" or "impacts of the drug war." I was there to walk in the shoes of Americans and their Mexican partners, driven to Juárez by another powerful force: a love deep enough that they were willing to risk their lives and livelihoods to be together.

Lauren & Carlos

Over paper plates of General Tso's chicken and fried rice at the Misiones Mall food court in Ciudad Juárez, Carlos Peralta told me about his season of waiting.

We were at the shiny shopping mall—a clone of the medium sized indoor mall in any U.S. city—because it felt safe. Around lunchtime on a crisp Saturday in January 2011, Carlos and his friend Martín, a Juárez local, took a series of buses to the brand new Ibis Hotel where I was staying. The three of us met in the guarded lobby and walked two hundred yards across the divided highway to find some food.

We spent the entire afternoon at the mall, hitting the indoor ATM, sipping espresso drinks and eavesdropping on a nearby binational couple that was also sipping espresso drinks and bouncing a stroller. We ogled running shoes and electronics and talked about cars, high school and politics. In the late afternoon we decided to catch *Tron 3D*, a Hollywood blockbuster about a man who figures out how to enter a video game world.

It was as if we had entered another world ourselves, donning 3-D glasses and sitting in the half-full stadium theater trying to relax in the dark in the murder capital of the world. Every time someone cleared their throat or rattled a cup of ice, we peeked over our paper glasses and looked around nervously.

We emerged from the theater two hours later to find that it was quickly getting dark. Carlos and Martín ran for a bus and I turned my collar up and walked quickly across the street back to my gated hotel.

Carlos took precautions in Juárez, without becoming as paranoid as I had become in just a few days there. He displayed an undying optimism during his two visits to the city while I adopted a morbid realism, which settled around me as the days passed and my urgency to get the hell out of there increased.

Carlos did not have a choice in the matter if he ever wanted to go home to his wife and family.

Almost 130,000 Mexicans visited the U.S. Consulate in Juárez in 2010 for immigrant visas, including 41,000 with American spouses. Fourteen thousand of those applicants had been living in the U.S. without papers, like Carlos, and were seeking a pardon of sorts—the I-601 waiver—to return home to their families.

Seventy-five percent of these I-601 visa waivers, on average, come through the U.S. Consulate in Ciudad Juárez (the rest are processed at other foreign consulates). Juárez is the only place that Mexicans and their American families can go to submit the waiver application. It cannot be done from the United States or from the U.S. Embassy in Mexico City or online.

In January 2012, the Obama administration proposed a change to the I-601 waiver process that would allow some immigrants to apply in the United States, before touching back to their home countries to pick up the visa. Carlos might have taken advantage of a program like this, but it was not available at the time and did not take effect until early 2013.

While waiting for their visas, many families stay at the cluster of hotels around the U.S. Consulate, eating in the hotel restaurants, wandering through the mall and going to bed early, not venturing out to see the sights in this historic border town. They lay low on the recommendation of their attorneys or their contacts on the popular immigrate2us.net or Juárez, Mexico Discussion Forum websites or just out of plain common sense. Most visitors take major precautions in Juárez, heeding the U.S. State Department travel warning that the region is of special concern: "You should defer nonessential travel to Ciudad Juárez and to the Guadalupe Bravo area southeast of Ciudad Juárez."

Nonessential travel is a relative term for Mexican citizens like Carlos, with American families and lives in the United States.

Carlos Peralta was born in Morelos, but his parents brought him to the United States when he was twelve, fleeing a violent situation in Mexico—a business feud that had gotten out of control. They landed first in Tennessee and then moved to Minneapolis. Carlos sports shaggy, longish jet black hair that hangs over his eyes conveying a clean-cut hipster look. He wears a gold earring in one ear; he is thin, not very tall and has a contagiously straight posture. He's into classic hot rods and knows how to rebuild an engine, yet he was never eligible for a driver's license. He speaks English with the barely perceptible trace of a Mexican accent.

There were about one million undocumented children in the United States in 2010, according to the Pew Hispanic Center. An additional one million young adults like Carlos grew up in the United States without papers. Carlos was in an ideal position to benefit from the Dream Act, a bill that has been introduced in Congress more than a dozen times since 2001. The Dream Act would provide visas to undocumented young people who grow up in the United States and want to attend college or enter the military. They are regular American kids who, because of circumstances beyond their control, grow up to eventually learn that they do not have permission to be fully American. During our afternoon at the mall, Carlos recalled a class trip to Greece that he had to sit out because he couldn't get a U.S. passport. Other Latino kids—Dreamers, as they now call themselves—skipped the trip as well: "They did what they had to do to survive," Carlos said.

Carlos finished his last year of high school in Arizona, completing three years of auto mechanic's curriculum in a year and taking over as crew chief at the school shop. Then he almost went to college. He was accepted at the well-known Universal Technical Institute in Chicago to continue his automotive training, but couldn't afford the $2,500 a month to attend and wasn't able to apply for federal financial aid because of his immigration status.

Carlos always loved cars. When he was two years old, in Mexico, he used to put his toy push car up on bricks and pretend to work on it. He owned a car in the States, when he couldn't even get a license. It was a '94 Ford Probe that he was none too proud of, but he dreamed of a '69 Camaro. All of those dreams—his dream of higher education, of a solid job and a good car—were not possible without his papers.

Carlos met Lauren Bernstein in the spring of 2008, just two weeks before he was supposed to move to Tucson to spend his senior year with his mom. He had already withdrawn from the high school in Minnesota and stopped by one day to say goodbye to friends. A buddy introduced him to Lauren. They struck up a conversation and he asked her out dancing, to salsa night at Famous Dave's.

Lauren ended up canceling that date, but she asked him to have dinner with her soon after, and they talked for hours. They hung out a few times during his last two weeks in town and Lauren actually accompanied Carlos and his dad and step-mom to the airport to say goodbye.

While he was in Arizona, Lauren and Carlos struck up a phone relationship, talking almost every day. Lauren visited Carlos in Tucson a few times and after he graduated, he returned to Minnesota to be with her. He stayed with his dad for about two months and then he moved in with Lauren, in her parents' basement where they each had their own bedroom. In November 2009, he asked for her hand in marriage.

Lauren and Carlos describe themselves as each other's *media naranja*, literally "half the orange," or better half. Lauren teaches high school Spanish and coaches the dance team at an international magnet school outside Minneapolis. She taught English in Guatemala for three summers after high school and considers herself bicultural, almost Latina herself, though she grew up Jewish in Minneapolis.

The Dream Act was reintroduced in late 2010 and again in the summer of 2011, but Carlos and Lauren were tired of waiting for a political solution. He wanted to start a career and a family; they wanted to travel together. And so they went to see attorney Michael Davis and took a chance on Juárez.

Davis told them about the I-601 hardship waiver process, which acts like a pardon for undocumented immigrants with spouses or parents who are either U.S. citizens or legal permanent residents. If you qualify for the waiver it is not a bad risk: Each year from 2007 to 2011, an average of 22,217 people applied for these waivers through the U.S. consulate in their home country or region. Seventy-two percent were approved, according to statistics from the U.S. Citizenship and Immigration Services, or USCIS.

Those seem like good odds, but it's still a large risk to apply. First of all, many couples do not even qualify for the I-601. Margo and Roberto each lost their chance when they returned to the U.S. that second time, incurring the permanent bar. Under the permanent bar, immigrants can apply for a different type of pardon after ten years—not a waiver but a discretionary readmission. That process has not been tested very many times to date.

The I-601 waiver is discretionary as well—it's up to an immigration officer whether or not an applicant qualifies. And it's a tricky case to make—one has to prove that the American relative would suffer an "extreme hardship" if his or her immigrant relative were kept out of the United States. Many couples do not understand how this works when they first visit an attorney or read about it online.

"They can't understand why the bad or the hard or the difficult things in their life would be a positive for their case," said Rosa Gaona, a paralegal in Davis' office. "I try not to get excited when I hear all the bad things in their life, but I know that actually the worse it is the stronger the case is going to be."

While in Juárez, I spoke with Warren Janssen, the top USCIS officer there for six years. USCIS is one of the three branches of the Department of Homeland Security's immigration apparatus. It is responsible for evaluating immigration applications and conferring citizenship. I asked Janssen what "extreme hardship" meant. He said that it was a "discretionary analysis" that is up to the immigration officer reviewing the case and that it has to include a burden beyond the consequences of a normal deportation.

"We're looking for a variety of things," he said. "We don't have a checklist. We don't have a point system. It's a discretionary decision and we weigh all of the evidence. But we look at financial issues, we look at medical issues, we look at emotional issues, psychological issues, we can look at the children of the qualifying relative and the applicant indirectly. If the children are having issues or problems, that can cause hardship to the spouse. So even though the children are not a qualifying relative, we can still look at that indirectly... it's normally a combination of things and not necessarily just one issue."

So the more medical problems or debt your American partner has, or the more financially dependent they are on you, the better chances you will have to return to the United States. Amazingly, the fact that you have American children together has only secondary bearing on your case.

Lauren, who is a pretty well-balanced, successful young adult, had to dig way back.

"Unfortunately on paper I look like a mental nut," she said. "A Humpty Dumpty mental woman."

Unfortunately for her, but fortunately for their case, Lauren was able to reach back into her medical history, citing asthma and allergy issues in the late 1990s, old neck and back problems and minor psychological issues. Davis also helped her build a case that she would not be able to practice her religion in Mexico. He had visited synagogues in Mexico that were not very welcoming to liberal, American Jews.

Lauren thought she knew something about immigration; she had international experience and a college degree.

"Having a degree in Spanish, they don't tell you anything about all this," Lauren said. "What I wasn't prepared for is that it is all about me and nothing about him."

She hated the process.

"I'm described as a woman who can't care for herself without her husband," Lauren said. "It made me feel useless and helpless, but I would do it again in a heartbeat because I got my husband back."

Lauren was the American sponsor, the "qualifying relative," and she had to show the government that banning Carlos would be an extreme hardship to her, whether she was forced to live without him or to relocate to Mexico with him. Carlos and Lauren considered this process and the advice that Davis gave them and decided to give it a shot.

In January 2010, the two married in a quiet ceremony. Lauren did not change her last name or relationship status on Facebook—that would wait until their "Big White" wedding, assuming Carlos got the waiver. Some people had judged her for her relationship with Carlos, and so she did not want to make their marriage public until they were certain of their fate.

"The whole world doesn't need to know what's going on in our situation. It's none of their business," Lauren said.

She kept wearing her engagement ring after the civil ceremony and they saved their vows for later. Lauren says now that having a simple civil wedding is not that strange. Many of her friends delay their own large wedding celebrations until they get on their feet and can afford the party on their own.

Soon after the wedding, the couple started the application process.

In February, Carlos and Lauren, submitted a visa application: the I-130,

Petition for Alien Relative, along with the $420 processing fee. With that application, Lauren petitioned USCIS for a green card for her husband. Based on their relationship, Carlos was clearly eligible. But because his parents brought him to the United States illegally, as a twelve-year-old boy, and he stayed more than a year after his eighteenth birthday, he was disqualified for the visa. Carlos knew that. His attorney, Michael Davis, had explained that to him and he was prepared to be rejected and then to file another petition, the I-601, in the hopes of reuniting with his wife. They had prepared the visa application and the waiver application and rehearsed all of the steps in the process. But these things never go exactly as planned.

Once they received a date for an appointment at the consulate in Juárez, Carlos started planning a trip back to Mexico—a trip that could very well end up being one-way.

Carlos left the United States on October 29, 2010, for his first appointment in Juárez. He took a bus to El Paso and Martín, the family friend who hosted him in Juárez, escorted him over the border. He stayed at the Holiday Inn Express, one of the shiny new hotels adjacent to the new U.S. Consulate. On November 1, he got up early and went for a required health screening at one of two large clinics certified by the U.S. Centers for Disease Control for examining prospective immigrants to the United States. The clinics see more than 100,000 patients in some years, about half of the them young men with lives in the United States and the other half seniors with kids in the United States, according to one of the doctors.

The clinics are required to screen for tuberculosis, sexually transmitted diseases, personality disorders and addictions. They also document tattoos. The exam cost $183. After his exam, Carlos waited a few days for the results of the health screening. It was ready just hours before his consular interview at the largest and busiest U.S. Consulate in the world. For that first appointment in November, Carlos expected an interview—and was ready to shine—but it turned out more like a bank transaction.

Carlos wound his way through the turnstiles outside the consulate, waited for his number to be called and handed his paperwork—the packet from the health clinic and a stack of documents that Davis had helped him prepare—to a woman who worked for the U.S. State Department, a consular officer. While the USCIS determines if immigrants are eligible for green cards so that they can stay and work in the United States, the State Department issues visas to people who want to legally enter the country. Carlos said his consular officer was not nice to him, but was, "not, not nice either." She checked his records and quizzed him on his addresses in the U.S. and his mother-in-law's name, and then she told him he did not qualify for a visa because of his year of illegal presence in the States after he turned eighteen. But he could qualify for a waiver, she added, and should call to schedule another appointment to submit the I-601 forms. He'd have to wait in Mexico for two months before his second appointment.

Carlos said he harbored some hope that the Consulate would just approve his visa at that point, but he knew it was unlikely. So he secured his second appointment for January 2011 and headed to his grandfather's home in Morelos, south of Mexico City, where he had not been since he was twelve. Lauren was home in a suburb of Minneapolis, living in her parents' basement, teaching high school Spanish and spending a small fortune on cell phone bills.

Laura & Arturo

For Laura and her husband, Arturo, the Juárez experience almost turned into a one-way trip.

Laura and Arturo, who asked that their last names not be used to protect their privacy, packed their '91 Subaru wagon and moved to Ciudad Juárez in December 2005. They went on advice of their attorney in Denver—perhaps the sixth attorney they had seen. The attorney knew that Arturo had a complicated case that would probably be slow-tracked. He had gone to the United States with a false Border Crossing Card, or Laser visa, for temporary visitors—and so she suggested they move to Mexico and establish themselves before they even got a date for a first appointment.

"We kind of figured out that he was going to have to leave and that was pretty upsetting," Laura said. "We made the decision that whatever happened we were going to go together."

Laura and Arturo were married and had an infant daughter when they moved to Mexico. Arturo had not been home for six years. After departing the United States—essentially driving across the border hoping not to be stopped by the Border Patrol along the way—they made a stop in Chihuahua to pick up his brother, sister-in-law, their two kids, his sister and uncle. Ten people piled into their Subaru wagon and another car followed for a twenty-hour caravan to Veracruz on the Gulf Coast.

Laura was excited to meet Arturo's family and to see what his child-hood had been like. She reveled in the short visit and cemented a lasting relationship with her mother-in-law, but she would later use that visit in Arturo's waiver application to argue for her husband's return to the United States, citing the lack of clean, running water, central heat or refrigerators, the $120 a month the family lives on and the dangers of disease and infection for her and her daughter.

After visiting Arturo's parents, Laura and Arturo moved into a small, furnished apartment in Juárez. It had hot water and was in a relatively nice part of town, on the street where the popular Mexican singer Juan Gabriel lived. It cost $250 a month—American dollars. The last couple that had lived there was also binational and "doing time" in Juárez.

On their first night in the new apartment, someone stole all the CDs out of the car, took the radio faceplate, which was useless without the radio, and grabbed the rear license plate. Every day after that they had to unscrew their remaining license plate and bring it in the house, only to screw it back on in the morning. The neighbors' groundskeepers were constantly painting over graffiti.

Laura planned to get a job across the border in El Paso, Texas, so they could pull in a U.S. wage. She had worked teaching English to adults and as a parent liaison in Denver schools and had experience at her mother's travel agency. But she quickly learned that being bilingual was nothing special in El Paso, and that there were not nearly as many jobs as in Denver. So she ended up delivering pizzas in El Paso. She had experience in that too.

Pizza was what brought Laura and Arturo together in the first place. Laura delivered pizzas in high school and eventually became assistant manager at a Pizza Hut in Denver. She learned street Spanish working at the Pizza Hut with a crew of Mexican guys, including Arturo for a while. But they never expressed an interest in one another while they worked there together. Arturo moved on to a long string of restaurant jobs, often holding two jobs at the same time. Laura finished college and went to

CHAPTER 7

Mexico to study Spanish formally.

When Laura returned to the States in 2002, she went back to work at Pizza Hut while looking for a more career-oriented job. Arturo came in to get some food one day and they started talking in Spanish. She learned a lot about him—stuff she did not have the language skills to ask him before—but it was a busy Friday at the restaurant and once Arturo got his food he disappeared. Laura tracked him down at the restaurant where he was working and gave him her phone number. They set up a dinner and dancing date and then started dating formally. Arturo surprised Laura by actually asking if she would be his girlfriend. And she surprised herself by agreeing.

Before crossing the border in 2000, Arturo spent a year working in Ciudad Juárez, making money to send home to his family in Veracruz. He lived in a dangerous neighborhood called East Salvarcar, but said he was not scared. He kind of liked it, as it was his first urban experience. He definitely liked the money. Nothing bad happened to him during his first year there, but he lived by certain rules as well. He only went to work and went home. He never went out, except to buy a few essentials, and never met up with friends after work.

Arturo had a friend from Veracruz who kept bugging him to go up to Denver. He told him he could make seven times what he was making in Juárez. He didn't fear life in Juárez, but he realized it would be safer in Denver. He would make more money. So he crossed the border in 2000 and headed to Denver.

For those first two years in the United States, Arturo was only interested in making money. He lived in cramped quarters with other migrant workers at first and then got his own place but had a roommate to help cover the rent. He did not bother with dating.

Then he met Laura for the second time, in 2002, and she changed his life. He took care of her house and dog when she returned to Mexico to take another Spanish course and then he gave up his own apartment and stayed with her. He quickly fell in love. Arturo says he was not concerned with a green card then—it was easy enough to find work anyway and he was making plenty of money. Plus, neither of them understood the process of sponsoring a spouse who was in the country illegally. But after they talked about it, Arturo began to realize it would be important for the future, when they had kids.

When their first daughter, Alma, was born, they put all of their immigration questions on hold for a few months. But Laura had already decided that it was worth the risk of moving to Mexico with a young baby in order to try to get papers for her husband. She was also eager to see the other side of Arturo's life and meet his family.

"She was excited," Arturo said. "She wanted to see how my country was."

The excitement did not last long: "Having visited Mexico as a tourist on numerous occasions, I assumed the transition would be a mild inconvenience. After several months, the situation had become so emotionally and financially trying that my daughter and I returned to Colorado in August of 2006," Laura wrote some two years later, on behalf of Arturo's waiver application.

"By the time I had lived in Juárez for a while that letter was no problem to write," she said. "These are basically just term papers and the evidence is your life."

During the nine months that Laura and Alma spent with Arturo in Juárez, they heard nothing from the USCIS. They were still waiting for that first appointment for the spousal visa that they knew they were going to be denied. Laura left her husband and baby at home every day to cross the border—wasting hours at the checkpoint into El Paso—to deliver pizzas. She often returned late at night. She was somewhat scared but mostly annoyed at all of the waiting and hassles at the border.

Though Arturo knew his way around Juárez from his time there five years prior, when he moved back with his wife and baby, their rules were even more rigid. They pretty much stayed in the house all the time, save a handful of daytime visits to a park or the zoo. Laura made no friends. There was one old man in the neighborhood whom they trusted. He helped them on the first day when their car was broken into. But other than that, they had no friends.

"I was worried because of her and because of my baby, because of crime," Arturo said.

In August 2006, unable to cope with life in Juárez or crossing the border anymore, Laura and her daughter went back to Denver, crashed with her mom and then her dad and then her sister and found a job at a call center. Two months later they finally received a date for the first appointment: October 30, almost a year after they had applied. Laura decided to go down to Juárez to be with Arturo when he went to the consulate, even though she did not have to. He was denied, as expected, and then she had a month to finalize the waiver letter.

It took another year of living apart before they got a response on their waiver. Another year of Arturo working in the *maquilas*, the border region sweatshops that flourished after the North American Free Trade Agreement went into effect in 1994. These were throwaway jobs for Arturo. He made $50 to $100 a week and literally quit every time his wife and daughter came to visit, confident he could find another one as soon as they left.

Laura, after she returned to Denver without Arturo, visited as often as possible, enduring many eleven-hour, overnight bus rides on the Los Paisanos Mexican bus line from Denver to El Paso with her young daughter. On one trip they got caught in a blizzard in the bus station and she thought they might die. It took eighteen hours to get to Arturo. Another time, the taxi driver belittled her during the ride from El Paso into Juárez, assuming she was Mexican and implying that she was up to no good, traveling at night in a bad neighborhood.

Arturo insists it was not exactly fear he felt in Juárez, whether Laura was with him or after she returned to Denver. But he held to his rules. He stayed home. And he does not aim to go back to Ciudad Juárez or the border region again.

"It's my country but I couldn't live there anymore," he said.

Laura and Arturo had trouble wrapping their heads around the concept of a waiver application. At first, people advised Laura that Arturo had to write a pardon letter saying he was sorry he came to the country illegally. But that's not the idea at all. They sought advice from several attorneys before the concept clicked and Laura ended up writing the ten-page letter herself, with help from the active online community at immigrate2us. net.

Immigrate2us.net is a forum for people with questions about immigrating to the United States. The vast majority of its users are going through the waiver process. There is even a Frequently Asked Questions thread with the title, "Help! My foreign spouse or fiance is/was present in the US illegally. What do I do?" The site boasts almost 21,000 members with about 2,000 active at any time. Every time I log on, there are dozens of people participating, asking questions about where to stay in Ciudad Juárez, how long it takes to get a decision on a waiver application and how to get along better with a Mexican mother-in-law. The forums have accumulated more than one million posts since the site's founding almost ten years ago.

Some immigrate2us users have uploaded their waiver letters—both successful and unsuccessful and Laura found those examples invaluable. She trolled the website ten times a day, checking when the other couples that had applied for waivers around the same time as Arturo were getting responses back from the government.

"I feel I put everything into that letter," Laura said. "I call it my second baby."

In the letter, Laura explained that she could not take her daughter to live in rural, southern Mexico, citing U.S. government statistics on the standard of living and health conditions there. She explained that the only way they could survive with a modicum of comfort in Juárez—like hot water and a refrigerator—was with her leaving her husband and baby daughter to cross an international border every day so that she could deliver pizzas at minimum wage plus tips in El Paso. And she argued that living separately was not viable either because of her need to support Arturo and herself from Denver, essentially maintaining two households.

Then she discussed the health care consequences of living in Mexico, her depression and isolation during the nine months she spent in Juárez, the effects of Arturo's separation from Alma on her young psyche, her daughter's prospects for education and opportunity south of the border, the impact of her absence from and then her sudden dependence on her parents when she moved back to Denver without her husband and the higher rates of crime along the border in Mexico.

The waiver letter included some reassurances of Arturo's good character and potential in the United States, but it's almost all about her, an argument for the extreme hardship of both her moving to Mexico or living apart from her spouse.

Finally, Laura cited her pride at being an American: "If forced to move abroad, I would be unable to fulfill my duties and responsibilities to the United States of America, as well as depriving our daughter the opportunity to know and value the freedom and responsibility of being an American."

Beth & Carlos

Choosing the right hotel in Ciudad Juárez is a key decision. When Beth Corona met Carlos there in October 2008 for his waiver appointment, they chose well: The old Holiday Inn Express near the old U.S. Consulate was full of spouses of Mexican citizens seeking waivers and pardons. It was a security conscious American hotel that catered to many travelers with business at the U.S. Consulate, before the consulate moved to an even more secure block in the southern part of the city.

The Los Cedros Inn is on the other side of the old consulate from The Holiday Inn, just blocks away. It has more of a Mexican feel to it, a bit less security and it's more affordable, especially for people who need to stay in Juárez for weeks at a time. Carlos did not choose Los Cedros, or more accurately, Beth did not choose it for them, based on advice she read online. And it was a good thing because the same afternoon that they checked in to the Holiday Inn, two Mexican police officers were gunned down at Los Cedros in broad daylight.

The event was most likely first reported on the immigrate2us website, even before authorities or news cameras showed up. Several Americans were staying at Los Cedros with their Mexican spouses waiting for appointments at the consulate or visa packets from the government or waiting for their spouses to return from Mexico City so they could go home together. Beth read about the shooting on the online forums in real time from her hotel, a few blocks away. Members of the forum offered advice on whether or not the woman reporting the incident should stay in her room, go out to see what was happening, change hotels, or cooperate with detectives. Dozens of Americans either in Juárez or getting ready to travel to Juárez, were watching out for one another, virtually experiencing the trauma of witnessing a police assassination at a nearby hotel.

The forum discussion, which went on for eighteen pages, was at once a practical stream of advice on what to do after witnessing a murder in a foreign country and a philosophical discussion on violence and immigration and the Mexico border. Many frequent posters, those with experience in Juárez, maintained that it was only police officers being targeted in this situation and that Americans and Mexicans who were just minding their own business were not in danger. Some stated how violence could occur anywhere, at any time and no hotel is safer than any other. Some made generalizations about violence in Mexico but other writers disagreed, insisting on the concentration of violence in places like Juárez and Nuevo Laredo.

Several posters asked why the U.S. government continued to force people to spend time in Juárez to do business with the consulate in the face of skyrocketing violence in the area.

An April 2011 article published in both *Mother Jones* magazine and at *Forbes.com* asked the same question: Why are tens of thousands of Mexicans with American relatives forced to go to Juárez every year to file paperwork with the U.S. Consulate? The article detailed the kidnapping and murder of a Mexican man who was in Juárez in 2008 to apply for a waiver. The man's wife posted to immigrate2us as she learned of his death.

The danger was not isolated to Juárez. Three men married to U.S. citizens from Minnesota were killed in El Salvador, Honduras and Guatemala in recent years, according to a report on Minnesota Public Radio. But Juárez had the most consular traffic and the highest risk. And in March 2011, a U.S. citizen, Denver native Jake Marlowe Reyes-Neal, was beaten and killed in Juárez where he had joined his high school sweetheart and their young son as she waited for her waiver to be processed.

The *Mother Jones* article quoted an anonymous State Department official saying that visa processing for Mexico was consolidated at the Juárez Consulate in 1992 for administrative reasons; other consulates around the world also underwent similar consolidations. That was before violence along the border had risen to its current levels. Now Juárez is home to a brand new U.S. Consulate, the largest in the world, specifically designed to process large numbers of applicants. Only a small number of sibling visas and adoptions are processed at the U.S. Embassy in Mexico City.

I asked Thomas Rogan, the number two State Department official at the U.S. Consulate in Juárez, what he tells Americans whose spouses are nervous about visiting Juárez to process their visas. He said American petitioners can file all of the paperwork from the U.S. Only foreign nationals are required to go to the consulate in person.

"Americans don't have to come here. Many of them choose to come, that's their choice," Rogan said.

I told him that many U.S. spouses, like Laura and Beth, feel compelled to join their husbands and wives in Juárez for the minimum six weeks it might take to obtain a waiver.

"It's a choice," Rogan reiterated.

I told him that I was nervous after just one day in Juárez.

"You're right to feel a little nervous here and people should exercise caution. And generally I would say if people don't need to be here, it's better not to come," he said.

Beth Corona did not get involved in the online debate, but she was in Juárez for the same reason as all of the others: to support her husband as he put himself at the mercy of the U.S. government, asking for a visa to return with his American family. Beth traveled to Juárez with her mother, Alice, and her young son, Diego, to reunite with Carlos and hand deliver the waiver packet to him just before his second appointment. An American woman from the immigrate2us forum picked them up at the airport in El Paso and delivered them to the hotel. During the drive it started to rain and her bag with the waiver in it got wet, but the paperwork survived.

Once settled at the hotel, they ventured out a bit, hitting a *mercado* where Diego's grandmother bought him a soccer jersey and shopping for groceries at the S-Mart. They also walked to the consulate, but turned back after a short stroll because they felt uncomfortable.

Beth had worked really hard on the waiver package. She had to pull up old doctor's notes on a bout with depression and obtained affidavits from her parents who wrote about their close-knit family, colleagues who testified that her work in special education required a partner to come home to at night and vent to, and a priest who testified that they had a good marriage. She also cited $27,000 in school loans that she would be unable to repay if forced to relocate to Mexico.

"Who isn't depressed?" Beth jokes now.

She chalks up their success with the waiver to it being well written and well organized.

"They have fifteen to twenty minutes to read that fat document," she said. "It's really a mystery."

Their attorney in Denver, Nancy Elkind, said that all of the evidence added up: Beth's history of mental health issues, her family's concern for her should she be separated from Carlos, and, even though it technically makes no difference, Carlos' clean record and diligence at learning a trade and studying English.

And Elkind said they clearly had a solid marriage: "With Carlos and

Beth there was no doubt about the marriage."

"My job is not to investigate a marriage," Elkind said. "There are a lot of real marriages that I would not want to deal with… there are lots of shitty marriages that are not entered into for immigration purposes."

Elkind said that in almost thirty years of practice, she has never encountered a bicultural marriage with a Mexican partner that she found suspicious.

Rosa Gaona, at Michael Davis' firm in Minneapolis, said she mostly sees couples with real, heartfelt relationships, often rural Mexican men marrying rural women from Northern Minnesota. She has spotted a few marriages of convenience while doing intake interviews, but they are usually weeded out. She provided Spanish interpretation for one couple that the immigration authorities had separated and she had to translate as they provided different answers to simple questions.

"It was really hard for me just watching them lie and shoot themselves in the foot," she said.

Beth and Carlos, Laura and Arturo, and Lauren and Carlos all demonstrated solid relationships and deep, bicultural, family ties. It was then up to a single Department of Homeland Security bureaucrat to determine whether or not they had demonstrated adequate hardship.

* * *

Laura visited her husband Arturo again in September 2007. It had been almost two years since they moved to Juárez together and a year of living apart after Laura and her daughter returned to Denver. She tried to visit him every other month or so.

Arturo was getting pretty discouraged.

"I was really sad and frustrated," he said. "I was tired of the situation, it seemed stupid. I was tired of waiting."

After a few days' visit, they said their goodbyes and Laura took the bus home to Denver over night, arriving at 6 a.m. and heading in to work. At lunch she went by her mom's house to check the mail and there was a letter from USCIS: They got the waiver.

She flipped out, but had to go back to work. Her boss, who knew their situation, winked at her and suggested she looked a bit sick. Laura took off, hopped back on a bus at 6 p.m. and was in Juárez again in the morning to pack. Arturo got his packet—a thick envelope with his passport, now stamped with an entry visa for the United States, and took care of all of his affairs in Juárez. By that evening they were back in the United States, together.

Laura and Arturo's two years of limbo were not all in vain. They had finally obtained the waiver and would be able to live together in the States with peace of mind. Their relationship was strengthened through the ordeal, as they were totally alone in Juárez, with no one else to rely on but each other. Laura lost sixty-five pounds in Juárez—taking off her pregnancy weight and a little more from the poverty, the stress and her busy days crossing the border for work. Laura's Spanish and knowledge of her husband's culture grew by leaps and bounds. Their two daughters speak and read Spanish and Laura is the *doña*, or respected den mother of their circle of binational couples in Denver, including Beth and Susie. She even taught the other wives how to make Mexican hot chocolate at their first get together (the key, according to Laura, is to cover the chocolate triangles with just enough milk to melt and make a thick syrup).

Beth, who was inspired by Laura's success, had an easier time of it. Carlos was not sure he wanted to take the risk of returning to Mexico and applying for a waiver in the first place, but in the end, he did. He drove to Juárez with Beth's father, Terry Kelly, in a pickup truck filled to the brim with televisions and clothing and supplies for his family in Mexico. They stayed at the Holiday Inn for two nights and then Carlos moved to Casa Tabor for a few days, getting to know Father Peter and Sister Betty. His visa was denied, as expected, and he got a date for his second appointment to submit the waiver some six weeks out.

Carlos is deeply religious, but in a very independent-minded way. He recalls a group singing the rosary every morning outside his window when he was a little boy in Tequisquiapan, Querétaro (fondly called Tequis). He likes to pray and attended two masses with Peter while in Juárez. But he also holds many of his own beliefs and interrogated the priest during his baby girl's baptismal classes, challenging him on conceptions of heaven. He was so inspired by Peter and Betty's selfless sacrifice for the less fortunate in Ciudad Juárez that he shed tears when he left Casa Tabor.

While waiting for his waiver appointment, Carlos went home to visit his family in Mexico for the first time in nine years. Carlos has three kids in Tequis from a previous marriage. He had supported them during his decade in Denver and still calls them every week and sends child support every month. On this visit back home—it had been a long absence—he took them gifts from the United States, and left them his truck.

Carlos then returned to the Holiday Inn in Juárez a few weeks later, bringing with him a huge box of *gorditas* his mother had made for Peter and Betty. The *gorditas* spoiled on the long bus ride back to Juárez and Carlos was crushed not to have anything for Peter and Betty.

Beth, Diego and Beth's mom, Alice, flew down to meet him. The next day, Carlos went in at 10 a.m. to submit his waiver and did not get back to the hotel until 4 p.m. He applied during the peak of a special pilot program at the consulate in which some easily processed waivers were decided in a day.

"I knew by the way that he was walking that he got it," Beth said.

Beth flew home the next morning, and Carlos took care of some more paperwork and flew home in the evening.

As he approached the boarding gate in El Paso for the first air flight of his life, two immigration officers spotted him and beckoned him over. They asked for his green card and he replied, with a straight face, that he did not have one. Then he pulled out his Mexican passport with the ninety-day temporary visa. A huge weight lifted off of his shoulders as the agents examined the visa with an infrared lens.

"My world changed," Carlos recalled. "Now, I'm not afraid of anything."

When he got back to Denver, Carlos Corona called his American mother-in-law for a ride.

"I'm at the plane station," he said.

Lauren Bernstein's husband, Carlos Peralta, was chopping wood at his friend Martín's place, a few weeks after we had met in Juárez, when he got the call.

He actually did not hear the phone ring. His mother-in-law called ten times and then left a message. When he finally got the message that his packet was ready—he didn't know if he got the visa or not, only that the response was ready for pickup at the DHL office near the consulate—he hopped on a bus. At the DHL office—the global delivery company that has a contract with the U.S. Consulate—the family in front of him got a really thin envelope. He presented his ID to the clerk and she produced a thick envelope, opened it and handed him his visa. He was ecstatic.

Lauren was teaching and had her phone on vibrate. She had told her class that she might get a very important phone call that day and she might answer it but that does not mean they can use their phones during class. When the phone buzzed, she picked it up and Carlos said simply, "Guess what, I got it."

"I did slap the desk," Lauren said. "I scared my students. I'm not a screamer."

She told the class that it was good news and that Carlos was coming home.

"I did think, 'How would I get through the day if the answer was no?' The kids aren't idiots," Lauren said.

Carlos took his DHL package, including a sealed portion that he had to present to the Border Patrol, and went back to Martín's to pack. Martín's mother joked with him that he had not finished cutting up the tree. Carlos actually felt badly about that, even though he knew she was joking. He had tried to help the family out while he stayed there, paying for some groceries. But they would not accept gifts from him, including a space heater he wanted to buy them. They couldn't afford to pay for fuel for the heater.

Lauren's mother booked him a hotel room in El Paso and arranged a 6 a.m. flight the next morning, but he did not make it over the border that night. He had to go to the Zaragoza Bridge, close to where he was staying, to get his visa stamped, but then to another bridge to cross to El Paso and get a ride to the hotel. It got too late and too dangerous to go to the bridge. So instead he stayed one last night in Juárez, got up at 3 a.m. and proceeded to the border. The Border Patrol kept him waiting for a few hours as they processed a group of visas at the same time. After about ten weeks in Mexico, never really knowing his fate, Carlos Peralta had just one long walk over a bridge and then a cab ride to the airport to go.

And then he was home.

Chapter 8

Split by Deportation

~

Nathaniel Hoffman

CHAPTER 8

Juan & Veronica

On Thursday, December 4, 2008, Veronica Mason was finishing up some Christmas shopping. She was about to call her fiancé, Juan Diaz, during his 9 a.m. break, and glanced at the cell phone sitting on the passenger seat of her truck. The phone registered several missed calls from her babysitter and her sister-in-law.

They were looking for Juan because when the raid first went down, no one could find him.

Veronica happened to be driving on the interstate near Idaho Truss, the wooden framing factory where Juan worked. She noticed a helicopter and a bunch of police cars near the warehouse. As she pulled off the highway, her sister-in-law was on the phone telling her that there had been an immigration raid at the factory and they were not sure where Juan was.

"I got off the Franklin exit as she's telling me this and I'm seeing a chopper and four cop cars—but I'm sure there were more—and a van where they come in and out with the wood. And I thought 'I know exactly what's going on,'" she told the *Idaho Press-Tribune* a few days after the raid. "I was in shock."

Veronica knew what was going on because everyone who worked at the plant had heard the rumors about this raid. The company had been under investigation for more than a year and the employees had known about it for months. Juan and Veronica had even sought legal advice before the raid from the advisor who suggested they just leave town. Immigration and Customs Enforcement had warned the owner that some of his employees were working under counterfeit social security numbers, and managers had spent a week photocopying employment records to forward to ICE. But no one working there expected the raid that day. No one anticipated the scale of the raid.

Veronica pulled off the highway and parked at a pet and garden store near the factory, watching the police action and manning her phone.

It was a cold December morning and the doors to the warehouse were closed. The crew was about to stop for the 9 a.m. coffee break when all of a sudden someone yelled, "Run!" Juan saw men in bulletproof jackets coming in through the front door and sprinted for the back with several other workers. He couldn't get out so he hid instead. Juan says he "hid a little," behind a large wood cutting machine, against the wall, but an agent found him pretty quickly.

The workers had joked around with each other for several weeks about the raid, even going so far as to pick out hiding places in the dusty, sprawling warehouse where they cut and assembled large wooden trusses. Some ran into a dark storage loft built of two-by-fours and metal shelves and littered with boxes of paper and hardware. Some sprinted up a roughed out staircase, behind a half wall that doubled as a closet and into the heating ducts. Others scrambled up a wall into a hole over the offices. There are still footprints halfway up that wall where ICE agents crawled after them.

One man was in the back corner of the outside lumberyard when the cops came screaming up to the back gate and he managed to get away, over the fence, along the railroad tracks.

The agents ran in with guns drawn—some of the workers hoped that they were loaded with rubber bullets, but ICE agents use live ammunition in law enforcement actions such as raids.

The agent who detained Juan seemed fresh faced—perhaps it was his first raid—and Juan quizzed him in Spanish on how they knew there were so many unauthorized workers there. ICE later confirmed that it had received three complaints from former Idaho Truss employees that the company employed unauthorized workers.

Juan suspected he knew who the three were. Some time before the raid, three white, U.S. citizens and two Mexican nationals with green cards were laid off. Juan said he told the supervisor, a man from Juan's home state of Michoacán, that it was not wise to lay off only workers who had papers and keep all of the undocumented staff on.

As the agents rounded up sixteen of the twenty-two employees working that day, using dogs and infrared glasses to find the eight who ran, Juan and the others were handcuffed and made to sit on the ground. It took about two hours to sweep the entire factory and detain the sixteen men. Juan said it was just like the movies, like the raid scene in *Born in East L.A.*, where the Chicano man played by Cheech Marin is rounded up and deported to Tijuana. There were more uncanny similarities with that classic Mexploitation flick than he knew.

Juan did not give the officers his name at first. He never volunteered his name when caught at the border either, always making up a new name before being sent back to Mexico. Juan wasn't even on ICE's list of people to detain on the day of the raid. He had used his own, real social security number and his California driver's license to get the job at Idaho Truss. His father obtained a real social security number for him in 1980, before Juan ever came to the United States to work.

But Juan had a record from his previous illegal crossings and ICE figured out who he was and that he had been deported in 2005. So from the ICE perspective, Juan was a lucky grab. One agent asked him why he ran if he had legit employment documents. ICE spokeswoman Lorie Dankers told reporters that three of the men arrested had prior deportations and three had criminal records. She never specified the crimes.

Juan worked at Idaho Truss for six years, making $11 an hour at the time he was arrested. Many of the other workers were loyal, longtime employees as well and the president of the company sort of backed them. He told the local paper that they were some of his best workers and that they had all provided work authorization documents that appeared to be authentic and legal.

"It's a disruption for sure... but we'll pull together and get the job done," company President Kendall Hoyd told the *Press-Tribune*.

Hoyd also told the paper that the raid came as a surprise, but ICE contradicted him in a press release, saying that the company had been warned that some employees had provided counterfeit social security numbers. Many of the rounded up workers felt betrayed.

The next day, some two hundred people applied for the sixteen jobs.

The Idaho Truss raid came during the final month of the Bush administration, after two years of high profile workplace raids in places like Greenville, South Carolina; Laurel, Mississippi; and Postville, Iowa. After the Bush administration's efforts at comprehensive immigration reform failed in 2007, a new regime of workplace enforcement ensued.

During Bush's last two years in office, ICE arrested more than 9,000 people in made-for-TV workplace raids. Hundreds of black-clad ICE agents would storm a chicken plant or rural factory, guns drawn, backed by helicopters. Terrified workers ran screaming. Armored buses staged near the raid site to cart arrestees to immigration detention centers. Local police led television satellite trucks to the best vantage points. Spanish radio stations issued alerts and families fled *en masse*, fearing *la migra*.

The day after the raid at a huge kosher meatpacking plant in Postville, Iowa, ninety percent of Latino students—half the school district— skipped school, according to the *Washington Post*. The raid devastated the company town, which revolved around the plant. Hearings for many of the workers were ironically held on the grounds of a livestock pavilion, and some remained in legal limbo in detention centers for years following the raid.

In Laurel, Mississippi, ICE detained almost six hundred people at a transformer manufacturing plant, releasing about a hundred juveniles and mothers, who were sent home with GPS ankle monitoring bracelets. ICE arrested more than three hundred workers at the poultry processing plant in Greenville.

None of the raids should have been complete surprises. Supervisors at the factory in Greenville had been indicted months before for labor and immigration violations. The meatpacking plant in Postville had faced serious labor and environmental charges for years and was under investigation with allegations including child labor violations. In Laurel, union workers harbored open resentment for the undocumented workers at the factory. But in all of the raids, while quiet charges were pursued against the employers, the workers and their families felt the overwhelming brunt of the government action.

That action included, for the first time, charging immigrant detainees with federal crimes, including aggravated identity theft and false claims of citizenship, rather than administrative violations of immigration law.

In Idaho, at the relatively small Idaho Truss raid, attorneys and social service providers jumped into action. The Idaho Community Action Network contacted many of the detainees' families and organized a candlelight vigil at the Idaho Anne Frank Memorial. The newly established Mexican Consulate in Idaho obtained a list of the men arrested. Initially, ICE refused to release their names to attorneys or to the press, stating that they were arrested on administrative charges. But the Consulate argued that if they were Mexican nationals, they should have access to consular assistance, and then helped facilitate a team of pro bono lawyers to interview the detainees.

About a week later, all sixteen were indicted on federal felony charges, including possession of counterfeit alien registration receipt cards, misuse of Social Security numbers, illegal re-entry after deportation and identity theft, which carried a two-year minimum sentence. The workers' names were released to the media, appearing as a list of long, generic-sounding Mexican names in the local papers—five were named Juan. There was very little follow-up reporting on the families or the mood of the Latino community after the raid.

Twelve of the men took a plea bargain, admitting to misdemeanor illegal entry and accepting deportation. Three, including Juan Diaz, went to trial. Juan Martínez, who attorneys believed was an American citizen (again, a la *Born in East L.A.*), convinced the judge to turn his case over to an immigration court and drop the criminal charges.

Martínez told the attorney who interviewed him soon after the raid that his mother was born in the United States, but he grew up in Mexico and came to the United States illegally. He did not know that he might be eligible for U.S. citizenship. His mother had to have lived in the United States for three consecutive years in order to convey citizenship to her son, so the attorneys got to work doing research.

They asked the immigration judge for a cancellation of removal based on his lengthy time in the United States and hardship to his family, including four U.S.-born children. Martínez was released from detention after about six weeks and, based on information they discovered, his attorneys submitted an application to U.S. Citizenship and Immigration Services, requesting a certificate of citizenship.

It took more than two years for attorneys to prove that Juan Martínez was eligible for U.S. citizenship when he was arrested at his job in Nampa. Paralegal Mariella Diaz who works for Andrade Legal in Boise found an archivist in Orange County, California, who was able to find Martínez Gonzalez's grandparents' entries in the 1932, 1933 and 1934 Orange County Directory. The directories proved that his mother, born in 1931, lived at least three years in the United States after she was born. The archivist signed an affidavit to that effect and Martínez was certified as an American citizen just as the judge was losing patience with the case.

In May 2011 Juan Martínez and his eldest son went back to Zacatecas to visit his American mom for the first time in more than a decade.

As she watched the raid outside the factory where Juan worked, Veronica heard from his sister-in-law that he had indeed been detained. She had an appointment with her obstetrician that day. She had asked Juan to accompany her to the appointment that morning, but he went to work instead because the factory seemed to be slowing down and he wanted to get in as many hours as possible. So Veronica pulled out of the parking lot and headed toward the doctor, full of dread.

"I knew I would eventually be hearing from Juan and he'd want to know how the OB appointment went," Veronica said.

The baby was doing well. Veronica came home with one of those small black and white ultrasound printouts of the fetus that she would wield a few nights later at the candlelight vigil for the detainees.

Veronica was able to speak to Juan after a few days, but she could not visit him for nearly a week, until their wedding day. She dropped off a bag of clothes and some cash for him and for several other detainees whose families were scared to go anywhere near the Ada County Jail.

Ed Keener, the minister who married them, recalled that jail officials were cooperative, though they had to perform the ceremony over a phone, through a thick glass window.

"When you marry somebody they are going to go off and live happily ever after," Keener recalled. "When you marry these two they were going to go off and maybe never see each other again."

He was not able to counsel Juan prior to the ceremony, but trusted in the attorneys and activists who helped arrange the jailhouse wedding. Juan and Veronica's enthusiasm and appreciation also encouraged him.

Juan fought the charges against him at first. How could it be identity theft if he had a Social Security card and driver's license in his own name? But in the end, he accepted the same deal as most of his co-workers, avoiding federal charges and almost certain prison time. Instead, the court turned him over to ICE and he was deported.

Veronica was crushed and vowed to join him in Mexico or get him back somehow. But there were other, very practical consequences of his deportation as well. Juan had helped Veronica out with bills for a while, paying her first month's rent on a new apartment that he sometimes shared and helping with grocery shopping. Veronica was still working as a home health-care provider, and was only a few months pregnant, so she started to plan ahead. When Juan was deported, she moved in with her sister, saving $300 a month, cashed in a 401K and eagerly awaited her 2008 tax refund.

In April, Veronica wrecked her truck. She had to quit her job because she could not get to the clients' homes anymore. She was seven months pregnant by then and pretty sure she could not get another job. So she sent the insurance money for the truck to Juan in Mexico and hunkered down. She was already on Medicaid and using food stamps and holding the rest of her savings to live off of when she joined Juan in Mexico.

After Victoria was born, Veronica took her and her older daughter, Mercedez, to Mexico for about ten months. Mercedez thrived there, making many friends and quickly learning Spanish. Veronica had a harder time, suffering through periods of intense loneliness. She had to rough it with the small kitchen and bathroom in an outbuilding and no central heat. She also found the cobblestone streets and steep hillsides of La Virgen difficult to navigate. When she found herself pregnant again, she and Juan decided it would be best to return to the United States to deliver the baby. Veronica did not like the hospital and private care in Mexico would have been prohibitively expensive.

"We were thinking at that time about our babies, not about ourselves," Juan said. "I never thought it was going to be that hard for her to be separate from me."

So Veronica returned home to Idaho with her two daughters after a horror of a trip that included missing the first flight because her Mexican visa had expired, then missing a connection in Mexico City.

Then she was back at her mom's house, pregnant again, still unable to work and separated from her husband.

"Juan was helping me stay off of the welfare system," Veronica said. When she came back from Mexico with $300 in her pocket, it was a different story. Veronica headed to the welfare office in Mountain Home, Idaho: "You took somebody away that was helping me stay away from the system and you know what, shabam, here I am with three kids."

After the raid, Kendall Hoyd, president of Idaho Truss, was basically shut down. He lost most of his workforce in one morning and could no longer operate.

"When you are an owner of a small business and everything that you own is on the line everyday that you operate and you're going through a construction market crash that is threatening everything you've built in your entire professional life, it's very personal," Hoyd told me some three years after the raid.

While not quite blaming the ultimate shuttering of Idaho Truss on the raid, Hoyd, who is now working for another truss company in Texas, said it was another nail in the coffin. The company had struggled through the recession and closed up shop a few months after the raid.

Hoyd reiterated that he never expected the immigration raid at the plant.

"It's just a little bit terrifying when there's a bunch of guys in flak jackets and drawn weapons in your factory," Hoyd said. He had showed up a bit late on the morning of the raid, and most of his employees were already in cuffs. The others huddled in the lobby, trying to figure out what was going on.

The Social Security Administration had sent Hoyd several "no match" letters over the years, indicating that some of his employees had potential discrepancies with the social security numbers they had provided. The letters were accompanied with instructions that Hoyd notify the employees, but did not seem to require anything else of him.

About the same time, Idaho Truss had combined with another local company, taking on some of its employees and picking up a large contract for military housing at Mountain Home Air Force Base an hour east of Boise. The base required enhanced background checks for contractors, which flagged one of the new Idaho Truss workers, setting off the ICE investigation. This may have been in addition to the tips that ICE received, though it's not completely clear.

Hoyd said that ICE contacted him during the summer of 2008 and requested employee records, which he sent. He didn't make a big announcement about it, but all of the employees knew what was going on—it was not a secret.

Hoyd had worked with many of the men, including Juan and his brother, Alex, or Alejandro, a foreman, for years. He said there was a language and cultural barrier between them, but that he had warm feelings for his Mexican employees and respected their contributions to his company and the work they put in. He paid the factory workers $11 to $13 dollars an hour and provided full health benefits. He sponsored a soccer team that some of the guys played on. And he kibitzed with them from time to time.

"I speak enough Spanish—enough to give them a hard time when the U.S. beats Mexico in a soccer game," Hoyd said.

Hoyd's best hires came through the informal recruiting network of his existing employees. Factory leaders like Juan's brother, Alejandro, who married an American and got his papers through 245i, brought good people in because it helped the company and gave them a personal boost with management, Hoyd said. He said the Social Security letters did indicate that some of his employees might not be authorized to work, but he did not know for sure who was and who was not.

One of the main criticisms of "no match" letters and workplace immigration audits is that they put employers in a position of enforcing federal immigration law, a position that few employers are qualified for or interested in dealing with. It also puts them in a position that is ripe for racial profiling, heightening suspicions of any new Spanish-speaking hires.

Hoyd described the raid and the ensuing media coverage of his company as painful and traumatic. An interesting thing happened the day after Hoyd lost sixteen workers: he fielded more than two hundred job applicants—mostly white or Mexican American—a phenomenon that warranted another story in the local paper.

ICE spokeswoman Dankers told the *Press-Tribune*: "When U.S. citizens and other legally permitted residents line up to do this work, it does fly in the perception that Americans won't take these jobs."

But Hoyd didn't see it that way. He said that two years before the raid he had always had problems filling job openings.

"None of those people would have answered that ad, not one," he said. "That kind of factory work, it's pretty hard to fill those jobs."

Hoyd, an American citizen, an entrepreneur who was born and raised in the conservative bastion of Southwest Idaho, takes a long view on immigration reform.

During the housing boom, the nation basically invited tons of unauthorized immigrants to take the tons of available jobs, he said.

"When the bubble popped, that invitation is withdrawn and now they are criminals," Hoyd said. "It's disingenuous at best."

∗   ∗   ∗

On January 21, 2009, I wrote an open letter to freshly inaugurated President Barack Obama that was published in *Boise Weekly*. It was a crowd-sourced wish list from Idaho for Obama's first year in office. This was the seventh plank:

> *Within your first year, see to it that the millions of immigrants who managed to get into the country without permission slips are made right: green cards, citizenship, amnesty, whatever it takes.*

> *The undocumented population of this country is already part of our national fabric, and millions of naturalized citizens voted for you.*

Now you must give others a chance to thrive as Americans, too.

And you must eliminate the conditions that created this huge immigrant underclass in America. Give our immigration system the tools to work again. Separate it from the Department of Homeland Security (consider disbanding the department, or even just changing its name; we didn't used to have one). Let people into the United States to work and study without having to wait a decade or more for a visa. Reunite families.

More than half of U.S. voters identified with Barack Obama on some personal level. He was our contemporary, even if he was a bit older than we thought. His background in law and community organizing gelled with our interests in civil rights and progress. He had fancy college degrees, too, even fancier than ours. We might have hung out in New York or Boston or Chicago, had our paths crossed at any point. He also had daughters and a liberated wife.

He was to be our first black president.

I voted for Obama on the strength of his global worldview. He was an American who had lived abroad, whose immediate family included Kenyan aunts and uncles and Indonesian stepsiblings and even Irish cousins. He had come into contact with all kinds of people from all over the world in his travels and studies at Columbia and Harvard. He was an antidote to American parochialism and xenophobia, especially in those years after September 11.

In retrospect, I wish I had read Obama's books earlier. Obama had an interesting but fairly conventional American childhood. He was worldly, to be sure, but his detractors also reinforced this impression of Obama as an internationalist by disingenuously painting him as a foreigner.

Obama's ideas on immigration—perhaps skewed by his handlers' modern reliance on polling data—are presented in a very clear, simplistic way in his writing and speeches. In *The Audacity of Hope,* he acknowledges that he has not always been comfortable with immigration, particularly with immigrants from Mexico and in the context of job competition with some African-American communities:

Native-born Americans suspect that it is they, and not the immigrant, who are being forced to adapt. In this way, the immigration debate comes to signify not a loss of jobs but a loss of sovereignty, just one more example—like September 11, avian flu, computer viruses, and factories moving to China—that America seems unable to control its own destiny.

But he also recognizes immigrant rights as a form of civil rights, just a few pages later, as he recalls signing an autograph for a young Hispanic girl named Cristina:

My daughters will learn Spanish and be the better for it. Cristina will learn about Rosa Parks and understand that the life of a black seamstress speaks to her own. The issues my girls and Cristina confront may lack the stark moral clarity of a segregated bus, but in one form or another their generation will surely be tested—just as Mrs. Parks was tested and the Freedom Riders were tested, just as we are all tested—by those voices that would divide us and have us turn on each other.
And when they are tested in that way, I hope Cristina and my daughters will have all read about the history of this country and will recognize they have been given something precious.
America is big enough to accommodate all their dreams.

Obama ran a campaign that immigrant justice activists identified with. It was a high-dollar, corporate-funded, professionally managed presidential campaign, but one that was imbued with a youthful activist spirit. Many young immigrants worked on his 2008 campaign. He promised to "fix the broken immigration system" with comprehensive immigration reform, including a path to citizenship for undocumented immigrants within his first year in office.

It was a promise that he did not keep.

Obama also promised to "secure the border" and crack down on employers who hire undocumented workers. With that mix of campaign pledges, he won overwhelming support from Latino voters. Obama took sixty-seven percent of the Latino vote, bringing twenty-five percent more Latino voters to the polls than had voted in 2004. That included new Latino voters in key swing states like North Carolina, Virginia and Indiana.

In the first six months of his administration, Obama's Department of Homeland Security did mostly put the brakes on military style workplace raids in favor of quiet immigration audits. The new administration's immigration cops rolled out audits at 625 companies across the country in mid-2009. They requested employee files and reviewed I-9 employment verification forms and other documentation—including some forms that employers were not legally required to provide. Rather than going in with guns blazing, ICE put the onus on employers to check up on employee paperwork and in some cases, to fire workers who could not verify their work status.

Obama was also more willing to fine employers for hiring unauthorized workers than the Bush administration had been. Bush's Department of Homeland Security collected less than $1 million in fines from employers in five years, but Obama's collected more than $8 million in its first two years.

Many assumed that Obama's increased workplace audits, quietly growing deportation record and even his appointment of former Arizona Governor Janet Napolitano as Secretary of Homeland Security were political moves calculated to bring about immigration reform in the first half of his first term. If that was the strategy, it was looking more tenuous all the time, and creating new problems for immigrant communities.

These audits had similar, if less dramatic, impacts on immigrant families and on the economy than the previous administration's raid regime had. Primary wage earners were not deported as frequently, but they still lost their jobs, pushing families with American citizen and permanent resident spouses, like Juan and Veronica, to register for food stamps and public assistance to survive. Others turned to charitable organizations, day labor or panhandling. Often, workers who lost decent jobs simply went across the street to work for even more unscrupulous employers, accepting lower wages and worse working conditions. In this way, the I-9 audits potentially bolstered the underground economy, rather than eliminating the illegal workforce as the administration intended.

Yet for his first year in office and into his second, pro-immigrant groups continued to treat the Obama administration's tactics with kid gloves—perhaps he would still deliver a path to citizenship for some of the millions of people living and working in the United States without papers.

Then the Democrats lost control of the House of Representatives in the 2010 midterm elections and it became increasingly clear that no progressive immigration reform bills would make it through Congress. Republicans called for a return to workplace immigration raids, using the continuing economic recession as a rationale.

But Obama did not need high-profile factory raids in order to boost his deportation numbers. The Department of Homeland Security was already deporting people much more efficiently than any administration in history.

Jaime & Santiago

On the morning of March 18, 2009—a few months into Obama's presidency—a black SUV idled just up the road from Jaime Reynal O'Connor's house in rural Stillwater, Minnesota, near Minneapolis. Jaime was already out taking her daughter to school. Santiago Reynal O'Connor, her husband, was getting ready to go to work. As he pulled out of the driveway, the black SUV cut him off and ICE agents detained him. They booked him at Ramsey County Jail and prepared to send him back to Argentina.

Just one day before his arrest, on their sixth wedding anniversary, Jaime and Santiago had visited their lawyer and asked if Santiago could be arrested. They had just received a letter from immigration that scared them. The attorney assured them that there was no way ICE would come and arrest him because their case was still in process. They were supposed to be called before an immigration judge first, he assured them.

The attorney was wrong. When Jaime finally heard from Santiago on the morning of his arrest, she called their attorney again. He told her he had no idea what to do and gave her another lawyer's name—a guy who wanted $10,000 to try to get Santiago in front of a judge, an expensive and unlikely proposition and an offer she wisely declined.

This was the start of a two-and-a-half year nightmare for the Reynal O'Connor family. Santiago was separated from his wife and kids—at times Jaime did not know where he was. They were robbed in Buenos Aires. They lost their home and their successful business. Their children could not understand why Santiago hadn't said goodbye to them. And even though they are now reunited, they have not recovered as a family.

"He's here, he's present but it's like his spirit has just been so damaged that I don't know…" Jaime said. "I will never know what it was like for him, it was just the darkest time in his life."

From 1996 to 2002, Argentines were part of the visa waiver program, meaning they could enter the United States for business or pleasure without applying for a visa in advance. Visitors from visa waiver countries can stay for up to ninety days. They are not supposed to work for U.S. companies, but they can conduct some business. Visa waiver countries are mostly highly developed European and Asian nations. They must meet certain U.S. economic, security and intelligence sharing criteria. In 2002, in the wake of an economic crisis in Argentina, USCIS determined that too many people from Argentina were overstaying and ended the program for Argentines.

One quirk of the visa waiver program that Jaime and Santiago's attorney should have known about is that you also waive your right to appear before an immigration judge if you enter on a visa waiver.

Santiago came to the U.S. in September 2001 on a visa waiver. He found work in Minneapolis laying television cable, though he was not supposed to work. He stayed at the youth hostel in Minneapolis. Jaime had just gotten back to Minnesota after traveling for a while, staying and working at youth hostels. She was staying at the hostel in her hometown while she got back on her feet, helping clean it to earn her keep. One day, in December, Jaime returned to the hostel late and the door was locked. Santiago let her in. They started dating a few months later and quickly started talking about a family.

"He stayed beyond the ninety days because we met," Jaime said.

More than a year later, on St. Patrick's Day, 2003 they got married and soon after, their daughter, Kaya, was born. In 2005 they went to their first attorney and applied for a marriage visa and adjustment of status. They thought they were doing things the right way, but they gradually realized that their attorney was not competent. He lost paperwork that they sent him and he never quizzed them on Santiago's immigration history—if he had, he would have known that Santiago could not adjust his status in the United States because he was already subject to a ten-year bar. His application was rejected, as was the hardship waiver they filed.

Santiago is tri-national. He was born in Argentina, but also has a Spanish passport from his grandparents and a Brazilian one from his mother. In 2003, Santiago and Jaime had visited Argentina for a few months. This visit triggered a ten-year bar for Santiago, but he didn't know it. When they returned to Minneapolis, Santi re-entered with his Spanish passport, also on a visa waiver. USCIS did not flag him as banned until he applied for adjustment of status.

After their first rejection, Jaime realized the immigration process was going to be more complicated than she thought. She found a different lawyer who seemed to know what he was doing. They wrote a much more detailed hardship letter—the first one had extolled the virtues of her husband's native country—and submitted an appeal.

Then they waited. They had spent $15,000 by now on Santi's case, between legal fees and application fees. The appeal took more than two years to process. Meanwhile, Santiago had to check in with the DMV every few months and find some way to convince them that his immigration status was still under review. Santiago had work authorization, and he and Jaime were building a very successful cable installation business. Jaime ran the business end and Santiago managed the job sites—they had ten to twenty subcontractors working for them at a time, burying underground cable through people's back yards.

In January 2009 they got word that the appeal had been denied and a few months later the black SUV came for Santiago.

Before he was deported, the *St. Paul Pioneer Press* did a story on Santiago's case.

"Yes, we've made mistakes, but we are in love," Jaime told the paper. "I can't fathom why it has to be so difficult for two people from two different countries to be together. I feel like we've paid our dues."

Jaime took Kaya and their younger son, Mateo, to see their father in jail. They had to communicate through a video screen. After the first traumatic visit, Jaime had to bribe Kaya to go another time. Jaime scrambled to find a foreman in order to salvage their business through the busy summer season. None of her elected officials seemed to be able to help— Michele Bachmann, her congressional representative, wanted nothing to do with her, Jaime said. Other members of Congress were sympathetic but declined to help because she was outside their district. The attorneys and the Argentine Embassy and the immigration agencies had little to offer as well. Jaime was on her own. The best they could do was to expedite the deportation so that Santiago did not spend too much time in jail.

After twenty-six days in jail—twenty-six trying days that Santi still won't tell her much about—he was sent home to Buenos Aires and moved back into a small room at his grandparents' house. Just before he left, a deputy who had read about Santi's case in the newspaper allowed them to spend an hour together in a jail conference room—a secret meeting that she was not to tell anyone about, but that she still cherishes to this day.

Then Santi was 6,000 miles to the south, and she was alone with their two children. Jaime described this period in the third hardship letter that she later wrote:

> *I watched every door of possibility close in my face, which just left me alone with a child in each hand. I cried myself to sleep every night. Santi had no criminal record, he was a taxpayer, a productive member of society who wanted nothing more than to support his family and watch our children grow. Yet, there he was, in a jail with murderers, rapists and child molesters. He was ripped away from everything he/we had worked so hard for...*

> *...I cried myself to sleep every night since the arrest. The toll this was already taking on my children and myself was daunting. My deep anguish when Kaya started telling me that she doesn't feel like a family anymore, her bewildering confusion about what had happened, asking when we will see Papi again, why can't he come home... the list goes on and on.*

Kaya described her anguish at losing her father as, "black bubbly goo that churns inside of her all the time." Her drawings were dark and she blew up at her mother and infant brother all the time. She snuck food, which Jaime realized later was a classic response to losing her father. And so Jaime and Santi came up with a plan to see one another. Canada has a policy that is similar to the U.S. visa waiver program, so Santi flew to Winnipeg and entered on a six-month visitor visa. Jaime made the eight-hour drive with the kids, not telling them where they were going to make it a surprise. They had a great weekend and Jaime left Kaya with her dad for the week.

The next weekend when she drove up, she brought lots of luggage and told the border guard that she was going to visit Santiago. They thought that was suspicious and denied her entry to Canada. They told her she'd need to demonstrate that she was not going to enter the country only to stay there with her foreign husband. Jaime was denied entry to Canada at 10 p.m. after a three-hour wait at the remote Pembina crossing between Grand Forks, North Dakota, and Winnipeg. She had no cell reception and Santi and Kaya were expecting her and Mateo. Then her rental car died in the no-man's land between the United States and Canada, full of all the stuff for Santi, like clothes and household goods. A Canadian official gave her a lift to the U.S. side. The U.S. Homeland Security agents would not let her wait near the crossing for a taxi and dropped her at a truck stop at 2 a.m. with her baby.

This was her new life after deportation.

The next day Jaime gathered a bunch of documents to prove that she had a business and house in Minnesota and was waved through the border. Thirty minutes after she arrived at the hostel where Santi was staying, three Canadian immigration officers knocked on their door. They interrogated Jaime and Santi for thirty minutes in front of the kids, playing good cop/bad cop and trying to catch them up in a lie. After a half an hour the agents acknowledged that they had done nothing wrong—they were both legitimate visitors to Canada. But as they left, one of the officers told them not to use Canada to solve their American immigration problems.

The Canada trips could not continue. Jaime was exhausted from the drives and the emotion and the risk. She went up alone one more time and told Santi it was not going to work. He flew back to Argentina and she went home to Stillwater in a dark mood.

Santi went to Spain for a month with his grandfather and when he got back to Argentina he called to say he was going out to a rural province and might be out of cell range for a while. That was September 2009.

Jaime waited a few days and beeped Santi's Nextel to see if he was back in range. Santi actually answered—he was in a hotel room in Nogales, Mexico. Desperate to see his family again, Santi had traveled to the Mexican border, hoping to cross over and attempt to reach Minneapolis in time for his and Jaime's shared birthday, September 6. Jaime reached him by phone in Nogales and begged him to go back to Buenos Aires.

By this point, their business was ruined and their house foreclosed. So Jaime sold most of their stuff—she let the kids keep a few treasures. They packed twelve suitcases and flew to Argentina, leaving their friends and family in Minnesota behind.

At first it worked out really well—for a few months. The family was together again and excited to explore Argentina. But then things started to break down again. Santi was not working and Jaime was unable to get a work permit. Their car was burglarized multiple times—the stereo, GPS and tires were taken—and Santiago was almost car jacked. The police did nothing. Jaime and the kids had a hard time acclimating to the foreign city and were often taken advantage of as ignorant Americans.

In November 2010, after almost a year in Argentina, Jaime decided she had to return to the U.S.—she had to work. She and the kids needed familiar, safe surroundings. They agreed that once Jaime got settled, they'd keep trying to get a waiver for Santiago, now with a third attorney.

"Saying goodbye to Santi was gruesome," Jaime wrote. "I had to hold myself together, knowing that once Santi was out of my teary sight, that I would be faced with a very long, hard journey, alone. I waited until my kids were finally asleep that night on the flight to quietly cry myself to sleep."

Jaime moved into her brother and sister-in-law's basement. She got a job waiting tables and applied for welfare—Medicaid, food stamps, medical assistance, cash assistance—anything she could get her hands on. Jaime had never sought government assistance in her life and kept reminding herself of all the taxes they had paid into the system before, when their business was prospering.

The new attorney, Michael Davis, told them they'd need to do a double waiver now. Santiago would need a waiver to return after a deportation and a hardship waiver for his ten-year bar. The third hardship letter to USCIS was much easier for Jaime to write after her time in Buenos Aires and living in her sister's basement on public assistance.

"This has been very trying on our relationship and I told him a long time ago that I would never give up," Jaime said.

While Jaime was home with the kids and had to keep moving forward for their sake, Santi was back in Argentina, estranged from his friends and family, living out of a suitcase. Alone.

"That's what he ended up with after working his ass off for years," Jaime said. "He has had the hardest time coming to terms with that."

$$* \quad * \quad *$$

In several ways, Jaime and Santiago's ordeal was the collateral damage of a complex political calculus that four successive presidents failed to solve. For more than twenty-five years, Democratic and Republican administrations and national immigrant rights organizations have supported comprehensive immigration reform. But figuring out the politics of such reform has proven an impossible task.

During the Reagan administration, conservatives saw comprehensive reform as a way to further seal the borders. The 1986 Immigration Reform and Control Act is the closest thing to comprehensive reform that has passed Congress in the last generation. IRCA is generally viewed as punitive to immigrants, but the punitive measures were balanced by a large-scale amnesty for undocumented immigrants with deep ties to the United States, winning bipartisan support in Congress and the signature of President Ronald Reagan.

Ten years later, a Republican Congress approved the Illegal Immigration Reform and Immigrant Responsibility Act, and President Bill Clinton signed it. The 1996 bill was not comprehensive. It focused on border control, made deportations easier, criminalized many immigration violations and established the bans that now prevent so many people from "getting in line for a visa."

After losing the IIRIRA fight, immigrant rights advocates unified around a "new" version of comprehensive immigration reform. Civil rights groups joined big business, agriculture and some labor interests to come up with a legislative framework that included some legalization, more guest workers, border security and workplace enforcement measures in an attempt to build support among both Democrats and Republicans. President George W. Bush embraced all of these planks by his second term, as did many Republicans in the Senate.

Bush began his presidency with a cautious line on immigration reform, mostly calling for a new guest worker program. He was willing to work with reform advocates and even discussed a new immigration bill with Mexican President Vicente Fox. Then the September 11, 2001, attacks ended any real discussion of immigration reform for a few years.

In Bush's second term, the debate picked up steam again, but a radicalized conservative flank in the Republican Party, fueled by anti-Islamic and anti-immigrant sentiment, went head to head with the president. A 2006 proposal by Wisconsin Republican James Sensenbrenner, H.R. 4437, read like a laundry list for immigration restrictionists: border fences, large fines for undocumented immigrants and their employers, mandated computer database checks for employment verification and measures intended to link the threat of terrorism to immigration.

The portion of H.R. 4437 that drew the strongest reaction—and drew people like Nicole and Margo to protest in the streets—prohibited any-one from assisting, transporting or harboring an "illegal alien" inside the United States. Millions of people marched against the Sensenbrenner bill in cities across the United States because it would have left any mixed-status family—tens of millions of people, at least—open to prosecution.

The Sensenbrenner bill passed the G.O.P-led House of Representatives and overshadowed a more comprehensive, Bush-backed reform package making its way through the Senate. By the fall of 2006 it became clear that Bush would not be able to claim victory on immigration reform.

In response, Bush pursued a scorched earth policy, viewing immigrant families as collateral damage in his attempt to appear tough on illegal immigration. Bush theorized that if he appealed to the right flank of his party by stepping up immigration raids across the country and patrols along the border, more Republicans might be willing to compromise on guest workers and even eventually deliver a path to citizenship for undoc-umented immigrants.

Juan, Veronica, and their three daughters were victims of this new po-litical tactic, and Santiago, Jaime, Kaya, and Mateo bore the brunt of the same politicized enforcement early in Obama's first term.

The failure of immigration reform during the Bush years left immi-gration advocates licking their wounds and retreating to their corners to figure out a new strategy. The failure of reform also emboldened groups of self-appointed Minutemen—armed militias that patrolled the border looking for illegal crossings. And it led, in part, to the Tea Party move-ment during the 2008 presidential race, which held anti-immigrant sen-timents at the core of its platform. Some states began to pass their own punitive immigration laws, including Arizona's S.B. 1070 in 2010 and Alabama's H.B. 56 in 2011.

At the same time, the 2006 marches and Obama's rise to the White House empowered a new generation of immigrant leaders. The Dream Act had been one of the major planks of comprehensive immigration re-form since 2001, and immigrant youth who would qualify now emerged with a new strategy for achieving immigration reform. They sought to break the Dream Act away from the wider realm of comprehensive re-form—if no grand compromise was to be had, at least some piecemeal reforms could be considered. The Dreamers, as they began to call them-selves, changed the terms of the debate by talking about their own experiences rather than continuing to let high-powered lobbyists or Washington, D.C., advocacy groups do it for them.

Both Democrats and Republicans originally championed the Dream Act, but every year it was caught up in the larger politics surrounding immigration reform. Finally, at the end of 2010, before Republicans took over the House, young immigrants successfully lobbied for a stand-alone Dream Act vote. Throughout that summer and fall, undocumented students and youth made their immigration statuses public, telling the world their stories on radio and television, in print and via the internet. In the final tally, the Senate came up five votes short of stopping a filibuster on the bill—five Democrats had voted against bringing the Dream Act to a vote.

In the next year and a half, the movement kept up a constant barrage of pressure on the White House. They used sit-ins, demonstrations, marches and "coming out" ceremonies to show that they were "undocumented and unafraid." They targeted specific politicians—courting Republicans as much or more than Democrats. They got arrested committing civil disobedience and dared Obama to deport them. And then in June 2011, a Pulitzer-prize winning journalist named Jose Antonio Vargas outed himself as undocumented in the *New York Times* Sunday Magazine, insisting that he was perfectly American, save one piece of paper. Thousands more undocumented youth who did not choose the way they arrived in the United States followed suit, declaring their status and that they too were part of the American fabric.

In June 2012, Vargas appeared on the cover of *Time* magazine with other "undocumented Americans" from all over the world. The headline proclaimed:

We Are Americans*

*Just Not Legally

Within a week of the Time cover, the Obama administration announced that it would grant two-year temporary stays of deportation to some immigrant youth who would otherwise qualify for the Dream Act.

Matias & Lindsay

Matias Ramos was one of the first undocumented students to go public with his status. In April 2009, he appeared on national television in a suit and tie and told CNN anchor Heidi Collins that he just wanted to officially be part of American society as he'd felt he'd been since coming to California from Argentina at thirteen years old.

"When my parents decided to come to this country, they told me... that we wanted to be in a place where we could work hard and be rewarded, and that is what the United States has historically been," Matias said on national television.

I spoke to Matias in December 2010, just before the Dream Act went up for a vote in the Senate.

"First you feel all alone, then you feel like other people have your back," he said. "The voice of the student in asking for the Dream Act has really changed that."

Dream activists mobilized thousands of supporters, particularly via on-line petition drives. Whenever a Dreamer received a deportation order, thousands of supporters signed petitions and flooded local ICE offices with phone calls.

In Matias' case, 7,000 people signed a petition on his behalf when he was detained at the Minneapolis International Airport in February 2010. Matias believes that the support and public attention to his case helped delay his deportation.

"It has a huge positive impact... in as far as I'm able to bring attention to the issue." Matias said. "It's not just me against the government; my removal would have an impact on other people's lives."

One life that would have been seriously affected by his removal was that of his American girlfriend—now wife—Lindsay McCluskey. Lindsay had been dating Matias since before he was detained.

"There is a whole community of people who feel it's in their self interest to not have him deported," Lindsay said. "He's changed me a lot in that regard. I didn't used to see the struggle of undocumented youth as my struggle at all."

Lindsay is a fellow activist working in the student and labor movements. The two met in August 2009 at a trivia night at a D.C. bar, though Matias' reputation preceded him.

"I knew about Matias before I actually knew him," Lindsay said.

Of course, he knew about her as well… they had met a few months prior, but Lindsay had forgotten about it.

Matias' attorney mentioned his American girlfriend in appealing the deportation order to demonstrate that he had strong ties to the United States. The two had discussed marriage, but Matias also hoped for the Dream Act to pass, or to have his case put aside after administrative review. And Lindsay never felt he needed her to get a green card.

"I've never felt that it was my job and Matias has never put pressure on me to do anything for his case," she said. "For him it's more than about his case. It's about the relationship of undocumented people to the U.S."

Matias struggled with his role in the movement and his personal life for a while, but in the end, the decision was easy.

In October 2011, when Lindsay was out of town on a work trip, Matias bought a ring at a jewelry store near his office. When she got back they attended a gala event together and after the event went for a walk around D.C. Lindsay noticed Matias was being a bit awkward and then he got down on one knee and asked her to marry him.

"It felt right," Matias said of his decision to pop the question. "I felt there was an uncertainty, but that uncertainty was never going to go away. Parts were about immigration and parts of it are in general about committing and building a life with someone, which everyone thinks about. The task of getting married is daunting enough for the regular person."

In December, they had a small ceremony with family at City Hall in D.C. Once he was married to an American citizen, Matias filed for adjustment of status. He had a hearing in August 2012, his deportation was canceled in late March 2013 and then USCIS notified him that his medical records had expired and would have to be updated—at a cost of $160—before they could issue a green card. Lindsay associates with many social activists and comes from a liberal, politically aware family. But even her circle is bewildered by the complexity of Matias' case.

"Most of my friends and most people in my life who don't know about immigration reform have often times said, 'Why didn't Matias just apply for citizenship,'" she said.

Matias and Lindsay celebrated Obama's announcement of deferred action for Dreamers, continue to watch immigration reform closely and believe that Obama wants to be on the right side of history. But Matias vacillates between feeling hopeful and dejected about the prospects for immigration reform.

"My beliefs may not be represented," Matias said. "But what comes through will benefit a lot of people."

The immigration movement has expanded, Matias said, incorporating new voices from places like Silicon Valley and evangelical churches. There is no doubt that youth activists like him moved the tactics forward. Families split by immigration law—including Dreamer couples like Lindsay and Matias—appealed to the public to stave off deportations throughout 2011 and 2012.

And their message was simple: We are Americans.

✳   ✳   ✳

The Obama administration's legacy on immigration remains unclear.

Obama entered office promising to champion immigration reform, including specific support for the Dream Act. But after two years, he was unable to accomplish anything in Congress. Obama said that Congress refused to act on his immigration initiatives, but many observers feel he failed to push them strongly enough.

In the second part of his first term, Obama was more willing to make limited, bureaucratic reforms without Congressional action. In June 2011, he directed ICE to exercise "prosecutorial discretion" in deprioritizing deportations of people who have strong ties to the United States and no criminal records. In January 2012, he reached out to mixed-status couples, promising to allow some to file their hardship waivers from within the United States, decreasing their risk in leaving the country without a guaranteed return. Throughout his term, Obama fought the anti-immigration measures passed in states like Arizona and Alabama in the courts—and won. And then he announced the administrative relief for some Dreamers in June 2012.

Meanwhile, overall immigration numbers continue to rise. As Princeton demographer Douglas Massey and former Mexican Foreign Minister Jorge G. Castañeda pointed out in a June 2012 *New York Times* op-ed, 160,000 Mexicans earned permanent residency in the U.S. every year since 2005. Almost 1.5 million Mexicans came with temporary work, business and exchange visas in 2010.

Illegal immigration from Mexico reached a net zero in recent years as well, as more Mexicans returned home and fewer crossed over without visas. The U.S. economy, stepped up immigration enforcement—including Obama's deportation record—and changes to the labor force and economy in Mexico have all contributed to this stabilization causing Massey and Castañeda to wonder if, "time, and common-sense decisions by Mexican migrants, have brought us nearly everything immigration reform was supposed to achieve."

Perhaps this result is Obama's real end game on immigration reform—visa reform through bureaucratic efficiency and a status quo limbo for the undocumented population.

But despite the apparent political and demographic gains for immigrants under Obama, immigrant families continue to feel the brunt of the administration's enhanced enforcement policies. Obama boosted the number of Border Patrol officers, built miles of new border fence and deployed drones along the border. ICE's prosecutorial discretion initiative was largely seen as a failure, even within the White House. During the first eight months of ICE reviewing its deportation case backlog—meant to identify people with strong ties to the U.S. and no criminal record—only 1.5 percent of cases were dismissed.

Obama also expanded Secure Communities, a federal program that provides data to ICE whenever local police and sheriff's departments detain suspects. Many advocates, including some local police officials, view the program as an immigration dragnet that lands minor criminals and even noncriminals in deportations proceedings. An estimated 88,000 immigrants with U.S. citizen spouses or children were detained through Secure Communities between 2008 and 2011, according to the Warren Institute on Law and Social Policy at the University of California-Berkeley.

There are no good statistics on how many Americans like Veronica Diaz and Jaime Reynal O'Connor have been separated from their spouses because of workplace raids, routine traffic stops, risky trips over the border or run-ins with ICE, because the number of immigrants with American citizen spouses is not tracked.

Only recently did the Department of Homeland Security begin to track American kids separated from their parents through deportation. Between 1998 and 2007, the government deported an estimated 100,000 parents of U.S. citizen children. In the first six months of 2011, DHS deported 46,486 immigrants with at least one U.S. citizen child, according to ICE statistics.

A hard-hitting 2011 study by the Applied Research Center, a racial justice think tank, estimated that at least 5,100 children were placed in foster care and prevented from reuniting with deported or detained immigrant parents.

These separations clearly have long-lasting psychological implications for the families involved and for society at large. Not a lot of research has been done on the impacts of detention and family separation, but Denver psychologist Donna Peters said that many of the immigrant families she sees are clearly experiencing trauma.

"People are still in a little bit of shock," Peters said. "There is some sense of disbelief—there is some thought that if you marry a U.S. citizen it will be okay."

Peters evaluates couples who are filing hardship waivers to determine the types of trauma the U.S. citizen spouse is likely to suffer if separated from his or her spouse or forced to relocate to another country. Immigration attorneys frequently include a psychological evaluation in their hardship waiver applications.

"It's been my impression that having a psychological evaluation can't hurt and in many cases it's helpful," she said.

The first thing Peters notices is that some families regret applying for the waiver in the first place because they had no idea of the bureaucracy they would be up against.

"There is some anger. The U.S. citizen is angry at the government for making the process so difficult," she said.

Many couples have grown used to living under the radar and are unsure how to navigate the system again, whether encountering government officials by choice or when caught up in deportation proceedings. The U.S. citizen partner often experiences adjustment disorders, anxiety and depression, Peters said. They feel fear and have difficulty with future planning, Peters added.

The difficulty planning is compounded by constantly shifting policies. It takes years for mixed-status couples to figure out what to do and once they make a decision the political climate may have shifted again. Nicole and Margo spent years debating the merits of moving to Mexico together, as they will do in deciding where to settle in the future. Beth and Carlos struggled over the decision to ask for a hardship waiver. Susie and Roberto are still not sure which route to take.

Jaime and Santiago tried to access the immigration system, but were thwarted by poor legal advice, bad timing and a federal agency tasked with mass deportations. In August 2011, Jaime and Santiago finally won their third appeal, and it happened quicker than they expected. Jaime flew to Buenos Aires to pick him up.

Upon landing in Minneapolis, Jaime drove Santiago to their old house in Stillwater. He got out of the car and walked up the street, stopping at the exact spot that immigration had picked him up two years prior. He sat for a while, considering his place in the world, his changed role in the United States, his family.

"That's where we began again," Jaime said. "Coming back together and trying to meld those changes and try and have a relationship again is and has been for us very difficult."

Santiago moved into the basement apartment with his family, trying to fit in to the life they had assembled in his absence. He found work, in cable installation again, and they eventually moved into their own house.

Jaime shared their story hoping that others might learn from their struggle. Santiago has not been willing to talk about his experience yet. He won't talk about it because even though he has a green card and is reunited with his family, the deportation weighs heavily on his psyche. Their story is not over.

Veronica and Juan continue their struggle to stay together. They had few choices after Juan was deported. They did not have the luxury of planning ahead—they had very little savings, little family support and did not appear to be eligible for any type of immigration relief. The separation really hurt Veronica, especially after she returned from Mexico pregnant and exhausted. She moved into her mother's cluttered house in Mountain Home. She had a long recovery after her third pregnancy and injured her knee. She put on too much weight—the doctors told her to lose 200 pounds before they would operate on her knee.

She ended up placing her hopes in Mexico, with its fresh vegetables, beans, and rice.

"I'm better off if I just go to Mexico," Veronica said. "It will take a while to lose all that. I can't just drop fifty pounds a month. I have to lose weight and tone at the same time."

In November 2011, Veronica and her three girls loaded up her red minivan and headed south again, first to visit family in California—her family and Juan's family—and then to continue on to Mexico. Juan still had seven years left before he could appeal to the U.S. to return with his wife and children.

"I'm actually really excited to be with Juan and for him to meet Sara," she told me just before hitting the road. "As long as I have Juan by my side, the girls are going to sprout up into neat little human beings. Look at Juan: He's turned out awesome and he grew up in Mexico."

Meanwhile, as Barack Obama announced new immigration initiatives for immigrant youth and mixed-status families, the deportations continued. By September 2011, just three years into his first term, the Obama administration had deported more than one million people. One million—a record deportation rate for any U.S. president. By the end of his first term, Obama's Department of Homeland Security had deported 1.5 million and was on track to deport 2 million people at the end of 2013, even as Congress began to debate comprehensive immigration reform again. George W. Bush deported 1.6 million people in his eight years as president.

To many immigrant families, Obama remains the Deporter in Chief.

Chapter 9

Alienation

~

Nicole Salgado

CHAPTER 9

Under the Radar (Spring 2003-Fall 2004)

I eventually began to lose faith in a political solution to our problem and decided it was time we steered our own course. Margo had grown tired of living invisibly, the complications it entailed and the headaches it created for those who cared about him.

I'd forgiven him for waffling over our engagement. I understood his worry. Margo was so concerned about ruining my life because he loved me so much. I just didn't buy the basic equation that me + Margo + moving to Mexico = my life, ruined. And I did my best to convince him of that. I felt like we just needed to work on our relationship more, in order to overcome all these challenges. It may have been naïve, but it was better than splitting up. We made up and moved forward with a plan.

Margo was going out of his mind in the U.S. and missed Mexico. But I wasn't ready to go south yet. In the early summer of 2003, I took my third trip home to New York since we'd started dating—the third time that Margo stayed behind while I visited my family. He hadn't seen his family for over two years. Neither of us wanted to have a long-distance relationship, but neither did I want Margo to cross the border by himself again.

I had just started the new job at the high school, and I'd also applied to graduate school to get a master's in science education. When I received a grad school acceptance letter in December, we came up with a "plan." I'd pay off my school loans and my car, we'd save up for a house down in Mexico, and once I graduated from my program, we'd move. In the meantime, we'd keep on, "under the radar."

Half Moon Bay, our former residence, is an agricultural town on the south side of a crescent shaped bay that also attracts tourists. Princeton, the town on the north side, is a quaint and functional village with a harbor, restaurants, and an Air Force station. Living in the area for a year gave me some insight to the living situations of the undocumented immigrants who worked and raised their families there.

Margo and I would often go to the harbor in Princeton, on the north side of Half Moon Bay, to buy live Dungeness crab, grab dinner at Mezzaluna Italian Restaurant, or take a walk on the beach path. Beyond Princeton's outer breakwater, the mighty Pacific meets rocky Pillar Point, marking the offshore location of Maverick's, which in high season boasts fifty-foot-plus monster waves and world-class surfing. Margo's former co-worker, Salinas, lived not too far from the beach.

When we visited Salinas on the weekends, I would often join his wife Magda (I've changed their names to protect their identities) in the kitchen. One time when we were making tamales I asked Margo, who often cooks at our house, if he was going to join us. He looked at me innocently while the rest of them broke out in peals of laughter. "These ladies don't let men into the kitchen," Salinas joked. When I frowned, Magda just smiled, showing her two silver front teeth, and showed me how to properly strain the red sauce.

Margo had relied on Salinas to hold the title and registration on his truck. Salinas was also undocumented when he first arrived from Michoacán, but because he went to the States much earlier than Margo, he was present for the 1986 amnesty. And so Salinas had a driver's license, which helped with official dealings with the DMV. He probably would have been happy to continue registering Margo's truck in his name, but by that point it made more sense to put the truck in my name. So when Margo decided it was time to sell his '84 *Professional* Nissan, I showed him a few tricks for browsing cars and VIN records online. He settled on a white 1995 Ford Ranger, paid for it in cash, and the seller signed the title over to me. I would later renew the registration for that truck and others we owned.

Margo and I stopped by Magda and Salinas' to show off his new wheels. They had two boys who both attended public school in Half Moon Bay. The older one spoke very little English but was an American-born citizen, while the younger one was born in Mexico but was boisterous and friendly, often chatting in English with me. Although Salinas had used his green card to get a driver's license, he'd later sold it. Magda had no papers at all.

I often pondered how they managed the logistics of a family with several different immigration statuses. When I heard that they had gone home to visit family, I wondered how they justified taking the risk, or what would happen to their boys if one of them got caught.

Another friend of mine also lived in the neighborhood. I had met Leticia (also not her real name) in the house we rented in Half Moon Bay. She was 19 years old and had come a year and a half earlier from rural Guanajuato, a state neighboring Querétaro. She didn't speak a word of English, which meant she taught me how to make *tinga* in our landlord's kitchen entirely in Spanish. About a month after we moved in, she went to live with her sister's family.

One day I stopped by to visit and, seeing how much energy her sister's boy had, I asked them if they wanted to join me for a walk up on the trail. They didn't look enthusiastic. I asked if they ever went out to walk, living as close to the beach as they did. "No, Nicole, we never go out," her sister responded. "Things can happen to people. It's not safe." I couldn't help but feel a little surprised. I was confused about whether she meant it was unsafe as a woman, as a person without papers, or both.

While I still had all the rights of an American citizen, having an un-documented partner and friends opened my eyes to what ostracism felt like in my own country. I'd considered driving without a license as the biggest risk for immigrants being apprehended by the authorities, but Leticia and Magda worked in greenhouses, which were subject to work-place raids. Their fear of the *migra* probably confronted them every time they stepped out of their houses. The handful of other Mexican families I came to know, were only a small fraction of the people living in our town who maintained invisibility like Margo, eking out a living every day and contributing to the U.S. economy, while essentially hiding in their homes.

Our Christmas gift that winter was to finally meet each other's families. My parents and my brother flew out to visit us for Christmas, and I went down to Mexico for a visit over New Year's.

My family was excited to finally meet Margo after two years. We hit all the classic tourist spots in San Francisco that Margo had never seen be-fore: Alcatraz, Chinatown, and the conservatory and gardens at Golden Gate Park. We visited Margo's job sites, showing off his skills, and Margo picked up the bills while we were out and about, demonstrating his mag-nanimous personality. But ultimately I was happy that Margo and my family finally spent some quality time together, and they left assured that I was in good hands.

When it was my turn to meet his family, I flew to León, Guanajuato. Margo's brother, whom I'd met in the States, picked me up and took me to the house where they grew up in Querétaro, two hours away.

Before I left for Mexico, Margo tried to prepare me as best he could. He described the city's landmarks and the approach to their neighbor-hood. But nothing could fully ready me for the overwhelming sensation of walking into his childhood home where his large family greeted me all at once in Spanish. Meeting the in-laws is hard enough as it is, but having to meet more than a dozen of them by myself in another country in another language made my nerves skyrocket. My head spun and I needed to sit down. I was temporarily mute.

They were amazingly perceptive though, saying that I needed some chamomile tea and time alone to rest. I was grateful that they understood. They took my bags up to the room one of the sisters loaned me. The surroundings were so different than anything I'd ever seen—from the patterns of stones and tiles on the floors, to the jagged cracks, exposed rebar, and mélange of pastel colors on the walls, to the flowerpots and children everywhere.

I spent a fun week touring Querétaro and the surrounding towns with Margo's family. I got a chance to really connect with them, and they seemed genuinely glad that I was there. The hardest parts were explaining why Margo couldn't also be there with me, difficulties with the phone, and keeping track of all his relatives' names. I teared up when his mother cried that she couldn't see her son.

I also experienced my first culture shocks—even though I'd been to Mexico a half dozen times before. I had the impression that the way Margo's family did certain things was unusual or irrational. But I really enjoyed all the artistry, dancing downtown on New Year's Eve and the desert landscape. I could see why Margo missed home. Perhaps most importantly, I was able to empathize with how difficult it was for him to be in the United States.

Not too long after I returned, in the spring of '04, we started looking for another place in the Bay Area to rent. We were saving money renting from the Oaxacan family, but it had become an uncomfortable living situation. There was a rather unequal domestic arrangement between the forty-something husband and the twenty-something wife. Besides his authoritarian personality, the husband had papers, and enjoyed many privileges over his wife. He could leave the house whenever he pleased, drove three cars, held a job, flew back and forth to their home country of Oaxaca, and ultimately made the final decisions on just about everything.

It created cultural gaps we were simply unable or unwilling to bridge. Our different family styles ultimately led to an inescapable conclusion that we were better off not living in the same house.

We couldn't find a good deal in terms of size and price on the Coastside, and at least for the time being, both of us were working on the Peninsula. So we looked into renting an apartment on the Bay side. When we finally submitted a rental application and I had to tell the landlord that no, my partner didn't have a valid driver's license for a background check, I thought we had run into the ultimate deal breaker. But in the end, he accepted our application and we soon moved into a one-bedroom flat in Redwood City, our last rental in California.

It seemed like the farther we moved from San Gregorio, the coastal town where we met, the closer we got to D-Day—departure to Mexico. I still missed my home in New York, and now I could already feel myself starting to miss California. But I was having so many inhospitable experiences in my own country, such as not being able to fly home with my partner, needing to register his vehicles for him and realizing how hard it'd be to buy a home together.

Life was good in our new apartment, and my first year of graduate school and teaching high school was hectic but satisfying. Still, Margo's discontent was growing. It had been a year since he first started voicing a desire to return home, and in the summer of 2004, he dropped the bomb on me that he wanted to move back to Mexico within the next six months.

As upset as his announcement made me, it wasn't unfounded. I was up late every night studying or grading, probably neglecting our relationship and being more impatient than normal. He'd been having frustrations on the job with his boss who'd often leave him in charge of the job site and with irresponsible coworkers and client relations for a long period of time. He was slipping into depression, saying he was "bad" and "bad for me." But this time I took his mood less personally. Frankly, I was too busy with school and work to freak out too much.

Instead, I decided to convince him to come with me to New York to visit my family that summer. I'd seen his home finally, and it dawned on me that it might be one of the last opportunities for him to see where I grew up. I figured if we drove instead of flying and I did most of the driving, we'd be less likely to run into problems. Margo loathed taking time off from work and never wanted to travel more than a few hours from the Bay Area. But to my surprise, he agreed.

It was an epic trip. We hit a ton of great places and Margo got to meet my grandmother and stand under the majestic hardwood trees I climbed in my youth. I think he mostly enjoyed himself, but he could never quite relax.

For example, we took a family jaunt to the beach on northeastern Lake Ontario, not too far from the Canadian border. It's a beautiful region where I made countless visits as a child and teenager, and I was delighted to take Margo there.

We stopped at a candy store that had totem pole-like pillars on the porch. I was looking at the pictures in my digital camera as we drove away. Suddenly Margo slid down a bit in his seat and hunched forward as he looked out the window. I looked out myself and saw a Border Patrol Jeep less than 100 yards away.

"Mom, I think we need to get out of here," I said urgently, and after explaining, the whole group was nervous until we were out of sight of the Jeep. The experience left us a bit shaken until we got home, but Margo's nervousness never totally diminished. It even affected his driving, and I'd have to take over the wheel once in a while when he was feeling shaken.

We found some relief in wild places like Yellowstone, the Little Bighorn Mountains, the Badlands, Salt Lake City, and Lake Tahoe. They sparked emotions I hadn't seen before in Margo. Seeing all that wildlife in so much abundance delighted him—especially in Yellowstone, but even in museums. I have a snapshot of him with a kidlike-grin on his face, waving from behind a dinosaur skeleton. Ultimately, I decided the trip had been worth the risk.

It also had long lasting implications. We hardly had a single disagreement for an unusually long period of time. Margo dropped the topic of moving back to Mexico for quite a while. Tahoe had impressed him so much that not too long after we got back, we decided to return to camp with friends, two of whom had been working undocumented in the U.S. for years.

During the camping trip we chatted about a lot of things, especially the differences between life in Mexico and the States. After we dropped them back off in the Bay Area, we lingered at dusk in the cul-de-sac by their house. They were another mixed status family with a U.S. citizen daughter and undocumented mom who'd had an unsuccessful attempt at adjusting status, and now had an undocumented boyfriend. Somehow we'd gotten on the subject of accidents and wills. One of us commented that if something happened to one of us, not having any legal say for the other meant we wouldn't be able to make sure our partner's desires were carried out. The conversation impacted Margo and I deeply, and we continued discussing it on our way home.

It had been almost three years since we'd started dating, and a little less than that since we'd gotten engaged, but that night we made a decision. It was unlikely that our marriage would have any impact on Margo's immediate immigration status, but our lives were too linked for us to justify putting off getting married. We soon planned a date for December of that same year. Our love and commitment to each other would go under the radar no longer.

Our Wedding (December 2004)

My dress wasn't white, but silver, for the Aztec goddess Tonantzin. Margo wore no tie, but a suit with a white rose on the lapel. It was a magical day, perfect in every way—like the times when we first met—all about love, and love only. It was both a respite from and a rejection of the kinds of worries that had confronted us since we'd gotten serious. From tasting wedding cakes to picking out balloons, it was so much fun to finally get to celebrate our love.

Our wedding was a fusion in every sense. Our entire circle helped with the preparations and attended our special event. Although Margo's immediate family was unable to join us, some of his cousins, friends, and coworkers were present, plus my family and friends from New York and the Bay Area, even some colleagues and students.

The ritual had many different cultural roots. After walking into the historic Pacifica firehouse to the music of Joanne Shenandoah, my parents gave me away under a Jewish chuppah made of a Guatemalan weaving. Rudi rang the Tibetan bowl next to Sue, who officiated. Halfway through the ceremony, which was based on a Native American prayer, my brother played "Imagine" on his acoustic guitar. I'd had the phrase *"amor sin fronteras"* engraved on Margo's ring, and after handing my bouquet of roses to my best buddy Sara, we sealed our vows *para siempre*.

It was a sun-drenched day in the middle of the rainy season, and surfers dotted the ocean in the background of almost every picture. After everyone ate their fill and took turns on the mic, live belly dancers whisked us to the dance floor for an evening of revelry.

At one point the back of my dress was accidentally soaked with tequila even though we only served wine and beer. But I hardly batted an eye. It's hard to think of a time when I'd been more thrilled. Sometime around midnight, we signed our California State marriage license, making the best day of our lives "official."

The Last Straws (2005-2006)

After the wedding, Margo and I still hadn't planned exactly when we would move. We just knew that the day was coming. In the meantime, we made the most of our lives in the States.

Although my days as a teacher and a grad student were filled with grading and research, my thesis project fascinated me. I was developing an innovative environmental stewardship class at the high school for my master's degree project. During the 2004-2005 academic year, I had to recruit enough students to the new class to launch it during the next school year. It was a rewarding project that led me to imagine how I could continue my work when we moved to Mexico.

Margo was busier than ever at work. He eventually split with the boss who had hired him when he first started working in the States. He'd become too frustrated to continue working for him. In the fall of '05 he began working with an energetic Coastside builder who owned a small construction company. They developed a particularly rewarding work relationship.

We were enjoying so much of what the Bay Area had to offer: good friends, incredible landscapes, great food (our favorites were Thai and Indian), and of course, salsa dancing. The music was a bridge that deepened our bond and helped me to not only embrace Margo's Spanish-speaking culture as my own, but also inspired me to embark on a new journey together.

August 2005
[From a note to Margo] After this year, I will be so ready to join you, in any endeavor you choose, should it be [move to Mexico or] stay in the U.S. and attempt citizenship should the bill up for passage actually

pass... Last night when we danced salsa at Club Barcelona to Celia Cruz, I felt like I was spinning on air. Whirling about dancing with you, I lost [track] of time—united with my partner and ecstatic... There are very few experiences as enjoyable to me than being surround-ed by loved ones and good music. I am so blessed with both. Thank you for everything you've given me.

Thanks to Margo's help, I finally paid off my college loans and my car, and started to save money. Things were going great with my new environmental stewardship class, my master's project was approved, and I was also presenting teacher-training workshops around the state.

Margo's new job also yielded great results—both for him and his boss. When he first started, Margo observed that his new boss was often overly impatient and demanding with the work crews, which made them work even more slowly, so he immediately pointed out the self-defeating behavior. Rather than ignoring Margo, or worse, retaliating, his new boss thanked him for bravely providing that insight and rewarded him with his trust and esteem.

When I was about to graduate, I had to make good on a decision I'd made with Margo a couple years prior: that once I graduated from my master's program, I'd accompany him to Mexico. And yet even Margo, who for so long had been dying to go home to Mexico, was torn about leaving. Our successes had given us a false sense of security, and the idea of staying in the U.S. to continue all that we'd cultivated was attractive. But nothing had changed politically—in fact, the atmosphere was going downhill for immigrants in the U.S.

That winter, the California State Assembly passed a new law that would have allowed individuals such as Margo to apply for a driver's license. Former Governor Gray Davis had signed such a bill in 2003, a ray of hope for us in that it could have decreased Margo's chances of running into problems on the road. But the 2003 law was repealed and then our hopes were promptly dashed again when Arnold Schwarzenegger, who had replaced Davis in a recall election, vetoed the bill.

A couple of my coworkers in the religious studies department at the high school recognized how deeply involved I was with the Mexican cul-ture and the issues our family was dealing with, and invited me along on two volunteer service trips for students to Mexico. By participating, I realized how far I'd come in terms of language and cultural understanding.

On the first trip, our students grappled with the subject of border injustice. At a section of the border in Tijuana painted with tombstones, the girls unabashedly climbed up the corrugated metal fence to argue with a Border Patrol agent about why we were able to visit Mexico so easily but Mexicans who wanted to work in the U.S. couldn't find a safe way to do so. My co-leader and I hung back at first, not wanting to get the group in trouble, but when we saw that the agent was actually engaged in a meaningful discussion with them, we joined. In the end, the agent couldn't come up with a winning argument, admitting that it was "just a job."

The years of being unable to obtain political legitimacy for my husband in my country had taken their toll on my once optimistic spirit. I had been a brave changemaker in the environmental field, but even so I was extremely nervous revealing my personal immigration story to my students on the trip. But they had empathized so deeply, and were so genuinely concerned about our fate, that it galvanized me to do something for undocumented immigrants beyond the walls of my home. In the trip's aftermath, I became more politicized about border issues. Activism was a concrete antidote, albeit small and temporary, to my feeling of powerlessness.

At the time, controversy was swirling regarding James Sensenbrenner's draconian House Bill 4437, which would have, among other things, made it illegal to simply drive with an undocumented immigrant as a passenger in your vehicle. The idea that just living with and going grocery shopping with my husband could soon be considered a felony was, to say the least, morally abhorrent to me. My first action was to circulate the following petition, which many of my high school colleagues and students signed:

March 29, 2006
An election year fight is under way in the United States Congress and in our communities. Millions have been in the streets demonstrating since Friday. Millions more will become acutely involved in what promises to be a battle for the political upper hand in the argument that has the power to divide families, parishes, workplaces, and friendships.

On one extremely polarized side are politicians who want to completely crack down on immigration into the United States, freeze our demographics, and make it a felony to enter illegally, have relations (pastoral, friendship, medical, etc.) with anyone who has entered illegally, and cease to give citizenship to infants born in the United States, if their parents are of "illegal" origin. This type of bill, sponsored by James Sensenbrenner, has passed the House of Representatives. It has created huge outcry in the immigrant, pastoral, and medical communities (...)

Unfortunately, nowhere in this argument does any side bring up the questions or realities that people are unable to voice about immigration in general:

- *How many times has our country done this before with an ethnic group?*
- *How can we refuse to give full rights to individuals who carry our economy?*
- *U.S. economic policies such as NAFTA have helped the Mexican economy to ruins.*
- *Have Christians forgotten their first edict, forgive and love thy neighbor?*
- *Have we forgotten that every one of us is an immigrant to this land?*

We are thankful that our Catholic bishops and Archbishops are speaking out already against the House bill 4437. We stand with these leaders and hope that they will incite us to demand more expansive protections. As one of our local or state leaders you have the power to become a beacon of safe-haven for immigrants. Many municipalities have already created "immigrant safe zones" where they will not have to worry if harsh and discriminatory bills pass Congress.

We ask for your assurance that under your purview, immigrants will not be arrested for feeding their families. Furthermore, we ask you for assurance that those who befriend, minister, treat, or serve immigrants will be protected, and not arrested. In contrast, we ask you that you proactively support the idea that as Americans we are all neighbors and family. None of us deserve to suffer and all of us deserve the dignity to seek a better life. We thank you for your support and hope to hear from you soon.

Sincerely,
The Undersigned

That spring, we weighed several different factors concerning our fate. Our plans to move once I graduated, the vetoed driver's license bill, budget cuts at the high school, a third (disappointing) opinion from a lawyer in San Francisco, and a recent promotion offer from Margo's boss.

Margo had initially suggested that I could stay to work for another school year while he went home to start building our house. Although I didn't want to ask him to stay in the States any longer, I didn't really like the idea because I couldn't picture myself happy in a long-distance relationship. But as I started to consider the logistics of moving, I also started to have misgivings, which I felt bad about sharing with Margo.

Two things contributed to our decision. First, my prospects at the high school were less than ideal: Despite success with my new class, I was only offered two sections. Moving on was my best option.

Next, we saw a reputable immigration attorney in San Francisco, mostly to make sure nothing had changed since we'd last checked in 2003. But the panorama remained bleak—Margo could not apply for a visa until at least ten years after our departure from the States. The attorney explained that after ten years, we'd have to submit a request for pardon and a hardship waiver. She did mention an esoteric Ninth Circuit Court of Appeals case that was testing the constitutionality of the permanent bar. But if we were to try to follow that precedent, Margo ran the risk of being held in ICE custody for up to a year while a decision was made, at which point he could still end up being deported. Being suspended in legal limbo for an indefinite period of time didn't sound like an attractive option to us at all.

Certain factors were out of our control, so we laid down the cards we'd been dealt, and, just like that, we made the decision to move.

April 30, 2006
May is upon us and we plan to march in support of immigrants' rights tomorrow in San Francisco. Rumors are spreading of mass sweeps but I highly doubt it. Today I walked 5K for brain cancer research and

donated $50. I also donated to Planned Parenthood. I am most likely not returning to Notre Dame and we are planning a move in the end of August. I sense Margo is genuinely anxious, as evidenced by what he said: He hasn't told family members, should he change his mind. I have told many but not consistently. The waiting game is not seeming so worthwhile when it's dependent on politics. I am ready for a change and attempting to deal with my grief earlier rather than later. I want to visit as many old wonderful haunts this summer before I go... I have a whole other list of academic to-do's... I am now off to Cultural Awareness Day at the school. I can't think of a better way to enter the mental and heart space of calling for free movement of people.

I'd never been as proud of Margo as when I saw him holding up a picket sign that I'd painted, high up and without fear, at the San Francisco rally that we attended with our good friend and her daughter, who'd been on our Tahoe camping trip.

Despite the relative ease with which we'd come to our decision, it felt bittersweet for quite some time. Soon after, I became unusually moody and we began bickering. It didn't take too much reflection to realize that approaching the precipice of our departure generated more anxiety than I was prepared to deal with.

In retrospect, I probably had some idea of what was in store. Underneath all the initial optimism I must have intuited the disillusionment that lay ahead. After all, why else would Margo have left his home and risked so much to move to the U.S.? Why would Margo, a person who rarely exaggerated, place so much emphasis on how difficult things were going to be?

The only thing that comforted me was the fact that I wasn't the only one with cold feet. Margo's boss had become so impressed with his skills and instincts that after less than a year working together, he offered him a partnership in his business, hoping he might convince Margo to stay in the States. Margo was seriously tempted, but the forces compelling him out of the States and back home were too strong. I sometimes still wonder about that offer, but as Margo says, "You can't live in the past."

My apprehension threatened to overwhelm me, but since our decision was based on love, I didn't want to act out of fear. But I'd be leaving everything I'd come to rely on, my entire comfort zone: friends, family, work, school, and a landscape that I loved dearly. In this case, friends' wisdom helped greatly. In my journal, almost exactly one year prior, I recalled a conversation with my good friend Sara. I was sharing how crazy the idea of moving to Mexico sometimes felt. She compared the move to the one I'd made in 1999 after graduating, and pointed out that back then, I was deeply in debt, with no job lined up, and in an off-and-on relationship. This time around, I was happily married, with significant savings, and a master's degree under my belt. Looking at things this way, it seemed so silly to be afraid… but as I wrote in my journal, "I guess the fear is that the move is irreversible especially if M can't [ever] get papers. That's what's so frightening, is the possible permanency."

I even got insecure about my relationship with Margo. Would he change when we got to Mexico? Would our relationship fall apart and leave me stranded in a foreign country, worse off than the last time I'd packed up and moved three thousand miles in a relationship?

To avoid a self-fulfilling prophecy, I consulted with a woman in our community named Maggi, a spiritual counselor and transformational guide. She helped me to see that a lot of my misgivings had to do with issues other than Margo. A lot of my feelings about moving were caught up with old emotional insecurities, missing my family, and not having had a celebratory ceremony after graduating. Experiencing a bit of catharsis and acknowledging that I'd missed an important rite of passage allowed me to regain my focus on the road ahead.

It was a busy summer as we prepared for our departure. We spent lots of time with friends, my family visited and helped me throw a belated graduation party and celebrate Margo's birthday. I led another volunteer service trip with the high school in Mexico, and traveled to New York to say goodbye to my grandmother.

The logistics of the move were intense. I had to sell my car and get my Mexican papers in order. We had to decide on our route south, sell our truck, purchase one big enough for all our possessions, make plans to legalize the truck in the town where we would cross the border, and pack and label everything for customs.

I got my *rentista* visa at the Mexican consulate in San José. It was my first time navigating this kind of red tape, and I got myself into more than one procedural snafu. But once I finally obtained the document, I was so happy that I got my picture taken with the agent who'd helped me through the process.

Legalizing the truck ended up being several times more complicated than my visa had been. Margo was in charge of arranging the truck paperwork in Mexico. We needed a federal permit (*pedimento*) at the border in order to get license plates in Querétaro, so Margo had to contact a *servicio aduanal* (customs company) to facilitate the paperwork in the town where we'd cross the border.

Deciding our route south was fun and a little like sketching plans for our future house in Margo's notebook. We finally decided on a route through Nogales, Arizona, which would allow us to hit Vegas and the Grand Canyon—two places I'd always wanted Margo to experience—"on the way." After crossing, we'd drive on to Hermosillo, and then further down the west coast of Mexico until turning inland to Querétaro.

Mexico only allowed current year models or vehicle models ten years or older to be legalized by individuals, and so we set out to find a ten-year-old truck and camper that was big enough to fit everything we had. We finally settled on a Ford F-250 long bed truck and camper that Margo painted bronze to match. But when I was away in New York saying goodbye to my family in early August, Margo called to say that he found out that Mexico only allowed trucks of that size class with diesel engines. Ours had a gas engine, so we wouldn't be able to legalize it. A week after we bought it, we had to turn around sell it.

We found the same model truck with a diesel engine for sale in Modesto, but going to get it was an ordeal in that Margo almost lost half of the $9,000 in cash he was carrying. Luckily, a pizza clerk found Margo's wallet and the friendly truck owner and his wife gave us a crash course in driving a full-sized diesel stick-shift truck while barefoot. We sealed the deal and could start packing.

Back home, we were almost ready to go, but I was in a weird mental space with lots of mixed feelings. Our friends, who were usually my rocks, were just as ambivalent.

September 3, 2006
… Labor Day weekend, weren't supposed to be here, finding ways to use the time, never finished preparing, leaving feels so far off, is it real? Seeing so many friends, receiving so many signals of their reluctance, almost a collective resistance… some make their own peace and wish us well, others know the risk and the price and refuse to say goodbye.

Myself, caught between the desire to feel every emotion, and the adventurer in me impatient to get up and go. The practical in me wondering just how this is going to work, and the fatalist in me wondering if I am gonna get kidnapped or all our things stolen...

Memories of the two weeks before we left are blurry—nowhere to be found in my journal, not even our going away party. A friend in Half Moon Bay hosted the *despedida* in the orchard behind her home. At the party, most of our friends managed to stay very upbeat, but our Mexican friends were the most pessimistic. A friend from Guanajuato told me it'd be hard for me to find friends I could trust. Jacobo (not his real name), Leticia's new husband from Guerrero, looked me straight in the eye and told me I was going to hate Mexico.

Back at the apartment, Margo packed the truck while I finished packing boxes and started a blog to update my family and friends on our move. In the end, I didn't need to give away as many things as I did because we ended up having a little extra space in the camper. But Margo was happy to be accountable for fewer possessions on a long road trip. He was even happier when we left the keys to our apartment on the counter, pulled the door shut and set off together.

The Road South (September 2006)

My first memories of Mexico stretch back to when I visited family in San Diego as a child. On the other side of the Tijuana River, a concrete channel covered with green scum, was a little girl selling bracelets. Everything about her image still haunts me—so young, unkempt, and alone.

I later made Spring Break forays with friends as a college student. In Mexicali, I danced with a one-legged man, and I journeyed to Guerrero Negro in search of grey whales.

I'd co-led the high school service trips to Tijuana and Vicente Guerrero. I'd even been to the city we were moving to, Querétaro, to meet Margo's family by myself.

But nothing could have prepared me for the life that was awaiting me in Mexico, and no trip affected me as much as the day I bid my country goodbye and my husband and I left the U.S. together. There was a lot riding on that southbound trip in our filled-to-the-brim Ford F-250 with no return date in sight. Never before had it been more important for me to be the perfect travel companion, for me to join Margo in the condition he'd lived for five years in the U.S. as an undocumented immigrant: perfectly invisible. The day we crossed from Nogales, Arizona, into Nogales, Mexico, I was no longer an American tourist. From that day forward Mexico would be my new home.

We spent our last night in the Bay Area at the home of Margo's best man from the wedding, Carl. After sharing a dinner of Thai takeout with him and his family, we slept on their futon in the living room. In the morning we said goodbye with lumps in our throats, walked to our truck, climbed in, and began our journey.

We drove through California and finally entered Nevada. Highway 15 was so windy that our F-250, packed with all our possessions and topping out at around six tons, swayed with each gust. When I could no longer stop the truck from veering into the adjacent lane, I turned the wheel over to Margo. Dust swirled in spirals across the freeway, reducing visibility. Just as conditions became too dangerous to continue, we approached the Vegas city limits, noted by the glow of thousands of multicolored lights. We quickly settled on the Excalibur as a place to stay, checked in, and parked in the back lot where we secured the tarp over the load on the camper roof.

We must have looked like a couple kids in a candy store as we walked through the back door. It was Margo's first time in a casino, and the slot machines transfixed him. Ascending in the gilded elevator, we saw ourselves grinning in the wall-to-wall mirrors. From our room's bird's eye window, you could see the fake castle facade lit up in a watercolor palette of floodlights. I'm embarrassed to say I actually took pictures of the gnome perched on one of the turrets.

The clock was ticking on our date with the city that never sleeps, so we quickly readied ourselves to hit "The Strip." We walked less than a mile down Las Vegas Boulevard, peeking into various casinos before we headed back in the direction of our hotel. I sensed an intangible distance from the people around us who were carrying drinks and having fun. We were there physically but unable to partake in the revelry, although we still had the pleasure of observing.

We must have lingered for more than an hour at one of those amazing casino buffets, literally savoring the last bites of the country we were about to depart. Inside the Luxor pyramid, Margo lingered again, staring up at the inner balconies of the rooms perched over impossible inclines. In a photo I snapped of him leaning on a rail and gazing at the lights of Paris and its imitation Eiffel Tower, there is neither happiness nor sadness on his face, just contemplation. When I asked him what he was thinking at the time, he recalled that he was simply happy to be there.

Arriving at the Grand Canyon was an exciting moment. Driving into the parking area, we passed an elk with an enormous rack grazing on the side of the road. Even Margo, who usually rejects my offers to use my binoculars, spent minutes staring into them at vultures spiraling up the thermals and at the intricate features carved in the rocks miles away on the North Rim. When he started getting antsy about getting back on the road, we left. Usually so cool and collected, he was clearly anxious about the trip ahead—part of him seemed to be elsewhere. His mood took me by surprise and only added to my own nervousness. It forced me to calm my own reactions, lest we both shut down at the same moment.

The leg from the Grand Canyon to Phoenix is practically blank in my memory. The most that Margo and I are able to recall is a Red Roof Inn, close to the highway, and in a run-down neighborhood with an open parking lot, which made him worry about the truck.

We set the alarm to get an early start on the road to Nogales. Neither of us got much sleep that night. Even our familiar irritability would have been preferable to the sort of robot-like behavior we both developed an hour before entering the city. We shared few words, and only then for trading logistical details. Adrenaline started to trickle in, but I didn't notice it until later when it surged through my veins like a garden hose with the nozzle off.

As much as I love the U.S. and the life I'd lived there for the last twenty-eight years, I couldn't help but perceive a sort of darkness as we approached the border zone. It wasn't my standard carefree road trip. On one hand, having been raised as a law-abiding citizen, I was terrified of the consequences were we to be stopped. Whether we were leaving or not was unimportant. I could have been charged with smuggling Margo into the country, or he could have been detained and served with a deportation order. But on the other hand, as my fear for our safety grew, I knew we were only doing what we had to do to survive. I couldn't expect anyone to sympathize unless they've lived through it themselves.

CHAPTER 9

The plan was to just drive through Nogales, Arizona until we crossed the border into the "safe harbor" of Nogales, Mexico. If we could pass through undetected, all would be well. So we developed a sort of tunnel vision "*al otro lado.*" Unfortunately, even the best laid plans sometimes go astray.

When we finally approached Nogales, I was driving. Through my jittery nerves, I maintained a sort of survival mentality: *No one is ever going to look twice at you guys; you just look like you're going on a camping trip.* My mind would not allow me to entertain any other possibility than us sailing through the border without any hitches. Despite the fact that we are usually so prepared, Margo and I had not discussed a back-up plan in the event that he was detained. Perhaps that possibility was too much for either of us to bear.

Everything had gone smoothly so far. I need to make constant pit stops, so I'd used a rest stop earlier, to avoid needing one mid-border-crossing. As we entered the final miles that represented the U.S./Mexico border zone, it looked we'd be on the other side in a matter of minutes. We slowed as the road narrowed from multilane highway to a two-lane road through town. The road gently curved down into a valley and a median separated us from the northbound traffic. Part of me grew excited as signs began to appear for the border, like: "International Border 1/2 mile ahead" or something like that. I noticed orange flagmen on the right hand side, waving their flags vigorously at us. "Don't slow down, keep going," Margo urged. "They're just trying to get people to park in their lots." So I ignored them. We probably had less than a quarter mile to go. But then my phone rang.

"My phone is ringing!" I exclaimed. Several thoughts ran through my head in an instant—*who could be calling me at this moment? Should we answer or not? Do we even have time to answer before we reach the border?* No cell phones were allowed at the border. I felt exasperated, but something told me not to ignore it, that the timing was too uncanny. "Answer, answer!" I told Margo, explaining where it was. He fumbled in my purse and pulled it out, flipping it open and putting it to his ear. "Hello?" He started to turn to me. I shook my head meaning to say, *I can't talk right now!* Instantly, I felt a sinking feeling that some wrench was about to be thrown into our plans. He held the phone away from his face. "You have to turn around," he said.

"What? No way!" I shrieked. This was not supposed to happen. But I slowed involuntarily. Then I saw the blue road sign: Last Return Before Border, 250 feet. My heart started pounding uncontrollably as my hands gripped the wheel. I'd taken my foot off the gas and we were coasting. "Nicole!" Margo's calm, but strained voice snapped me back to reality. "It was the guy from the *aduana*"—the service that would process our truck's legal papers—"you have to turn around and go back." As much as every fiber in my body rebelled against that command, I forced myself into the left-turn lane. "Where?" I asked, defeated. "Where do they want us to go?" *And how did they get my phone number, and how did they know where we were?* I wondered simultaneously.

"Turn into the Burger King up ahead," Margo replied. He spoke and I drove as if we were in a trance. *We should be crossing into Mexico,* I kept thinking, *why am I driving north?* Up ahead, I saw the entrance for the Burger King and pulled in to the parking lot. I didn't even have time to ask Margo what was going on when a car pulled up behind us. A man got out and approached the truck. "Follow me," he said to Margo.

He pulled out, and we dutifully followed behind. We drove around the block and turned into an overgrown parking lot. Our mysterious leader parked and got out of his car and walked over to Margo's side. Margo rolled his window down, whereupon the fellow began to give Margo some instructions for processing the truck paperwork in Spanish. His normally steady hands trembling, Margo opened the glove compartment and took out the folder with the truck's title. He brought out his wallet, and fished out his Mexican voting ID. He handed them over to the strange man, who disappeared. Margo sat back and I looked at him, mouth agape.

"What just happened?" I demanded. "I gave him the title and my ID so he can start the *pedimento*," Margo answered nonchalantly, as if it made perfect sense that we'd be doing business in a parking lot overlooking the highway in the border zone, with someone we'd never met. "And what's he going to do with it?" I wanted to know. "He's going to send someone to take pictures of the VIN and GVWR in a while, and then afterward we will pay." Margo had never done this either and was only parroting what the fellow had told him. I sat back in my seat. This had *not* been part of the plan. "How did they know to call us?" I asked. "They knew we were crossing today—the flaggers tried to stop us when they saw our truck—we didn't stop, so they called us," Margo responded, as if it were obvious.

"But why do we have to do this here, and not once we get into Mexico?" I complained. "I didn't know we'd have to do this," he kept saying. "I don't know why." He told me that the fellow had said this might take a few hours. Oh great, I thought. But we had no choice. We settled in to wait.

The parking lot was on a knoll perched over the highway, removed from the main road by a short side street shared with the Burger King drive-through. From where we were sitting, you could see the dusty colored hills of the Mexican horizon beyond the border zone. For the first ten or fifteen minutes, it was bearable. But then Margo announced, "I've got to pee." "Well, you're not leaving this truck, so you're just going to have to hold it," I snapped. He was less than one hundred feet from the Burger King bathroom, but in order to avoid running into the Border Patrol, he'd have to wait it out.

After sitting there for more than an hour, we were sweating badly, and our legs and backs started to cramp up. My left arm was starting to get sunburned. Margo was trying to appear relaxed, but you could tell he was tense and feeling impatient. He gazed out the window. "*Tardan mucho, no?* (They're taking a long time, no)?"

We chatted the same lines over every ten or fifteen minutes, wondering aloud why we'd had to stop here, and if this was really going to work out. Just when I started to get seriously worried we were being scammed, a young woman approached the vehicle on my side. She motioned for me to open the door, which I did. She spoke to Margo in Spanish, which I thought I knew so well, but I didn't understand her. "She's going to take pictures of the sticker on the inside of the door," Margo explained. She pointed her lens toward the sticker with all the details like weight rating, recommended tire pressure, etc.

As she took the pictures, I wondered if she even noticed how odd we were acting. We must have appeared normal, because she didn't look at us strangely—in fact, she didn't even look at us at all. The *foto chica* disappeared as unceremoniously as the other fellow had. "Now what?" I asked Margo. I was getting fed up with the way things were being handled. "At least she came to take the pictures," Margo offered. I had to agree. That touch made the process feel more legitimate. "Now we just have to wait for him to come back and we will pay and get going," he mused.

Prior to and during our journey, I'd willed myself to not think about the "what ifs," since my fears were naturally of the disastrous sort. They were pretty easy to ignore while cruising down the highway at seventy miles per hour. But sitting still in the parking lot, my worries came flooding in. What if neither of us could hold our pee any longer? What if the paperwork process took all night, would we have to sleep in the truck? What if the Border Patrol noticed us and came over? Could Margo go to jail? Would I? What would happen to our things? Would I have to drive back to California alone? How would Margo and I contact each other? When they threatened to get out of control, something kicked in to cut off the train of thought, producing a sort of tingly, hollow feeling in my body, as if I was floating or careening down a zip line. Pure adrenaline.

September 18, 2006
Height of fear and trepidation. We had to stop here and stare at the border and hold our pee for two hours. We watched about ten or twelve Border Patrol trucks circle by, even pulling into the Burger King take-out line less than fifty feet from us... Our hearts were beating so fast that for a moment I contemplated how it would be if a Border Patrol officer came up to me, what I would say. I decided I would tell him or her the truth and try to talk my way out of it...

Sometimes when kids play hide and seek, they think that if they shut their eyes, no one will see them. That was my strategy. Keep looking straight ahead, and no one will look at you. Nope, no need to glance over at that American girl and the Mexican guy next to her. They are just taking a well-needed pit stop in the shade of a willow tree in an abandoned lot next to the Burger King drive through. They are not waiting for illicitly crossed northbound passengers to jump in the back. In fact, we can't see them at all because they are invisible. That was my hope. Especially when, out of the corner of my eye, I saw a Jeep with white lettering on the door pull up to the Burger King drive-through window.

For an instant, I felt a twinge of jealousy. It would have been nice to pop over to BK and go in to get some lunch, some drinks, use the bathroom, lounge in the air-conditioned booths while waiting for the paperwork to get finished up. But the risk was too great and I put the thought out of my head. Then the panic hit when I realized it was a pair of Border Patrol officers.

First my heart started to pound and my armpits and palms became dripping wet. When the Jeep's uniformed passengers received their order and settled back into their seats, I realized that the bags of food in their hands were distracting them from looking our way. "I hope that guy comes back soon," Margo sighed. He hadn't seen the Jeep. Trying not to scare him, I casually fiddled with the radio tuner dial. I watched out of the corner of my eye as they pulled out of the exit below us and disappeared down the highway. I let out my breath. "I'm sure he'll be back soon," I lied, as I slipped a CD into the stereo.

My heart was still beating in my ears, and my breathing was shallow. Only then did I realize my heart had been racing for almost two hours. I had to calm down. I found a relaxing spray that an herbalist friend had made me for the trip and spritzed it over myself. As I inhaled the sweet smelling mist, I reminded myself that soon the paperwork would be complete, and we'd be back on the road. I've never been a great meditator, but that horizon ahead and the desire to not lose my sanity was a pretty great focal point. The adrenaline didn't hurt, either. It's made little ladies lift cars off people, and in my case it made the unbearable waiting possible. Faith in a fortunate outcome became my only rope to reality.

Just when I started to dissociate, the first fellow reappeared at Margo's window with a handful of documents. After some brief discussion, Margo fished out his wallet yet again, this time to pay the fee for the legalization. But it quickly became apparent that things wouldn't be done just with forking over the cash. The man, whom we'd discovered was named Christian, explained in his maddening but compelling way that we needed to follow him to the "other" border crossing in Nogales (which I later realized was the commercial crossing), where he'd make the deposit and we'd be free to go. We nodded obediently, buckled up, and I cranked the diesel engine, pulling out in a hurry to catch up with him. *I sure hope this is legit*, I thought. Margo looked optimistic.

We eased onto the highway in the opposite direction again, made a few turns, and then the road began to roll gently downhill again and widened before us. Up ahead we could clearly see the border crossing kiosks marking the *frontera*. A number of different administrative buildings appeared on both sides of the highway. It had a different look than a "people's" border—no cars waiting in lines or pedestrians going through turnstiles—it looked industrial, and sure enough, a few tractor trailers rolled by as we slowed to park next to Christian in a triangle-shaped patch of gravel between a large government building and the main road.

But when I looked up and made out the words on the building in front of us, my heart leaped into my mouth. DEPARTMENT OF HOMELAND SECURITY read the blue, white, and red sign on the front of the mammoth compound before us. To my horror, dozens of Border Patrol Jeeps were parked in front, pulling in and out of the parking lot only meters away from our grill. No lovely willow tree shaded over us; there was no side lot to retreat to. Christian had delivered us directly into the worst possible place.

To this day I'm still not sure why we hadn't leveled with him from the beginning—probably our fear of attracting attention. But suddenly, my attitude of meek compliance shifted dramatically. Needing to take action, and not even consulting Margo, who looked too dazed anyways, I motioned to Christian to come over to my window. I took a deep breath and started out in halting Spanish. *"Mira, señor, es que mi esposo no tiene papeles, y no podemos estar AQUI."* I motioned toward the building in front of us, explaining that my husband was undocumented and we couldn't stay there. Then let out my breath and looked into his eyes.

The great love and respect I had for the man by my side, everything we'd shared, having come this far with him, was almost too much to bear. I was terrified to experience it shattered in an instant by officers of my own government who wouldn't take into consideration our history, our lives, our love.

All we needed was our truck paperwork—to do things the right way on our way out of the country and into Mexico. Christian immediately realized the gravity of the situation he had inadvertently placed us in and calmly but quickly walked over to Margo's side, where he climbed into the backseat. In Spanish, he told us to "just drive." Margo nodded and shifted in his seat—quietly aware of what was at stake in those few moments and grateful for my executive decision, despite the fact that words had temporarily escaped him.

At 28 years old, I'd only fantasized about becoming a mother, but in that moment I had a notion of what it felt like to want to give your life to protect your kin from harm—that's what I felt for Margo in that instant. I threw the F-250 into reverse, and as casually as was possible with six tons on board, I rolled backward, watching the Border Patrol Jeeps in my side mirror. As I shifted the gear to first, I pictured an invisible shield, and felt the cabin of our truck impervious to exterior eyes. I imagined for a moment, even believed, that we were just two ordinary U.S. citizens who were getting on with our late summer road trip to Mexico. It wasn't possible for me to be stopped. I was too good of a driver, too white to attract any attention. I didn't fit the profile. That's what I hoped. I just couldn't have handled it if something went wrong.

But I did handle it, driving while out of body. My gamble in exposing our situation to Christian had paid off, and now we only had one hundred yards to go. I don't know if it was divine intervention or dumb luck, but the next thing I knew, we were in Mexico. No fanfare, no turnstile, no sirens or flag wavers. The only reason I even realized we had crossed was because the colors on the official signs around us were almost like the colors of the U.S. flag, except the blue of the red, white and blue had been replaced with a dark *chile* green.

I looked back over my shoulder out the window at the Department of Homeland Security building behind us. Border Patrol Jeeps still swarmed around the entrance like worker bees flying in and out of the hive. Only five hundred feet of open space separated us and them, and although I couldn't see it or touch it, an international border separated us all the same. I laid my head and arms on the steering wheel and let out an enormous sigh of relief.

I turned to Margo, who had a shit-eating grin on his face, and shook my head slowly. Then, noticing the Mexican customs agent outside the truck waiting for us, his expression quickly morphed into his no-nonsense face. "Come on, it's time to go," he said, his hand reaching for the door.

Chapter 10

Legal Strangers: Same-Sex Couples and U.S. Immigration

~

Nathaniel Hoffman

J.W. & Gabriel

J.W. Lown is on his third Shiner Bock and about to switch to wine.

We are sitting on an elaborately staged but comfortable Victorian porch eating the best bowl of beans in the world, a mixture from two local barbecue joints. Just beyond a wall of sliding glass that frames in the porch, the sun sets on a meticulous grove of Texas live oak and pecan trees.

J.W. moves a heavy, velvet dining room chair closer to the wall of door-sized porch windows and slides one partly open. He lights a Mexican Marlboro, crosses his legs and blows smoke outside, steeling himself for an imminent brow beating.

I'm sitting between J.W. and one of his key mother figures—a San Angelo powerbroker and longtime political supporter. She is drinking vodka and has been since before we arrived. She's just getting warmed up.

"You don't go to attorneys with this kind of shit," she tells him matter-of-factly. "Transporting an illegal alien is a lot different than going to a fucking movie."

They have not seen one another for three years. This is a reunion and their first opportunity to review the facts of that fateful May day, three years prior, when J.W. disappeared, leaving the town of San Angelo, Texas, at the altar, or more accurately, at the podium.

An older man at the head of the table chews an expensive, unlit cigar, perhaps a Davidoff, his preferred brand. He's wearing a deep blue tracksuit and house shoes and wants to talk politics but can't get a word in. He declares several times, in a soft Texas drawl, that the partisan rancor in Washington is the worst he's ever seen. He gripes about the number of cars pulling up outside the gate to his ranchito, folks coming to gawk at the banks of the South Concho River, swollen after the recent rains.

This couple asked not to be identified by name, so I'll call them John and Kelly. He's a retired cable television pioneer who believes in historic preservation and bought several blocks of downtown San Angelo to save the old bank and brothel buildings. He recollects "riding a pedal horse in Ted Turner's office" some thirty years ago and agreeing to bring a fledgling CNN to West Texas. She's a retired fashion industry executive, perhaps twenty years his junior, who now runs a popular restaurant in town.

They were among J.W.'s first backers—financially and politically—when J.W. became the 26-year-old mayor of this town a decade ago.

This conversation has been a long time coming. When J.W. left town on the eve of his fourth swearing in, John and Kelly didn't know where he'd gone.

Only three people knew he was in Mexico.

J.W. won his fourth term in May 2009 with eighty-nine percent of the vote. By that fourth election, J.W. had locked up the San Angelo electorate handily enough that he had no serious opposition. He beat a high school teacher and a student, his only opponents. After the election, the local paper, which had endorsed him, ran a front-page photo of him hugging John in a celebratory embrace.

The swearing in ceremony would be two weeks after the election. It was a particularly stressful time for J.W. He remained busy, giving a big speech at the Angelo State commencement ceremony and maintaining his packed mayoral schedule. But he was also making lots of secret plans, getting his affairs in order. Kelly bumped into J.W. that last week and could tell that something was wrong. She invited him for dinner at the ranchito, but he declined the invitation. Three years later, on their porch, Kelly let J.W. have it:

"If you came for dinner that Friday night your life would have been different," Kelly said. He left his "mother" broken hearted, she told him; he made a knee-jerk decision to abandon his office.

"I can live with a little bit of failure; regret would eat me alive," J.W. responded. He remained convinced that leaving town had been his only authentic option.

Kelly was teary, emotional and forceful as she steered the conversation on the enclosed porch. J.W. spoke carefully, choosing his words, and tearing up a few times himself. John mostly stared out the window, speaking up only when necessary.

"I think you were getting tired of the mayor shit," John interjected at one point.

"I felt all alone and I know I wasn't alone," J.W. said, addressing Kelly as Mom. "Lots of people said we could have done X, Y, Z."

John and Kelly don't think of themselves as "lots of people." They know the system. They entertain politicians and university presidents and have practice exerting influence.

John and Kelly believe in the rule of law. They feel strongly about American sovereignty over the international border three hours south of their town. They are lifelong Republicans who had their picture taken with

George W. Bush a few months prior, at a fundraiser for the local Boys and Girls Club. They have a beautiful Victorian-style home on a small ranch with statuary and great paintings and large Persian rugs and a loaded gun rack on the wall of their bedroom.

And they feel that they understand human nature.

Kelly saw J.W. on that Friday and then he was gone on Tuesday.

"All you had to do was come out here," she told him. "It always gets down to one story—as an individual, we could have made shit happen."

A lot of people in San Angelo feel this way, actually. Texas is not a friendly state for gay people or for undocumented immigrants, but if you know a Texan, or at least if you know a San Angelan, the story might be different. You don't wave your *chones* in the air and get a brass band going, as J.W. put it. But West Texas holds a genuine "stay out of my bedroom and stay out of my pocketbook" kind of conservatism. This attitude was born of the tension between self-reliance and dependence on neighbors that made settling the Texas drylands possible. Or as Mario Castillo put it: at a very early age you learn to not piss in somebody else's pot because you might have to drink that.

"A lot of great things happened in San Angelo because you laid the groundwork for it." Kelly said. "The people wanted you for mayor. They fuckin' could give a shit that you were gay."

J.W. Lown had been stressed since mid-March 2009, when his relationship intensified with Gabriel, the undergraduate from Mexico who taught salsa lessons on the Angelo State campus. (Gabriel is not his real name.)

But his sexual orientation was not the primary source of his worry. J.W.'s orientation was the worst kept secret in town. In his third race he faced an opponent who tried to use it against him, blatantly campaigning as the "Christian, family" candidate. Editors at the *Standard-Times* knew the mayor was gay and many of his supporters knew. He never hid his orientation, nor did he flaunt it. Many others didn't care, as long as he kept taxes low and kept San Angelo on the upswing.

J.W. came to terms with his sexual orientation in his twenties. He had married his college sweetheart for a short time after she graduated and took her back to Santa Cruz, Bolivia, with him, where he was serving in the Peace Corps. They lasted four months before it was obvious it would not work out. She played on the computer all day and then returned to

England when he told her that the marriage had been a mistake.

But they remained friends. When J.W. crossed into Mexico seven years later, one of the first emails he sent was to his ex-wife.

J.W. believed in true love and in waiting for the right person to come along. He thought his ex had been the one and then when the marriage broke up he thought maybe he was just not meant to love, that he had been forsaken.

J.W.'s older sister, Alicia—his only close family—never imagined he was gay either. He never really came out to her—just started dating a few men, sometimes bringing them back to the ranch house they shared. The small gay community in San Angelo certainly embraced him, from prominent gay citizens who became his confidants and advisors to the Texas Dancehall Queens who showed up at public events to people he didn't even know. When J.W. took me out to the city putting green where he first learned to swing a golf club, two men drove by, slowed their sedan on the drive along the river, rolled down the window and thanked him profusely for everything he'd done for the town, begging him to return.

This affection was not limited to San Angelo's gay citizens. J.W.'s sexual orientation may have helped pave his political fortunes in a way. Never having experienced a deep relationship, J.W. sunk all of his drive and passion into work. He studied city issues hard and worked tirelessly and people noticed.

"Once elected he was everywhere," recalls Jack Cowan, a long time columnist and political reporter at the *Standard-Times*. "People thought he cared about them."

San Angelo is a mid-sized city of about 93,000 people in West Central Texas, about three and a half hours from anywhere. For decades, the town chugged along as a ranching hub along the Concho River. It found some prosperity during the short oil boom in the 1970s but remained a quiet university town with a couple of hospitals and a stagnant downtown.

J.W.'s paternal grandparents were Swedes who settled in San Angelo after living in Colorado and Dallas, and his mother was Mexican. J.W. inherited Mexican citizenship from his mother but never imagined it would be of so much use to him.

J.W. and his sister grew up in a large house with a tennis court in a leafy neighborhood near downtown. His father ran a successful foundry for many years, a family business that made oil tanks and other oil and gas industry equipment using the patented Lown Bending Roll, invented by J.W.'s grandfather. They led a comfortable life for the first part of his youth. But then his father lost the family business and floundered in dozens of get rich quick schemes—selling magnets, bedspreads for people with osteoporosis, Amway—until he weighed four hundred pounds and his mother feared he'd soon need a wheelchair to get around. They moved to a smaller house and his parents' marriage ended when he was a teenager. His mother died of cancer when J.W. was in his first year of college and his father died a few years later, when J.W. was in the Peace Corps.

In 2002, after he got out of the Peace Corps and failed to get into Yale Drama School, J.W. returned to San Angelo and decided to run for mayor of his hometown. One impetus for his sudden entry into politics involved a vision quest to Mexico and Central America, where he started out contemplating his future. That trip ended abruptly when he returned to San Angelo, and perhaps still inspired by his recent quest, took all of his family heirlooms out of storage and read the Bible front to back.

Another possible inspiration for his run was that J.W. had dreamed of becoming a congressman from the time he was a young boy. He went to a Christian Science college called The Principia, where he was exposed to politicians like Henry Kissinger, Jimmy Carter and Ralph Nader. He interned for Texas Congressman Lamar Smith, also a Christian Scientist, his junior year. And he had a libertarian streak as well—he voted for Ron Paul in the 2012 Republican primary in Texas via absentee ballot.

But J.W.'s sudden decision ultimately came down to the news that the incumbent mayor was bowing out of the race. A few good supporters encouraged him to run and he did not have any other great ideas about what to do with his career. In May 2003, J.W. was elected mayor, taking the town by surprise. His only pledges were that he would work full time as mayor—it was a largely ceremonial position—and that he would bring a "new perspective," a phrase engineered by one of J.W.'s neighbors, a marketing professor at Angelo State.

J.W. took his new job very seriously. He attended multiple community events every day—*quinceañeras*, school events, neighborhood meetings and international nights at Angelo State University. He formed new committees and brought scores of new people into civic life. He was everywhere. He took on large construction and real estate interests, making city contracting more rigorous and refusing to dole out business development money that some Chamber of Commerce types had come to expect. He worked on changing the politics of the City Council to support his initiatives. And he kept doing it, through three terms, winning the vote by larger and larger margins every two years.

By his fourth race, the *Standard-Times* opined that he was a good mayor who may one day be remembered as a great mayor. Downtown San Angelo had been revitalized and a positive, almost progressive vibe permeated the city. Everything was going right politically when all of a sudden, J.W. found himself in love, for the first time.

Kelly did not mince words on her porch that night, three years later.

"We've all had broken hearts. We didn't fuckin' run to Mexico," she told J.W. "Let's show up to the swearing in, let's start with that... You knee jerked in four or five days... It would have been the longest term ever."

"Timing was a bitch," J.W. half-agreed. "I've always tried to be absolute."

"Well that's worked out great," Kelly said.

J.W. tried to explain himself in a few different ways. There were lots of "woulda, shoulda, coulda's." His other key political advisor told him there was no way it could work out. It was a legal catch-22 for him to be mayor—to have police powers and maintain his political capital—and date an undocumented man. It was his first broken heart.

"It wouldn't have kicked me out of office. It would have made me miserable," he said.

But Kelly insisted that J.W.'s decision had been rash and cost him a fortune, and that "typical gay relationships don't last."

"He gave up nothing. You gave up everything," she said.

J.W. defended Gabriel, insisting that he paid a price as well. And he tried to defend his decision to leave in personal terms.

"I have my sanity," he said.

Gabriel was raised by his grandparents in the dry ranchlands south of San Miguel de Allende in Guanajuato, Mexico. His mother died when he was young. His father and three older brothers were in the United States working during most of his childhood. They rarely called—he only remembers speaking to his father once on the phone.

Gabriel finished ninth grade in Mexico, after which most of the young men he knew went north to seek their fortunes or join their fathers. But he had heard about *la migra* and the "clandestine" life in the United States—his father worked as a *pollero*, or *coyote*, for a time and served a five-year prison sentence in the U.S.

Because of that family history, Gabriel had other plans. He recognized the cycle of poverty and family separation that infused his community and he wanted to break the cycle. He wanted to finish high school in Mexico and go on to college, but that costs money and the family savings had been depleted when his father was arrested.

Still, Gabriel persevered, finding a government program similar to Teach for America, where he would teach in a rural school for a year and then the Mexican government would pay for his education. On the day of his graduation from *secundaria* (the end of compulsory education in Mexico), Gabriel was supposed to travel to another town for an orientation for his teaching gig. But he didn't have the money—or permission—to go, and his father, who had returned to Mexico after getting out of prison, disappeared again after a fight with his stepmother. He missed the orientation, and with it his best shot at continuing his education in Mexico.

Gabriel was still determined to go back to school, so he worked construction jobs, trying to save money for tuition. He worked from 7 a.m. until dark and spent most of his earnings on food and transport. After six months he decided he'd never save the cash to continue school and so, at fifteen years old, he set off for Texas.

Gabriel had lots of uncles and other family members in the United States; all of his uncles had green cards. His father had a green card until it was revoked when he went to prison. Gabriel didn't have a green card, but he had plenty of places to go, so he set off to live with his grandfather and finish high school in a small town in Central Texas. He saved enough money for a bus ticket to the border and, along with a friend who had made the journey before, swam the Rio Grande and walked through the night.

In the morning, his friend said, "I think we made it." Fifteen minutes later, the Border Patrol picked them up and deposited them back in Mexico.

They slept in the bus station and tried again in the morning. Gabriel had very mixed feelings about the adventure. He didn't want to leave his sisters behind; he didn't really want to leave Mexico. But he felt he had no choice. He was like a man seeking work and hoping he'd never find it, *buscando trabajo esperando no encontrarlo,* an expression normally reserved for the lazy, but in this case fitting Gabriel's reluctance to cross over.

On their second attempt, his friend and guide admitted to not really knowing where they were, and the Border Patrol picked them up again, dropping them back on the Mexican side of the bridge. Gabriel believes he was deported twice at the border, though it may have been voluntary departure and not recorded as a deportation. They spent another night in the bus station in a border town that Gabriel declined to name.

The third time, the group had to wait out a fire and didn't cross until morning. They made it through and kept walking but Gabriel was not optimistic and felt they would be caught at any moment. He had always had nightmares about snakes, but no longer.

"Once we were there I wasn't scared. I was scared, but not because of the snakes... I was scared of getting caught by the Border Patrol," he said.

They kept walking through one night and then another and another. They were walking through the Texas countryside, in the *monte*. Some of the guys' feet started to bleed and so they rested for a day and then kept walking.

They ate whatever provisions they found along the way and filled their water bottles with rainwater. They carried some rice and dried food, but they were hungry and tired and quite lost.

After about two weeks of wandering, the group—they were now five people—decided to give up and just walk to the nearest town. They spent that night at a ranch and in the morning, two Mexican ranch hands came by and offered to drive them to their destination for $150 each.

The boys took the ride—Gabriel got the cash from a relative—and in an hour and a half they were at his grandfather's house.

Within a week, Gabriel had a job doing yard work and taking care of animals and within two weeks he enrolled in English as a Second Language and art classes (the teacher spoke Spanish) at the high school. He also took home economics, though he did not really know what the teacher was saying.

Gabriel excelled in high school. He ran cross-country, played tennis and took tons of art classes. He learned English very well and made lots of friends. In his senior year, Gabriel was accepted at Angelo State. Undocumented students are not eligible for federal financial aid and have to find other sources of grants and scholarships to attend college. He got three scholarships—from the college and from the Hispanic community—for academics and running. Friends and even people he didn't know showered gifts on him—money and suitcases, proud that a Mexican kid from their town who had just showed up a few years before was going to college. A friend drove him up to San Angelo and he started his college career in the fall of 2007.

When Gabriel went to the registrar's office at Angelo State they asked for a green card. He didn't even bat an eye, telling them he was out of status. The registrar told him he needed to get a notarized letter certifying that he would apply for a green card as soon as the option was available—that is the policy for undocumented students who graduate from Texas high schools. And like that, he was a Texas college student, majoring in business.

"It's like I got lucky and I always met the right people and they helped me," Gabriel said.

J.W. always met the right people as well. When he decided to run for mayor in 2003, he had people like John and Kelly backing him. He had mowed lawns as a teenager, stuffing his lawn mower in the trunk of the family Mercedes Benz. Many of the prominent citizens whose lawns he had mowed remembered him as a responsible kid and remembered his parents as prominent citizens. After she got sick, his mother had been very involved in the Republican women's group in San Angelo and many of those women supported J.W.

Right after he won his first race, J.W. visited his godfather, Mario Castillo, in Washington, D.C., to seek advice. In an earlier life, Mario tended bar at the River Club in San Angelo, a place J.W.'s father, George, used to frequent. Castillo, a San Angelo native, studied in Mexico City, won a Ford Foundation internship in Washington, D.C., during the Nixon administration and stayed on, serving as chief of staff to the U.S. House Committee on Agriculture in the 1980s and later founding the Aegis Group, a Capitol Hill lobby firm.

Mario knew George from the bar and he knew J.W.'s mother, Alicia, from his time in Mexico City. He brought them both along on a European vacation in the late 1960s, where he rendezvoused with a fast-driving, hard-drinking, cigar-smoking countess. George met Alicia in Vienna, fell deeply in love with her as they made their way to Paris, and by the time they got to London she had agreed to marry him. But Alicia made George travel to Mexico City to meet his future mother-in-law and court her first.

Mario was the best man at their wedding. When George died, Mario promised to look after J.W. and his sister, a promise that he took very seriously, invoking both the Mexican notion of the stern *padrino* and a Texas high society notion of the godfather/mentor.

J.W. reveres Mario in many ways. He told Kelly that Mario was the reason for his existence, having introduced his parents. Mario is a godfather to J.W., both literally—he relishes the title—and in his enthusiastic sculpting of J.W.'s political career.

Still buzzing from the election night victory high in the spring of 2003, J.W. sat in Mario's D.C. home office on Embassy Row. Mario asked J.W. what kind of mayor he wanted to be: a ribbon-cutting mayor or a do-something mayor. J.W. said he wanted be a do-something mayor and Mario outlined the strategy of bringing new blood into city committees, working around a hostile city council and methodically building up an electoral base.

Then they had a tougher conversation.

"I said, 'Do you understand boy that you've got a hard, hard road ahead of you… You are gay, you're not going to find anybody of your equivalent in San Angelo unless you look really hard and are patient,'" Mario said.

Mario personally understands this struggle all too well. He is also an openly gay Latino Republican, who sat on the board of the Gay and Lesbian Victory Fund, helping bring Republican candidates into the fold of the largest LGBT political action committee. He now has a seat on the Log Cabin Republicans' board, the primary gay GOP group in the country.

For years, Mario had told J.W. the tale of the monkey in the mesquite tree.

"The way I explained it to my godchildren is that West Texans learned a long time ago the story about the monkey and the mesquite tree," he said. "The higher the monkey climbs up the mesquite tree the more you see of its ass. You have to be very careful how you scamper up that tree."

During J.W.'s D.C. visit, Mario invited several prominent gay political activists to his home to help J.W. understand what he would face. They went through an intense series of what-ifs to help him learn how to deal with homophobia.

"I wanted my godson to have as many comfort blankets as I could give him," Mario said.

Then Mario flew to San Angelo for J.W.'s first big speech as mayor, where he outlined Operation Take Charge, the strategy he had devised with Mario.

"I am a firm believer that empowered citizens are effective agents of change... My plan empowers the bottom rather than waiting for the top to take action," he told the downtown crowd at Kelly's restaurant, according to the *Standard-Times*.

Throughout that first term and the second and third, Mario was a constant advisor, using his government relations firm's resources to produce speeches and initiatives and bringing money into the campaign war chest. Mario kept a close eye on his godson from afar. People in San Angelo called him to let him know what J.W. was up to, who he was hanging out with, what folks were saying about him. Mario came to town frequently and headed off attacks and threats and innuendo. He was J.W.'s self-appointed wingman and his bagman at the same time.

For three full terms, this arrangement worked beautifully, and by almost all accounts, J.W. did a great job as mayor. But in May 2009, when J.W. called on Mario for advice on his relationship with Gabriel—even introducing his godfather to his boyfriend—he didn't like the answer.

"He was happy for me but he said you gotta end this," J.W. said. "You are an official."

Mario recalls that his advice for Gabriel was for him to keep his head down and hope the Dream Act passed. J.W. does not remember any mention of the Dream Act.

Yet, at first J.W. actually took the advice. He broke up with Gabriel. But then he made some calls on his own, searched his soul and decided to go it alone, without his godfather's endorsement. Mario did not like J.W.'s decision.

"His dick was guiding him rather than his head," Mario said.

On the porch, three years later, Kelly felt slighted that J.W. had sought advice only from Mario. J.W. said he allowed Mario to take over, to dictate his decision to leave. He said that Mario was the reason for his existence—having introduced his parents and jumpstarted his political career.

Kelly insisted that J.W. had other inspirations, other close advisors.

"No, no, don't you ever say that. What do you think the fuck we are?" she asked. "Were we not intimate? You let one man force you into packing your bags."

As his correspondence with Gabriel intensified in that last week before the swearing in, J.W. floated the idea of moving to Mexico. Gabriel agreed.

"He said he would go back if they could be *together,* and just that word together was so earth shattering," J.W. recalls.

J.W. started packing clothes, his computer, his golf clubs, whatever fit in the truck. He moved some money around and drafted a resignation letter. He had confided in his best boyhood friend that he was thinking of leaving, but told no one that he had decided.

They rendezvoused the night before the swearing in and J.W. told Gabriel to pack a few things. He told him he was ready to make a life together, but that they could not do it in the United States.

"One way I frame this was I felt like I had to choose between politics and my humanity. And I thought, if I don't give this a chance I will hate myself forever, and I couldn't live with that," J.W. said.

And so, in the early morning hours of May 19, 2009, J.W. swung by Gabriel's apartment in his loaded pickup truck and the two set off for the border, dressed in business suits, holding hands and listening to Robert Earl Keen's "Gringo Honeymoon."

"I said, 'I need you. As we're driving to the border, if for some reason you need to turn back I'll honor you but we can never be together,'" he said.

As they approached Del Rio, Texas, heading south, J.W. saw the Border Patrol and the German shepherds and it sent a shiver up his spine.

"Gabriel felt anger. I felt fear," J.W. said.

In Acuña, Mexico, on the other side of the border, J.W. called on another friend, the Mexican Consul General in Del Rio. The mayor had worked with the consul on several projects in San Angelo and he considered him a friend. The consul helped arrange paperwork for their truck and then they had a nice lunch in Acuña. J.W. told the Mexican official that he was resigning as mayor and moving to Mexico and the man teared up, wishing them the best and bidding them to stay in touch.

He then called the San Angelo city manager, a man he had recruited to the job, and left him a voicemail to look under the Kleenex box on his desk for a letter. The city manager later reported that he almost had a heart attack when he read the letter. He had to inform the city council before the swearing in ceremony that evening.

J.W. and Gabriel called a few close friends and family members to assure them that they were safe. One friend was concerned that J.W. was suicidal.

They stayed at a hotel in Monclova—the undisclosed location mentioned in many press accounts—for a few days, ducking intense press attention. J.W. spoke to his hometown paper and responded by email to the *Wall Street Journal*, but ignored other requests. He declined to identify his boyfriend, to protect Gabriel's privacy and that of his family. He told the *Standard-Times* in San Angelo that he did not want to take the oath of office knowing he was "aiding and assisting" someone who was not a citizen.

"I made the final decision when I knew it was the right decision to make for me and my partner and our future—and for the community," he told the paper.

A brief *Wall Street Journal* story headlined "Texas Mayor Trades Job for Romance in Mexico" stated that J.W.'s colleagues and constituents were rallying around him and quoted J.W. saying only it had been "hectic."

Gabriel and J.W. moved to Chihuahua for one semester, where Gabriel continued his studies, and then they settled in San Miguel de Allende.

Meanwhile, a few days prior, Mario had second thoughts. He consulted his colleague, the immigration attorney, again, and thought he had a plan that would eventually allow J.W. and Gabriel to be together. He called J.W. from the San Angelo airport, as he was flying back to D.C. and left a message. He called him again from Dallas and again from Reagan and he never heard back. He still has not heard back, three years later, save an annual birthday card.

"I'm not the one who never returned phone calls and a perfunctory birthday card once in a while does not cut the crap," Mario said. "That's the sign of a coward and you can quote me on that."

Mario refused to explain how he thought J.W. and Gabriel could have stayed in the U.S., but he was adamant that he had the answer. Kelly was adamant as well that she could have pulled some strings, gotten Gabriel a student visa or something. Hundreds of well-wishers at a reception J.W. held in May 2012 on his first return to San Angelo since resigning, wanted to know when they'd get to meet his "friend," when he was coming back to be mayor again.

But no matter how connected or rich or powerful J.W.'s friends are, the fact is his boyfriend is banned from the United States for at least ten years, a ban that was drafted into law by Rep. Lamar Smith, the very man for whom J.W. wrote book reports as a college intern. Smith, whose district used to encompass San Angelo, also co-sponsored the Defense of Marriage Act, the other main barrier to J.W. and Gabriel returning to the United States together.

"My opinion is you have immigration laws and they have to be orderly," J.W. said. "The injustice of the thing is if you're not hetero and you find the person you want to spend your life with, the immigration system rejects you."

He's only partly correct.

* * *

J.W. is only partly correct because the immigration system rejects many heterosexual couples as well. But the rejection of same-sex binational couples remains even more draconian. Until 1979, the Immigration and Nationalization Services officially viewed homosexuality as a mental illness and all "known" gays and lesbians were barred from entry. That is no longer the case, but the passage of the Defense of Marriage Act, or DOMA, in 1996, under Bill Clinton, specifically denied gay couples access to family immigration visas.

Gay immigrants were formally denied entry into the United States in the Immigration Act of 1917 as "persons of constitutional psychopathic inferiority." Congress clarified that phrase in 1952 to exclude immigrants, "afflicted with psychopathic personality." Then a 1962 decision in the Ninth Circuit Court of Appeals ruled that phrase too vague and allowed George Fleuti, a gay man from Switzerland to stay. The U.S. Supreme Court took up the case as well, but got hung up on the word "entry"—as in what constitutes an official entry into the country—and handed it back to the lower court. A few years later, the Supreme Court ruled in another case that Congress clearly intended the phrase "psychopathic personality" to refer to homosexuality and that Congress had the authority to exclude gay immigrants from the country.

In 1965, mainly in reaction to the Fleuti case, Congress added "sexual deviation" to the list of excludable conditions that public health officials review before an immigrant visa is granted. The exclusion of gays and lesbians was officially based on a medical examination, but in 1973, the American Psychiatric Association decided that homosexuality was not a mental illness. It took six years for the U.S. Public Health Service to catch up to the medical community and agree to stop automatically diagnosing gay people with psychopathic personality. The INS and the Justice Department adopted a kind of "Don't Ask, Don't Tell" policy for admitting gay people. If they were not outed as they entered the country, they were admitted.

In 1983, the Fifth Circuit Court of Appeals, which includes Texas, Louisiana and Mississippi, ruled that the Immigration and Naturalization Services could still deny gays and lesbians visas based on the sexual deviancy clause. That same year the Ninth Circuit in San Francisco disagreed, ruling in *Hill v. INS* that the government could not bar gay and lesbian people without the medical rationale.

In the Immigration Act of 1990, the exclusions for both sexual deviancy and psychopathic personality were eliminated and openly gay immigrants were finally eligible for green cards.

But the coast was still not clear. While some visa categories became available to gay immigrants, spousal and fiancé visas—the vast majority of family immigration visas issued—were still denied.

During the Clinton administration, the United States began to approve some gay and lesbian asylum cases. The government does not track the number of cases approved, but according to news accounts and law firms that specialize in asylum cases, it may be in the hundreds now. Asylum seekers must prove a well-founded fear of persecution in their home country, and many foreign partners cannot make that case. For a few years, the government granted asylum to a number of gay and lesbian Mexicans. But as evidence emerged that Mexico was becoming more open—same-sex marriage is now recognized in Mexico City and many Mexican cities have Gay Pride events—fewer asylum cases seemed to be approved.

In the 1990s, the movement for marriage equality was still in its infancy. As early as 1975, the city of Boulder, Colorado, had started granting marriage licenses to same-sex couples. One of these couples was Richard Frank Adams, an American citizen, and Anthony Corbett Sullivan, an Australian whose tourist visa had expired. The Ninth Circuit Court, despite having taken a liberal view on admission of gay people in the past, denied immigration benefits to Sullivan in 1982. The court found that Congress had a "rational intention" to deny immigration benefits to same-sex couples—whether because gay marriages "never produce off-spring," are banned in most states or violate "prevailing societal mores." Thus, same-sex couples continued to be denied access to spousal and fiancé visas.

In 1993, the Hawaii Supreme Court ruled that a prohibition on same-sex marriage was discriminatory and violated the state constitution. In reaction, Congress passed and Clinton signed DOMA in 1996. DOMA further codified that same-sex couples would not be eligible for more than 1,100 federal benefits that accompany marriage, from tax and military benefits to healthcare and immigration programs. DOMA makes it abundantly clear that a same-sex spouse is not a spouse in the eyes of the federal government:

In determining the meaning of any Act of Congress, or of any ruling, regulation, or interpretation of the various administrative bureaus and agencies of the United States, the word "marriage" means only a legal union between one man and one woman as husband and wife, and the word "spouse" refers only to a person of the opposite sex who is a husband or a wife.

So even if J.W. and Gabriel had met in Mexico, gotten engaged and applied for a fiancé visa together, they would have been denied. If Gabriel landed a job with a company that could sponsor him for a work visa, he would have had to return to Mexico, put his name in the queue and find out later that he was denied on the basis of his entering without inspection and then remaining in the country for more than six months. If Gabriel had been in the United States on a valid student visa and they were married in one of the six states or the District of Columbia, where gay marriage was legal, they would still be denied.

In 2013, this double standard between the states and the federal government is well on its way to being rectified. The Obama administration refused to defend DOMA in court and Obama endorsed gay marriage in May 2012. An increasing number of courts, including the First Circuit Court of Appeals in Massachusetts, ruled DOMA unconstitutional and dozens of challenges worked their way up to the Supreme Court. In March 2013, the Supreme Court heard arguments in one challenge to

DOMA, based on the inability of same-sex spouses to waive estate taxes. A decision on the constitutionality of DOMA was expected during the summer.

The denial of immigration benefits to same-sex couples became a major driving force in the marriage equality movement.

Victoria Neilson, the lead attorney at Immigration Equality, an activist law firm that advocates for same-sex binational couples, said that of the more than 1,000 rights denied to same-sex couples, it's hard to imagine one more important than that ability to live in the same country as a spouse.

"The American immigration system is based largely on the concept of family unification," Neilson said. "It seems especially unfair that families whose relationship is celebrated in the state where they live is not honored by the federal government."

According to an estimate from the Williams Institute at the University of California-Los Angeles Law School, there are about 24,000 same-sex binational couples in the United States; an unknown number of gay couples with one American partner live abroad. While striking down DOMA is one strategy that would allow some of these couples to get married and sponsor their foreign partners, it is not a complete solution. First of all, only a handful of states recognize gay marriage. And secondly, some gay couples—like many straight couples—are not married, though they have long-term, committed relationships.

The Uniting American Families Act, which grants immigration benefits to "permanent partners" regardless of marital status, is another partial solution. The bill, which has not gotten much momentum in Congress since it was first introduced in 2000, avoids the definition of "spouse" embedded in DOMA, granting immigration benefits to foreign partners of American citizens.

This practice of delinking marriage and immigration benefits is common in many other countries. Glenn Greenwald, the popular civil liberties blogger at *The Guardian* and a former civil rights attorney, earned permanent residency in Brazil through his Brazilian partner David Michael Miranda. Greenwald met Miranda in 2004, during a vacation in Brazil, as he contemplated getting out of lawyering and getting into journalism. Miranda, who grew up in poverty, had never been to the United States and had very little chance of getting a visa.

But Greenwald set up shop in Brazil, established his blog, and applied for same-sex partner immigration benefits. Brazil is, in many ways, quite conservative—it's an overwhelmingly Catholic country that was run by a military dictatorship until 1985. But since 2003, Brazil has allowed permanent partners, regardless of gender, to apply for immigration benefits. According to Greenwald, it was viewed as a humanitarian issue, not a gay rights issue. Denial of immigration benefits to certain Brazilian citizens was seen as discriminatory.

"Congress is not going to vote to even get close to issuing federal benefits to same-sex couples because it has the stench of legalizing same-sex marriage in their eyes," Greenwald said of the United States.

In Brazil, immigration authorities just want to know if you have a legit partner or not.

"You have to provide a ton of documentation to demonstrate that your relationship is the spousal equivalent of a married couple," Greenwald said.

Greenwald had to show that he and Miranda lived together, maintained joint bank accounts, appeared on one another's wills and had to provide sworn affidavits from Brazilian citizens who knew them as a legitimate couple. They also had a home inspection by an immigration official. Greenwald was able to stay and work for three years, while their application was considered and then granted.

In the meantime, Miranda is now in graduate school studying corporate communications, or "propaganda," as it's called in Brazil. He has obtained a tourist visa for the United States and can accompany Greenwald on short visits. Greenwald said that they would like to live in the United States at some point, as it would be convenient for his work as a frequent television and radio commentator. But they are also happy in Brazil. He also does not want to be a poster child for same-sex couples in exile, though he writes about it from time to time.

Greenwald, a frequent critic of President Obama's continued War on Terror policies and other federal issues, says that the Obama administration's refusal to defend DOMA is one of the best things the administration has done. The courts will overturn the law and immigration judges will be able to grant spousal benefits to same-sex couples, he says.

But granting same-sex couples immigration benefits will also bring gay couples parity on the exile front. Even if DOMA is overturned or if the Uniting American Families Act passes Congress, couples like J.W. and Gabriel—with three and ten year bars—will still be kept out of the country, just as Nicole and Margo are.

Ottie & Jenny

On April 17, 2012, Jenny Phipps and Ottie Pondman put on their newest threads, affixed "peachish-rose" corsages to one another and went to the City Hall in Zoetermeer. Zoetermeer means "sweet water" in Dutch. It's a town twenty minutes inland from The Hague in the Netherlands. It was Tuesday—free marriage license day.

They chose the short version of the ceremony in which a "lady of the law," as Jenny put it, legally bound them as a couple. They grasped right hands, exchanged the rings that Ottie's granddaughter delivered on a flower, kissed and then rushed out, just in time for the next couple's appointment.

After the ceremony, Ottie and Jenny returned to their flat, swept cat hair from the couch and set up for an evening reception. They laid out salmon on special Dutch rolls, made coffee and arranged the wine and juice. Jenny's daughter brought a wedding cake. Soft music played in the background and their closest friends and family mingled, congratulating the brides.

The wedding was mostly a formality—the couple had lived together for seventeen years. But it also affirmed their relationship in a new way.

"We felt real special for a couple of days, living in the clouds," Jenny said. Ottie said the wedding ceremony was emotional because it was such a long time coming. Travel and deaths in the family and life had always gotten in the way before. A month after their wedding, Jenny and Ottie went to Crete for a week, taking advantage of the suffering Greek economy for a relaxing honeymoon. It was their first vacation in years.

At 20, Jenny Phipps had gone off to the Netherlands, to Delft, to work as an au pair. During her year abroad, she met a Dutch man, a student at the university, and they struck up a relationship. He wrote to her once she was back in the States. Then he came to see her on the family farm outside of Wilmington, Delaware, and they decided to get married.

The young couple spent their first summer together out West, mostly in Vail, Colorado, where he did research for his thesis and she worked in a restaurant. Then they returned to the Netherlands, and Jenny found work as a typist and a desk assistant for the first few years. In 1986 their first daughter was born and 1989 they had a second daughter.

In retrospect, something had always been missing from the relationship, Jenny says now, an emotional richness that was lacking in her marriage and had been lacking with her high school boyfriend. In retrospect, she still recalls an elementary school teacher's nice legs. But Jenny was married and had two wonderful daughters in those days. She had a young family and an interesting enough life overseas in a progressive, Western European country, and she had never even had to think about the U.S. immigration system.

Then she met Ottie.

Ottie Pondman was born in The Hague. When she was fourteen, her mother died and her strict father made her drop out of school and take care of the house and her four brothers and younger sister. Even after she married, at 22, she would go back to the family home three times a week to clean and do the shopping. Ottie also had two daughters with her husband but not a very happy marriage. Her husband was older and a domineering man, she said. Her family was Catholic and fairly strict, and though she felt an attraction to women for some time, it was very difficult for her to acknowledge.

In 1992, Ottie's younger daughter was in playschool and she used to wait for her at the top of the stairs. One day she saw Jenny coming up the steps to pick up her younger daughter and thought to herself, "Woo!" It was love at first sight.

Both women were married, had their own families and Jenny had never really thought much about women. But they started spending lots of time together, at the playground with their kids, having coffee with other moms. Ottie taught Jenny to play guitar—that's where it really started—and Jenny gave Ottie watercolor painting lessons.

Jenny slowly realized that it pained her every time Ottie left her to go home, but she didn't really know why. One time, Ottie leaned in and kissed her and at first Jenny pushed her away. But then she realized she was falling in love.

Soon after that, Jenny told her husband that she was in love with Ottie and moved up to their attic. Jenny could not sleep next to her husband when she was in love with someone else. She knew she had to find a way to be with Ottie but she did not want to break up her family. Eventually she moved out and got her own apartment, taking the girls during the week. Then Ottie and her younger daughter moved in with them.

While it was a relief to be together, Jenny was also very depressed about breaking up her family. She went to a psychologist and took medication for about a year, trying to come to terms with her choice.

But the girls were already tight friends and viewed Ottie as a second mom. Jenny's ex was accepting of the relationship and remains supportive.

When the girls were about eleven and thirteen, Jenny decided to take them home to spend time with her family and learn about America.

"I just had to be in America to figure out what I needed to do," Jenny said.

The plan was to live with her brother and sister-in-law, a few minutes from the family farm, to get grounded again. The girls went to public school and spent a lot of time with their grandparents. Jenny got a job as a secretary at a mortgage company and then worked at a call center. But she missed Ottie terribly. Ottie came to visit for a few weeks in October and returned around Christmas time for a second visit.

When their year was up, Jenny had figured one thing out for sure. She had to go back to the Netherlands to be with Ottie. This time, she and her daughters moved into Ottie's home and she got a job that she loved teaching art to disabled people.

In 2004, Jenny's brother was diagnosed with cancer and, for the second time in her many years living abroad, Jenny felt a strong need to travel back across the Atlantic. She flew to Houston and donated stem cells for her brother. Jenny, her brother and her sister-in-law spent more than two weeks together, staying at a hotel near the hospital and eating out every night.

"We knew he was sick, but he didn't seem sick," she said.

The procedure was successful and bought him some more time, but in 2005, her brother died. His death at forty-eight years old shocked the family. Jenny and Ottie flew home for the funeral and then visited again in the summer. Jenny could see how much her parents, who were getting older themselves, missed her brother and she decided to talk with Ottie about moving back the States for a while.

Jenny and Ottie did not know it yet, but this decision to move to the United States together—the simple desire to be near family—was the first step toward a life in exile.

In 2007, Ottie left a good job and her kids and grandkids in Holland and entered the United States as a tourist. The Netherlands is one of thirty-six countries around the world that currently participate in the U.S. visa waiver program, which means that Dutch people do not need advance approval to visit the U.S. to stay up to ninety days. They kind of knew that Ottie could not apply for permanent residency, though they were not clear about the terms of the visa she would get. But Jenny's sister-in-law did some research and encouraged them to come together, with Ottie entering as a tourist, and to stay with her in Elkton, Maryland, near Wilmington.

Within the ninety days, Ottie applied for permanent residency and got employment authorization in the meantime, so that she was able to work. They still don't exactly understand why she got the work permit, but it was official and Ottie found a job at a retirement home, the same kind of work she did in Holland. Everything seemed to be going well. After a year, Immigration renewed her work permit and she stayed on at her job another year. But on April 22, 2009, Ottie received a letter that her permanent residency had been denied and that she was no longer allowed to stay in the United States.

"I had nightmares that these men in black were going to come and take her away," Jenny said.

They spoke with a lawyer who advised them to just sit tight. The letter did not have a date by which Ottie was supposed to leave the country and her work permit was good until November. So they sat tight.

In the summer another letter came with a summons and a date attached. They were to report to the Homeland Security office in Baltimore on September 14. Jenny, her sister and sister-in-law went with Ottie and as soon as they arrived things went haywire. Ottie was detained, finger printed five times and held with other foreigners who were being deported. Jenny and her two companions waited seven hours to see Ottie.

At first they thought she was going to be deported immediately, but Ottie and Jenny argued that they were trying to arrange housing in the Netherlands first and asked if she could stay through Thanksgiving. The immigration officer relented, giving Ottie until November 16 and requiring her to check in once a month.

Ottie had overstayed her initial entry under the visa waiver program by more than a year. She could have been deported and barred for a decade.

But the immigration officer agreed that it had been an administrative error to grant her a visa waiver when she arrived at the airport—she should not have been allowed to enter at all—and then later to allow her a work permit. A visa waived visitor is not eligible for work authorization, and if she had intended to stay longer than ninety days in the U.S., she should not have been granted the visa waiver. The officer promised them that Ottie would not face a ban, because of the agency's mistake.

In October, when she went to check in, however, a new agent read her case file differently and had her sign a paper that indicated she would be barred from re-entering the United States for a decade. The agent told her he didn't like doing it and that she should get a lawyer and fight it. But it was too late for them to fight it. They had already made preparations to return to Europe. Not only would Ottie be deported, but any future visits together were now in jeopardy. They had been in the U.S. for two years, all of their belongings were in the States. They both had rewarding jobs that they liked and they were close to Jenny's family.

"If Ottie was a man, we could have gotten married and she would have been able to stay," Jenny said.

If Ottie was a man, they could have left the U.S., gotten married and reapplied for permanent residency, or, more likely, they would have done that from the beginning. But now Ottie faced the same ban that anyone who overstayed a visa, entered without inspection or otherwise become undocumented would face.

On November 17, a plain-clothes immigration officer escorted Ottie onto an airplane. Jenny was on the same plane with her. They flew back to Holland together and moved in with a friend and her large dog.

"We were very, very sad. Very disappointed," Jenny said. "So many different emotions go through you but we had to put those emotions on hold."

They were only able to ship some of their things back from the United States. Their bed is still in storage in Jenny's parents' basement. When they returned to the Netherlands, Ottie got her old job back, but it took them three months to find their own apartment. It took Jenny seven months to find a good job. She worked in a bakery on Saturdays for a while, a job she did not like, and then she worked at a stressful science lab, labeling test tubes. Eventually she found work teaching art and other activities to people with disabilities.

When they first returned to Europe, Jenny had a problem with Dutch immigration as well. Jenny had lost her residency permit for Holland when she left for more than a year and she needed a Dutch citizen with a good income to sponsor her. They were not sure if Ottie's income would cover it, and they were in a financial bind. The total cost of the papers was 900 Euros, or about $1,100.

"I almost thought I couldn't live in Holland and Ottie couldn't live in America," Jenny said. "In Holland they don't give a crap who you live with, what sex you have, as long as someone could pay."

When she went into the Dutch immigration office, they noticed that her residency card had never actually been canceled and so she asked them to just reinstate it, which they did for a 40 Euro fee instead.

They were back in The Netherlands and secure, but now their exile from the United States was official.

Meanwhile, Jenny's parents were getting older and they had all grown rather close during the two years they spent together. Then, in 2010, Jenny's father got sick. He was diagnosed with Stage Four lung cancer, probably from working with asbestos at a chemical company for many years. But her life partner had a ten-year ban from the U.S. and there was nothing Jenny could do about it.

This is typical life for many same-sex couples in exile. First you just want the option to return home. Then you figure out a way home but experience the rejection of your own country in the deportation and denial of your partner. After that, something happens to necessitate a return—a death in the family, a change in career, a need for an America fix—and the personal becomes political. Jenny and Ottie are not political people. They don't follow every twist and turn in immigration policy, even as they live through it. But they know this rejection well.

And so Jenny went home to visit her father alone. Her father was a stoic weekend farmer who had worked with chemicals at a large company for his whole life. Jenny and her mom could not be too emotional around him. They had to joke around and put up a front. When Jenny got back to Holland with a doctor's note that her father had become terminally ill, they started asking around about what could be done.

Jenny and Ottie had discovered a local chapter of Love Exiles, a support organization for same-sex binational couples living abroad. One of their contacts mentioned that it might be possible to request a special visa to visit an ill loved one. Ottie went to the U.S. Embassy in Amsterdam, dropped some names at the counter, saw three very nice consular officials and within three weeks had a special visitor's visa, good for one year. In January 2011, they went together to see Jenny's dad for a short visit. His tongue had swelled from the chemotherapy and he was having a hard time eating.

In April, Jenny's mom called to say that they'd brought in hospice, so she started planning another visit. She planned to ask for a leave from her job on Monday. On Friday night she went to dinner at her daughter's boyfriend's house. All of a sudden the doorbell rang. It was Jenny's ex-husband bearing the bad news: Her father had died and no one could find her to tell her—it happened too fast.

"I was making plans to go home and poof, he was gone," Jenny said.

They went back to their flat and had tea with Jenny's ex and his girlfriend. She cried and drank more tea and cried again. Her ex paid for plane tickets to the United States with his credit card because Jenny and Ottie didn't have a high enough credit limit. They paid him back later. They took a flight to JFK, a taxi to LaGuardia, another flight to Philly and then were home for the funeral.

Jenny and Ottie stayed three weeks and tried to help Jenny's mother. They tried to make sure she was comfortable but it was hard to really do much, especially when they had to return to Europe so soon.

Now Jenny's mom is almost 80 and Ottie's special visa has expired. They are still living with one foot on each side of an ocean.

$$* \quad * \quad *$$

The widespread exile from the United States of some same-sex binational couples does not always feel like punishment. J.W. and Gabriel have established a good life for themselves in San Miguel de Allende. J.W. is a top selling real estate agent and Gabriel has finished his bachelor's degree in international business. He's done academic exchanges in Canada and Argentina. Glenn Greenwald and his partner David enjoy their life and their right to live together as a couple in Brazil and have not thought much about moving to the United States.

"When you don't have the option you actually don't seriously sit down and think about it," Greenwald said.

Jenny and Ottie have many dear friends in the Netherlands, enjoy a European quality of life and have rewarding careers. They are happy most of the time.

But love exile can also feel like banishment, undemocratic to the core in that these couples lose their political voices. They miss out on career and educational opportunities. They miss family and friends. They are often separated for long periods of time. There is no way for them to plan ahead.

"These are the people who kind of fall off the edge of the earth," said Martha McDevitt-Pugh, founder of Love Exiles, the online community for same-sex binational couples living abroad. Martha and her partner also live in the Netherlands and know Jenny and Ottie.

Many Americans find themselves in exile with their binational partners, without a voice in the U.S. or in their adopted land. For Martha, and her partner, Lyn McDevitt-Pugh, who is Australian, being stripped of a political outlet was very difficult. Lyn cannot vote in Australia—after several years abroad, Australians lose their franchise—and neither can she fully participate in Dutch democracy. Even though Martha got involved with Democrats Abroad, an arm of the Democratic Party overseas, and founded Love Exiles in 2002, she feels rejected by her own democracy.

"Lyn is treated there when we cross the border, technically as a legal stranger," she said.

Many of the couples that Martha and Lyn know—hundreds of binational same-sex couples in the Netherlands alone—never plan to permanently return to the United States. But they all need to plan for their futures, for their parents and for their kids. They need to plan for their careers. Not knowing when, or if, U.S. immigration policy will change for their partners leaves them in a terrible limbo. It distances them from family back home, who also live in limbo, only knowing their children, their children's partners, and even their grandchildren during one or two visits a year and maybe an occasional overseas vacation.

Then there is the stress of relocating abroad, sometimes to a third country unfamiliar to either partner.

"People don't tend to connect and reach out to each other," Martha said. "They are dealing with the language and culture and their new in-laws... A lot of people get in touch with us when they don't know what to do anymore."

Jenny and Ottie are back in Zoetermeer, surrounded by friends and stable. But they want some choices as well.

"If time goes on much longer, Ottie and I are going to feel too old to make that move again," Jenny said.

J.W. and Gabriel are not in a rush to move back to Texas, but they would like to go home to J.W.'s ranch and spend Christmas with his sister and many dear friends. J.W. is not in a rush to get back into politics either, but he would like the option and many of his former constituents would like him to return as well.

"It would be nice to have the flexibility to make a life with Gabriel in the United States, but this is the second best option," he said.

In many ways, same-sex binational couples have made more progress on the immigration front than any other group of immigrant families. They will most likely win access to immigration benefits and all of the other federal benefits that DOMA denies them in the near future.

But as long as the three-year, ten-year and permanent bars remain, it's still a race to nowhere for Gabriel and Ottie and their American families.

Chapter 11

On the Continental Divide

~

Nicole Salgado

The Second Floor (February 2007-Fall 2009)

Sometime in early 2007, I poked my head out of the brand new stairwell to the second floor of our house. The wind swirled around me as I approached the edge of the freshly dried concrete slab, and I got vertigo looking down on our construction site thirteen feet below. Stacks of concrete bricks lined a rocky driveway strewn with empty cement and *cal* bags.

From up high, I had a 360-degree birds-eye view of our neighborhood. On the highway into town, I could see the Pemex and OXXO, the local gas station and convenience store. The southern view went clear across the valley to Cimatario, an extinct volcanic peak marked by radio towers. Behind me, to the north, the scrubby dry forest stood dotted with organ cacti. The neighboring states of Guanajuato, Michoacán and Hidalgo appeared as grey-green silhouettes, distant mountain ranges.

A few raggedy *mesquite* and *huizache* trees dotted our open lot. Below a big *mesquite* was the firepit where we often had lunch. Sometimes my *suegro* would bring *elotes*, big, fat ears of corn still in their husks, to roast over flaming branches. One time, he dropped an armful, disappeared momentarily and returned with a soda bottle full of liquid, which he doused over the flames. They jumped higher and a foul-smelling smoke arose.

I asked, "*¿Qué es eso?*"

Margo replied, "It's diesel."

I flipped. "That's so toxic!" I complained. Everyone just laughed.

They also laughed at me at my birthday party that year. After they sang to me, my brother-in-law snuck up behind me and shoved my face into the cake. I got covered with frosting and swore at him. But when they told me it was tradition for the celebrated person to have a *mordida* (big bite) of the cake, I sheepishly apologized.

These lapses of propriety on my part—which were fairly common at first—occurred less often as my in-laws and I got used to one another's customs. Even so, frictions still occur on occasion, and there was a lot that I never got used to about living with Margo's family. Thus, we kept up the pace of our construction, and nine months from when we'd begun building, we moved into the first floor of our house.

The second floor of our house was "finished" over the course of the next year and a half, *poco a poco*. Two years is a snail's pace by some standards, but for our neighborhood, our construction project was lightning fast. It was a remarkable achievement for both of us, and a far cry from the conditions Margo's family lived in many years ago in San José el Alto.

Margo's family was one factor that drove him to the U.S. It's also part of what brought him back to Mexico. For better or for worse, his family is a part of our story, part of our life here.

The family's early dwellings in San José had humble dirt floors, and they fetched water by *burro* from a well over a mile away. They eventually moved to the city and Don Lupe and Doña Sirenia usually met their basic material needs, but Margo has told me of at least one time he went dumpster diving out of hunger. He was a middle child, so although he didn't have to care much for younger siblings, he had to fend for himself. Together with his family, he was also expected to work hard, to an extent that flies in the face of child labor laws. As a result, Margo learned to work as a team, and he prides himself on his self-sufficiency.

That same work ethic earned Margo great respect on job sites in the U.S., which, in turn, gave him much-deserved self-esteem and hope that his family would recognize his successes. He received some of that approval when they saw his abilities as a builder. Finally able to provide for his family in a way he'd never before been able to, Margo sent thousands of dollars home to his mother from the U.S., hoping to be able to help her even more upon returning. But when we arrived, his mother tried to give him back the money he'd sent. He considered her living situation bordering on neglect and her health substandard, so he invited her to live with us when we were done with the house. But she feared abandoning her adult children who still lived with her, or becoming a nuisance to us.

Margo's father had actually come into new money as a result of his *ejido* land sales, but it didn't result in much progress for his wife or their standard of living. For example, despite the fact that his parents could now afford private medical care, they clung to the inadequate state pension system they'd relied on for decades, allowing their health to worsen.

Further, Don Lupe tended to focus his attentions on a few opportunistic sons. Sometimes he complained to Margo about the lack of profit in his farming operation, or that his brothers were pocketing earnings without reinvesting in machinery. In response, Margo encouraged his father to put his money in savings, make a will, take some time off the farm, and to spend time with his wife, other children, and grandchildren rather than just focus on the farm and the few brothers who took advantage of him. Margo suggested getting back into organic farming instead of shelling out on chemicals and hybrid seed. He also argued that his brothers wouldn't learn to make a living if Don Lupe always provided for them. Even though his father readily accepted physical assistance, he would often ignore advice. In an odd compliment, Don Lupe told Margo that he didn't help him as much because he didn't need it.

It took Margo a few years to come to grips with the realization that the sort of progress he wished to see in his family simply wasn't going to happen. Some material gains were made for a handful of brothers, but equitable progress and emotional growth seem beyond the family's reach. I initially encouraged Margo's attempts to constructively reintegrate with his family, so it was hard for me to avoid the family drama. It's been disappointing for me to come to the realization that there won't be much, if any emotional closeness, with Margo's family.

We try to make the best of it. We tell ourselves that we're better off as homeowners and don't run the risk of detention in the U.S. anymore. That we "did the right thing." Margo and his relatives still help each other out when it's urgently needed. I've found a few special ways to connect with some of my in-laws. My *suegro* loves my baked goods and I make herbal remedies for my *suegra*. I'll always value what they've taught me about patience, endurance and generosity. We're sometimes able to enjoy each other's company for the occasional meal, birthdays and baptisms. However, some conflicts have worsened to the point where relationships with some of Margo's family members are unbearable.

Margo's kin really charmed me when I first met them, and I had high hopes for relocating south and becoming part of such a large family. But since their dynamics have proved so trying, with a few exceptions, Margo and I can now really only count on each other in Mexico.

On the last day of June 2007, we moved into our new house. We had painted walls, windows, tile floors, and a bathroom with a shower stall, but no doors, furniture, kitchen sink or cabinets. Those came over the next couple months. In the meantime we washed dishes on a plywood platform outside, rain or shine.

Our first guests, Annika, a former student, and her mother Colleen, joined us a week later and stayed on the living room floor. Their arrival was unconventional. Our driveway was too muddy to drive up after days of heavy rains, and they had to walk the last hundred feet with their luggage in the rain. Annika lost a flip-flop in the mud. But the next day we walked up the hill behind our home and picked *garambullo* berries—tree cactus fruit—while sipping wine.

Every guest who arrived over the next year represented a benchmark for our home. Sara was our next guest, in August, and helped us sand our dining room table right after Margo had finished the kitchen cabinets. Before my parents came in October, we finished an upstairs bedroom. By November, when Camly came, we finished the second upstairs bedroom.

It hasn't always been rosy living on the rural-urban fringe. It's a beautiful view, but we have regular power outages, water shortages, or neighbors burning trash nearby. For me, the odor of smoldering plastic is as bad as inhaling diesel fumes—dangerously unacceptable. But in our rural town, Margo is doubtful that I will ever manage to change our neighbors' ways.

Those who were adventurous enough to visit were curious about the different "living standards" of a developing country, and everyone has gotten their money's worth. It just so happened that one of the longest blackouts occurred the first time my parents came to visit.

October 12, 2007
We are emerging from a week-long "blackout" induced by paying the bill on the day it was due. It took that long for CFE [the electric company] to get their story straight and two cold showers and four nights of candles and a bonfire… 'til this morning at 5:30 a.m., when the lights miraculously went on. What relief. I had already lost quite a bit of spoiled food and wasn't looking forward to a finale to my parents' trip here without "luz." But it sure does make you appreciate it more once it's gone.

My folks, being good sports, said it was still better than booking a hotel room, even with the electricity debacle. For my mom's birthday we threw an unforgettable party, with a full house singing her *las mañanitas* and homemade *pollo en mole* that my sister-in-law helped cook.

We had twelve visitors in the first year and a half. In a way they allowed us to maintain a semblance of our former life, just transplanted a few thousand miles south. But finally the visits began to slow down, just as the house project wound up.

I remember the date when the house was finally finished, because Rudi and Sue, our friends who'd married us, came to visit with their son and his friend. With Margo's last piece of gold jewelry from the U.S., we made one last push to finish the second bathroom. It was Christmas 2008. To help our Jewish guests celebrate Hanukah, we made a menorah from scratch out of a *nopal*, bamboo and copper wire stripped from scrap electrical cable.

While finishing the house, we'd defied our own fears of bankruptcy and gainfully employed ourselves for over two years. But with that page turned, we were left with an inescapable question of "what now?" We had many reasons to be grateful, but I often felt otherwise. I loved my house but had few outlets and still complained regularly. I felt like a fish out of water.

I was isolated in a process of acculturation but didn't really know it. There wasn't much that friends or family could do. The situation was almost beyond help, and it was hard taking advice when I felt like nobody could comprehend me. The lack of internet and an unreliable Mexican mail system added to the vicious cycle, making friendships from back home drift apart, which left me feeling less support and less likely to reach out when I needed it.

I needed someone to commiserate with. One day while attending a niece's birthday party, I was sitting on a bale of hay near the corral, away from the others, with my sunglasses on because I'd been crying. I was feeling like an awkward foreigner again. I called my friend Michelle Myers in San José who was interning as a therapist. But I wasn't just looking for empathy—I intuited that her three and a half years of service work in Brazil might provide some insight into my experience in Mexico.

"I'm having a hard time feeling grateful for things," I told her. She could hear the conversations in Spanish and the cows mooing in the background, and said something along the lines of "being grateful isn't everything." Then she laughed heartily and her mirth wrapped around me like a comforter.

"Nicole, don't you know you're going through culture shock?" she asked candidly. I should have known, but it was an eye-opening moment for me. It was as if I couldn't really believe it until an "expert" acknowledged it.

Despite the relief of naming my problem, I still needed to gain control of my negativity. Everything irritated me. My old back pain started to come back in late 2007, and I intuited that it was a bit more than just culture shock. I felt continually buffeted by my emotions and circumstances, and so I needed to do something about it, or risk putting more strain on our marriage.

I began a sort of personal self-help course, starting with my Tibetan Buddhist books, such as *When Things Fall Apart,* by Pema Chodron, and *The Myth of Freedom,* by her teacher, Chogyam Trungpa. Although I'd heard about loving kindness, as applied in Buddhism this was the first time I'd really put it into practice. Getting some insight into our behaviors in response to the challenges we faced, whether Margo's or my own, compelled me into a more compassionate perspective.

July 11, 2008
After seven years of companionship, after a conversation with Margo about his father and the cow, I finally observed samsara [the cycle of suffering] before my eyes. I asked Margo what would happen in this hypothetical conversation: He would ask his father, "Why are you mad at me?" and his father would say, "I'm not, why?" then Margo would say, "Because you told me you'd move the cow last night and you didn't." Margo simply and candidly replied to me, "He would say nothing and walk away." And that's when it dawned on me, what's been driving most of Margo's behavior for most of his life and for much of our relationship… his unconscious repetition of his father's behaviors.

Tonglen, a meditative practice of giving and taking, also had a powerful effect. As I struggled to transform my annoyance into patience, my irritation with my in-laws started to diminish and I even experienced some relief from my back pain. It didn't solve all my problems, but it was a useful tool in my arsenal of survival and adaptation—what some books refer to as "becoming conscious."

Finishing our house had been a large, external accomplishment that we could rightfully feel very proud of. But my laborious task of inner work had only just begun.

Every year here meant a little more growth, a little more assimilation

Even though the initial terror of running out of money lightened up once we finished the house, we were still concerned with having enough income to scrape by. I was also feeling professionally aimless. Being un-employed for me was like being a bee without flowers. But there weren't any jobs in my field, at least nothing at a reasonable salary. My first "job" was teaching English in a local community center a few hours a week—for $1.50 (U.S.) per student.

The options weren't much better for Margo. He'd accepted a job with a science/industry consortium, and was hired entry-level despite the fact that he was more skilled than many of his coworkers and had actually trained one of them before leaving for the States. It lasted three months, after which his entire department was laid off. Finally, he took the plunge and began to work for himself, doing residential maintenance and con-struction—but it was slow going getting the business rolling.

I slowly began make friends locally, enjoy my adopted home, and locate business opportunities. Through friends in the U.S., I met another ecol-ogist in town named Tamara, originally from the D.F. She was studying the sustainability of the wild oregano harvest in the Sierra Gorda for her Ph.D. project. We became friends and she invited me to help with her fieldwork. I have fond memories of our trips to and from the Sierra in her blue Tsuru. We'd career around hairpin turns onto ridges covered in cat's claw and barrel cacti while swapping stories of our pasts in Spanish and her broken English.

We spent hours under the pounding sun and the clearest, bluest sky in the world, listening to the hawks cry above us, eating backpack lunches in gravel washes under majestic *mesquite* trees and trading calls with the wild burros across the canyons. When we'd come back down into the little pueblos, we'd down ice-cold *Barrillito* beer or sip fresh *pulque* (fer-mented *agua miel*, or agave nectar). Those times made me think: *Maybe I can do Mexico after all.*

Tamara introduced me to some other environmentalists in Querétaro. Through them, I had my first public event in Mexico—an exhibit of my wildflower photography. I began giving presentations, starting at confer-ences, about watershed education and climate change.

I soon discovered the Peace Corps Mexico headquarters in Querétaro and helped out in their library for a few months. I admired the volunteers who gave up their professions and families to serve in Mexico for two years. But I felt a twinge of envy for the support they received on cultural adjustment, when I'd had to just figure it out myself. Plus, my stay didn't really have an end point in sight like theirs did. When I found out that a volunteer stipend was more than what Margo made for a full-time salary at that company job, I even looked into applying for the corps myself. But since my husband was a Mexican national I wouldn't be able to request placement in Querétaro.

For the first time, I noticed some aspects of American culture that repelled me.

> *Spring 2009*
> *It's no wonder we Americans have the issues we do. We're conquerors at heart. One guy went for the jugular, wanting to know if I was a librarian or a former PC volunteer, in which case if I was neither, what was I doing there? Another woman made [a] comment about if I spent too much time in the library surely I was a glutton for punishment...*
> *I fell back to appreciating the cordiality of the Mexican coworkers...*
> *how much I appreciated the warm, affectionate hug of my dear friend Tamara a few hours later.*

The experience felt ironic because I'd initially been relieved to meet more foreigners in Mexico. It felt good to speak English and to relate to people in that familiar way. My irritations had long centered on things that bothered me about the Mexican culture, while I felt nostalgia for U.S. customs. Coming into contact with newly arrived Americans made me contemplate how much of the brash American attitude I kept in check since I'd first arrived.

But the truth was that there were positive and negative aspects of both cultures. I kept that in mind as I continued to make more and more friends, of both nationalities.

Through my contacts I managed to stay tangentially involved in my field. But I always had to take jobs like teaching English or translating to supplement my income. It left me hungry to feed my passion for the environment and social change.

In the latter half of 2008, I met an American art therapist named Naomi, who was doing domestic violence prevention work in Querétaro. She lent me *The Artist's Way* by Julia Cameron and I bounced some ideas off of her. It proved to be a turning point in my professional life—one in which I came to see the importance of cultivating my own capacity for creativity. As a result, I had a vision for telling a story of the human side of migration. My contribution to this book eventually followed.

But my vision would have to wait—my first creative writing project was of a much different flavor.

Every year after the summer rains, the first strands of cornsilk turn brown, starting the local craze for *elotes*. Some ears are left on the stalk, harvested when dry, and the kernels are shucked and stored in sacks. Then the women (typically) prepare the *nixtamal* for *masa*, corn dough used to make *atole, tamales, tortillas* and *gorditas*.

My *suegro* had maintained his heirloom corn varieties and nourished his family in this way for more than sixty years. In my first years here, a mountain of *mazorcas* would appear on our property in the fall, to be sorted into piles by color: reddish-pink, purplish-black, and sometimes white or yellow. But things were changing fast. Don Lupe's new, mechanized farming practices relied almost exclusively on hybrid white corn seed. And my *suegra* was also now too frail to prepare the corn and traditional foods by hand.

I was fortunate to be exposed to many of the family's traditions before it was too late. I didn't realize quite how much I'd learned until I heard our visitors' comments about my meals during their stays. When I found out how many Americans (and modern *mexicanas*) wanted to know how to make things like *tamales*, I held my first workshop at home in late 2008. It inspired me to start compiling Mexican recipes in English for friends. The number of recipes quickly grew to almost fifty—a collection worthy of a small cookbook.

The Bajio's Bounty, which I self-published on a whim in early 2009, ended up garnering more interest than expected. It even led to three Stateside trips for book talks and workshops, finally allowing me to return to California after almost three years away. The positive feedback helped me to develop more faith that my creative urges could result in economic opportunity.

Later that summer, buoyed by that self-confidence, I organized several organic gardening workshops at our home, which also received a surprisingly enthusiastic response. I started to think I just might be able to carve out a fulfilling professional life in Mexico.

I hadn't been that happy in a long time.

That December, my parents were coming to visit for the second time. I planned a trip for the four of us to the Guerrero coast, to Playa Troncones. It was our first real beach vacation since we'd passed through Mazatlan just over three years prior, and our B&B and the weather were a dream. The only event that marred our experience was Margo's inability to relax the first two days—he felt guilty that my parents were footing the bill.

Luckily, he finally warmed up to the idea enough to enjoy himself. It was a good thing, because we both deserved a vacation. After working on his own for over a year, Margo was finally building a good reputation and with my small book sales, we'd made enough to break even for the first time since arriving in Mexico. It was cause for celebration.

On our way back home, we passed through Pátzcuaro, Morelia, and finally the Monarch Butterfly Sanctuary. The last stop was magical. It was the winter resting place of the emblematic migrants that had enchanted me since I was a little girl and welcomed me to Mexico when I'd seen them flying over Margo's childhood home.

Deep in the heart of that migratory mecca we stood agape under towering *oyamels* dripping with festoons of orange and black wings, hearing the vibrations of millions of butterflies above us. These tireless travelers had inspired me during my hardest time as an *extranjera*, and now I was standing in the place they'd returned to for eons. For the first time since coming to Mexico, there was nowhere else on Earth I wanted to be.

Binational family

By 2009, Margo and I had been together for eight years and still had no plans to have kids. We had a lot of reasons, including environmental ones, but mostly we were doubtful that we could provide enough financial stability for a family. I think even our exile itself was one of the unspoken reasons for our hesitance. But as Mexico is such a family-oriented culture, we often received the question "¿*Y ustedes, cuando?*" to which we replied that we were happy "just the two of us."

Rather than recognize our conscious decision, some relatives thought we were cursed. One brother-in-law told Margo we should go to pray at San Juan de los Lagos, since he and his wife had finally conceived after visiting the chapel there. As diplomatically as possible, Margo replied that perhaps that was true, but it also could have been that his sister had been on birth control for a while before.

Nosy relatives aside, I often had little fantasies about having a child. I kept a running list of baby names I liked. I'd even printed out baby astrological signs that were compatible with Aquarius and Gemini parents. One time I wandered into the third, empty bedroom, and joked to Margo that our house was too big for just the two of us. He laughed and replied that he was making up for his crowded childhood, when they used to sleep four to a bed.

Some locals believe that children choose their parents, not the other way around. We never really did try to have a child. But while on vacation we had a conversation about being open to having one, were it to happen. A little "angel" must have overheard us, because she decided to come and join us.

Five weeks later, I realized I was pregnant. After years of false alarms that had always come up negative, I felt a rush of excitement at seeing the positive result. I quickly embraced the idea, despite my earlier mixed feelings.

The rush didn't last long.

January 15, 2010
Once I found out [I was pregnant], I thought that all my indecision would be sandblasted out of my field of vision. But just this morning I woke up practically in a panic attack of fright about impending motherhood. Granted, it's still eight months away. But a fearful moment it was, out of nowhere. Paralyzing. I couldn't figure out or analyze it, let alone decipher it, but I did remember... [to keep] breathing, remembered that it was an emotion... and it disappeared about as quickly as it arose. That kind of steady breathing... helped me through a rather challenging encounter with my OB-GYN today as well... I'd almost rather not recount the details for [how] distasteful that it was but needless to say she was defensive, condescending, crotchety, offensive, and slow to pick up on the fact that I was going to dump her as a doctor if she didn't make an attempt to be nice or at least joke around with me by the end of the appointment. She was telling Margo to give me a slap upside the head, for god's sake. When I told my friend Shannon who is also pregnant ... she told me flat out that I need to find another. I just hope my luck doesn't run too thin...

The next day, I woke up nauseous. I thought, *so this is morning sickness, just part of being pregnant.* But soon I was throwing up around the clock, and I began to lose weight and strength. I tried to research my problem but I didn't have internet at home, and constant vomiting made trips to cyber cafes complicated. Making it down a grocery aisle without heaving became difficult. I tried a homeopath for the nausea on the recommendation of a friend, but I was throwing up bile the morning after my first visit.

I took to camping out on the bathroom floor. I finally found another OB-GYN near where we lived. In a few weeks, I had lost more than twelve pounds. She diagnosed me with *hyperemesis gravidarum* (HG), severe pregnancy nausea and vomiting. She put me on medication for the nausea, which helped a little at first, but my symptoms soon returned.

I hadn't told my family yet in the hopes I could keep it secret for the first twelve weeks. But my resolve to keep going with the pregnancy was weakening. I had so little energy that I could barely leave the couch.

My doctor's best recommendation was to increase the dose, but the side effects of the meds were drowsiness, tremors and depression. But the alternative seemed even worse—in the worst cases of HG, women are hospitalized or fed through nose tubes for their entire pregnancies. I knew I couldn't handle that either. I wept when I saw women walking down the street holding their children's hands. I wanted that. I didn't want to miss out on bringing a new life into the world.

Margo supported whatever decision I made, but any legitimate fears I was having about motherhood had become mixed up with my illness, and I couldn't think straight. I hadn't eaten normally in more than a month. I finally told my mother, who suggested praying to something, no matter the deity. Prayer had helped me several times before. Now I'd been bestowed the greatest creative gift of my life, but it left not one but two lives hanging in the balance. I began to say some general prayers for my health and the health of my baby. My friend Maggi reminded me to ask for guidance from the spirit within myself.

I know it sounds impossible, but I got a response the next day, just like that.

I remembered a suggestion I'd seen on one of the HG help sites about eating in the early morning, so I took some crackers up to my bedroom that night. Starting the next morning, with one isolated exception, I did not get sick again for the rest of my pregnancy. It was as if a veil had been lifted.

> *February 15, 2010*
> *February 14th was an amazing day, a day where I woke up with no*
> *nausea, where I felt no fear, where my energies returned to me... I*
> *was able to spend a tranquil morning just cleaning the kitchen with*
> *Margo. Even the precious act of drinking a smoothie and [going] for*
> *a walk felt like ecstasy. Leaving the house, I saw the surroundings like*
> *a child, without prior judgment, without prejudices... I saw the coun-*
> *tryside around us for what it was, not for what it was lacking or for*
> *what I wanted it to be... it's time to start over. Allowing myself to*
> *dream of things like making clothes for a child, going to a baby shower*
> *or blessing. If that's what the future holds for me, so be it. I don't want*
> *to fear, but I also don't want to be alone. I'm not saying that my child*
> *is going to solve my problems of being isolated, not by any stretch. No,*
> *I see it more now as a catalyst for me taking stewardship over my own*
> *destiny and well being. Not just letting the reins drop and letting others*
> *determine my destiny, so to say.*

I never realized quite how cynical I'd become until I realized it made me doubt my potential as a mother. All the unspoken fears I'd had about parenthood felt even scarier in a foreign country, and made me forget that I had the strength within me to overcome them. But once I drew upon that inner strength, I could deal with my fears differently.

Most importantly, Margo exceeded my expectations as a very supportive partner who was with me every step of the way, from the physical preparations to attending prenatal classes. An American herbalist in nearby San Miguel de Allende that my doctor recommended became a new ally and resource. With the help of our circle on both sides of the border, we got ready to be the best parents we could possibly be, together.

I allowed myself to dream again. We dreamed of our baby, together.

And exactly four years to the day after Margo and I rolled across the Nogales, Arizona, border into Nogales, Mexico, with our lives strapped to our F-250, in the Year of the Tiger like her father, our daughter Bea was born.

The next day, happiness and rain poured over the roof of our house. *Y nuestra casa se convertió en un hogar.*

Becoming a mother coincided with some other major milestones for me. When Bea was four months old, I began coauthoring this book. During her first year, I went through the Mexican naturalization process. Just before her first birthday, I officially became a dual citizen—on Mexican Independence Day 2011.

Having a child has provoked a lot of growth for both Margo and I. Bea makes us happy in ways we've never known before. We've had the typical parenting ups and downs as well as some of the more unique drawbacks of parenting in exile. Some of my fears did come true. I experienced the kind of snafu that I dread from Mexican institutions during the birth itself. I had to switch my hospital at the last minute, and the one I went to just happened to not have hot water in my room that day.

Raising Bea in the local economy, without the physical support of our immediate families, is challenging. I had to sell my car to cover the expenses of the birth and Bea's first year medical appointments. Most of Bea's clothes and toys are the product of others' generosity. By tag-teaming childcare in am/pm shifts, we cobble together enough income to pay the bills.

Since my parents still work, they can only come visit once a year. We haven't been able to turn to Margo's family for help, as they're all either working or physically unable. His mother's increasing falls were actually undiagnosed mini-strokes, which went undiscovered until she suffered a major stroke when I was seven months pregnant, leaving her entire left side paralyzed. Although she recovered much of her mobility, she needs regular assistance. Margo's father is still caught up with his farm and *misa*.

But even if his relatives were free to help, trust is an issue. Margo's own childhood experience was harsh discipline bordering on verbal and physical abuse, and I have my own differences with the way children are raised in traditional Mexican culture. We do have a babysitter, but we don't rely heavily on her. Perhaps other fears aren't far below the surface. Although gun violence is rare in Querétaro, kidnapping and extortion are more common types of serious crime.

I'm not sure what Bea's educational future holds—my encounters with the Mexican education system have left mixed impressions. I've taught both students and teachers in rural, urban, public and private schools here. I've certainly met dedicated individuals working in the public sector, but resource-poor public schools simply can't compete with private schools. We recently heard of a public elementary school classroom that had one teacher for *eighty* students. Having attended excellent public schools as a youth, I'm not happy with the degree of class segregation or having to afford private schools. Lately though, the media snippets I hear about the direction the American education system are uninspiring.

My social circle has naturally expanded since having a child with play-groups. A surprising number of families of different nationalities raise kids in Querétaro. When I hang out with my *gringa* friends who are also raising their children here, we can commiserate in that same way I probably would with other mothers in the U.S. Or we laugh about the idiosyncrasies of our *suegros* or the prying comments like "you're not going to give her formula?" or the even more hilarious superstitions like the one where our children will get upset stomachs (*empachar*) if we dab drool off their chins with a washcloth.

Many of my counterparts have a different perspective on life here. Those who have live-in maids or nannies and abundant leisure time lead a comparative life of luxury, one which makes them prefer their life in Mexico. One friend, who isn't wealthy *per se* but lives comfortably, has built her entire career here and can't imagine returning to the States. She says she can't understand why I'd want to go back. In her opinion, we have it so much better here than in the U.S. We own homes and enjoy a rich local cultural heritage. It's not the first time someone has implied my daughter would have a "better" childhood in Mexico.

I struggle with these commentaries because they contain a grain of truth. There are some really great things about raising a child in Mexico. For example, it's a very family-friendly culture that really embraces kids. We can take her with us to restaurants and not even get a single glance, much less a dirty look, if she has a temper tantrum in the middle of dinner. That's a relief coming from the land of shame should your kid make so much as a peep on an airplane.

And even Margo says, "I think it would be a lot harder to raise a kid in the U.S.—it would be a lot more expensive."

On the other hand, for me, it boils down to a matter of choice. Sure we can chart our course to a certain extent here in Mexico, but as long as we have no choice but to be here, we will have a sense of an interrupted trajectory and unattainable fulfillment—the absence of personal sovereignty. Paolo Coelho writes, *"Man needs to choose, not just accept, his destiny,"* and this rings true for me. There's a difference between making the best of a forced situation, and having the autonomy to raise your family wherever you most want to be. Ten years in exile will of course blur the line between the two, as we further discover what it means to live our dream regardless of geography.

Flora, Fauna & Choices

Taking our story public became a personal necessity, a desire to turn an unfortunate situation into something meaningful and an obligation to share my voice where others cannot or will not. The idea became reality when my coauthor Nathaniel visited us in January 2011 after reporting from Ciudad Juárez. While showing him around Querétaro, an art gallery downtown happened to have an exhibit on pan-North Americanism. It was a serendipitous trail marker on the path to making my personal matter political.

The artist, Erika Harrsch, expressed a belief in the arbitrary nature of country citizenship and the heartlessness of immigration policy. She had created a beautiful green passport with a golden Monarch butterfly on the cover. Her concept really captured my feelings about what it means to be citizen on the North American continent.

I'm a bioregionalist who's believed in natural—as opposed to political—boundaries, as well as indigenous rights, for a long time. Living in Mexico has only deepened my appreciation for how inextricably linked the lives on this continent are.

I grew up in Syracuse thinking that beans, squash and corn—the three sisters, planted by the Haudenosaunee people—originated in New York, or perhaps in New Mexico. But later I learned that corn originated in Mexico, almost 8,000 years ago in the Tehuacán region southeast of Mexico City. I can only imagine the wealth of knowledge that's migrated across Turtle Island since then. Or what's been lost along the way, as people themselves became a commodity.

Even California and Querétaro are linked by the fabled El Camino Real, or "The Kings' Highway," named by the first Spanish who arrived in Mexico. The original El Camino Real wasn't a Californian boulevard for low-riders, but an ancient trail of tears in Aztlán, a path for the forcible spread of the mining industry, Christianity, and the concentration of resources into the hands of a few. Catholic missions were later established along the route, spreading an ironic mixture of both healing and harm. The same Fray Junipero Serra who traveled hundreds of miles erecting Californian missions began his career converting Otomi and Chichimecs in the Sierra Gorda of Querétaro, only a few hours north of us.

In reflecting on how our past has contributed to our current situation, I've come to see that people and wildlife face indistinguishable struggles, whether we're migrants or permanent residents. I often lament that we consider arbitrary borders and rampant development without regard to the natural balance with the land, or with each other, to be progress.

My mother-in-law fondly called the scrub-covered slopes behind our house *La Bolsa*. It was a special place where she and her mother used to go to forage, in the ancient tradition. There, they gathered cactus pads—*nopales*—and their fruits—*chilitos, pitahaya, guamishe, garambullos*. Decades later, I, too, eagerly tried these foods—and you can still find them in local markets.

Although I still longed for the salty Pacific breezes and the deep green northern forests, the irresistible array of desert flora seduced me, and like every new bird that perches in our *mesquites*, local nature is ultimately what sustains me. There's nothing more I'd rather do than walk these hills covered with dry forest, among the *huisache, palo dulce, palo xixote, palo bobo, granjeno* and *yucca*, or in the shade of the ancestral *encinos* (oak) of the highest ridges.

The scene changed when the new highway behind our house was completed. Aptly named the Anillo Vial Fray Junipero Serra, it conveniently connects one side of the city to the other, but poses a new danger in our neighborhood. A six-lane highway with high speed through traffic and no shoulders, crosswalks or bridges, it restricts local pedestrian traffic, and caused the death of two bicyclists within the first few months of operation. For our family, it meant no more weekend bike rides behind the house, no more walks in *La Bolsa* to pick cactus fruits. My *suegro* sold his last two horses.

The urban fringe was hurtling toward us. Margo had already watched Querétaro quadruple in size. He talks about running the cows in what's now the Costco parking lot. And while I'm no stranger to suburban sprawl—I watched my own favorite childhood forest razed when I was eight years old—I was shocked to see square kilometers of desert scrub obliterated in a matter of months.

The breakneck speed of development in our city—less than three hours from Mexico City, one of the largest cities in the world—seemed inevitable in that master plans made years prior were being carried out in all corners of the region simultaneously. But I found myself losing one of the few things I loved about Mexico—nature—and it affected me deeply. As a recent immigrant, I felt helpless to do anything about it.

In a dream, the boundaries blurred between people and animals caught up in the wake of progress—some were free to flee, while others could only sit passively and watch it move like wildfire, consuming everything in its path.

> *Early 2011*
> *A pair of earplugs muffles the nighttime noises. I squeeze my eyes shut and soft warmth surrounds me. I try to unplug from the visions of the day, songs in my head. Colors appear in my internal view, squiggles of yellow criss-crossed on a purple background, almost like midnight. I am seeing its skin close up, pixelated on my screen. Then I see it curled on the ground, looking at me, safe in its home. The lights of five thousand new homes on the horizon or is it grassfire? Approaching quickly. I am afraid of when she [my own daughter] is old enough to notice, and there is nothing left to see. All of them, huddled in quiet solitude, witnesses to those scurrying by in darkness, headed for the border. How I will forget all of this in the morning.*

I wish that the growth of the conservation movement could catch up to the pace of development, but Querétaro is one of the fastest growing cities in Mexico, and our community's quality of life hangs in the balance.

There are always contraband birds for sale at the local markets—colorful songbirds in cages, most of them migratory or threatened species—many that I'd only seen in books before. They were either being poached from the hills surrounding our city or brought in from other states. When I first got here, I filed complaints to the PROFEPA, Mexico's environmental protection agency. They successfully followed up on one of them, but then I became concerned about retribution when I saw my house address on the letter.

One time I found my brother-in-law parading around a snake he'd killed on a strand of baling wire and I berated him for his behavior. His excuse was that it had spooked him, slithering out from under a tarp, but

I explained that it was completely harmless, a threatened species, and had only been hunting mice that were nibbling their stored corn.

To be fair, some of our local fauna does make even me take notice. I want Bea to be as safe as I was growing up, but the poisonous animals in our yard are more threatening than the poison ivy of my childhood. Margo was hospitalized for a scorpion sting this year, and his brother has been bitten by a black widow. But Bea is also sharpening her senses. She calls us when she sees strange bugs, even feigning "ouch" when she points to them in picture books. And my delight in watching her spot wildlife outweighs my anxiety.

Back in the U.S., two separate lawyers told us that ten years after leaving the country we'd need to file a hardship waiver with Margo's visa application. I remember feeling like 2016 would take forever to arrive, but now it's only three years away. Since we arrived, "extreme difficulties," the kind that go beyond "minor inconveniences" go into an Excel file called my "Hardship Log." The file includes all my bouts of depression, back pain that's now spread to my hip, dermatitis, gastrointestinal infections, irritable bowel syndrome and appendicitis, among other problems.

My gut has had a hard time adapting to its new home and has been vulnerable to both parasites and stress. Intestinal parasites are naturally more prevalent in a developing country, but something's wrong when you get food poisoning and say, "*Well, at least it's not amoebas.*"

It messes with your head, too. When I was teaching English at a local high school a few years ago, I started to have stomach cramps for more than a month. At first I was convinced it was just another case of amoebas, but it turned out to be IBS (irritable bowel syndrome)—from stress.

That diagnosis made me question similar symptoms two years later, when a pain in my stomach wouldn't go away for almost a week. I kept trying to will it away, but finally my concerned mother worried me into thinking it might be my appendix. As it turned out, it *was* appendicitis and I had emergency surgery the next day. So much for all in my head.

When I had Bea, I prayed that I'd confer all the antibodies I'd built up my first five years here through breastfeeding. To our great fortune, she is rarely sick. But then last year she and her father both came down with *Giardia,* to my horror. It's the kind of thing that can be cleared up fairly easily with the right medicine, and I've found some great practitioners who help me keep my family healthy, but it's a never-ending battle against poor hygienic and pollution standards.

Separation from my family, underemployment in my field and our below-the-U.S.-poverty-line income also go on file. As for personal safety, Querétaro is a low-crime state compared to other states in Mexico, so I'm not sure if that will make the list—although the situation could certainly change with the new presidential administration.

It feels weird to keep a journal of all my problems, but I've maintained it with the hope that maybe someday it'll help Margo to return to the U.S. with us.

Honestly, even before I moved to Mexico, I always considered the idea of submitting a hardship waiver after living here for ten years to be kind of paradoxical. I'd say, "If I can make it ten years in Mexico, I just might not need to move back to the U.S." After almost seven years here, I've changed so much that this isn't actually far from the truth.

Hardship waiver or not, I've asked myself these kinds of questions: Am I supposed to focus entirely on the negative aspects of being here and build the best case possible for a return bid? Or do I live these ten years to the fullest, not look back, and actually try to enjoy my life, put down roots, try to become happy living here permanently? There's something pathetic-feeling about living my life looking for ways out, despite all the hardships, all the desire I have for things back "home."

I'd love to imagine the three of us back on a California beach, the ocean breeze whipping our hair against our cheeks, watching elephant seals together. I fantasize about getting back into my professional field in a fulfilling way that also pays the bills.

It'd be so nice to be able to visit my family and our old friends *together*. As my brother lamented recently, in anticipation of his wedding this fall, "Geez, I wish Margo could be there."

Margo would love to entertain that dream alongside me, to reclaim those work opportunities he so relished in the States. I'm reminded of that daily by his broad grin in a photo hanging in my office. He's standing shoulder to shoulder with his work crew the summer before we left. But that would mean pinning his hopes on the fickle decision of an anonymous government official who doesn't know us, who might not like Margo's accent or his answers to questions. Margo's pragmatic cynicism doesn't allow him to entertain the possibility of a second chance, of a pardon.

So when that visa application gets submitted, I'll be the main advocate, the 24/7 secretary who makes it happen. I'll have to convince him that it's worth a try, and that even if we fail, we're still golden—a cruel joke. Part of me thinks it'd be easier to just become satisfied with the life I've wrought with my own hands here, to not shoot for the moon, to stay grounded.

The irony of these "hardships" is that although they stress me out to no end, since I'm so proactive, they force me to take more and more of my happiness into my own hands.

Since my pregnancy, I have become even more proactive about my family's health. I see the value of friends and family in a new light, and keep seeking that elusive equilibrium for us as a couple, and as a family—now that we are parents.

When I began writing *Amor and Exile*, I sought therapy as emotional support for revisiting the heavy topics from my past. It was in therapy that I discovered that my experience of having to leave my home country against my will was essentially a trauma that I am still grieving. But as any survivor of trauma knows, there's a point where you have to reclaim your life and move on. That's why although I'll continue to keep my hardship log updated, I'll be damned if I'll let it define me.

During one of those weeks when the highs and lows intermingled as naturally as ocean waves, I contemplated if we'd be lucky to have no choice but to remain stuck in Mexico.

Pinning our hopes on a visa is a natural thing to do. If they did approve a visa, it'd be wonderful to finally be able to travel as a family. But beyond visits to the U.S., the choice about where to settle won't be as easy as it seemed five years ago. Dr. Daniel Gilbert, author of *Stumbling Toward Happiness*, writes that we often feel worse about our decisions when we have too many options.

On the one hand, I can't overlook certain things that deeply disappoint me about Mexico. But many of those issues aren't unique to this society, and the U.S. has its share of troubles as well. Further, a lot will have happened between 2006 and 2016. We love the home we built and have put down new roots. We've started a family, made friends, and eked out a living. I have a lot to offer locally in terms of experience in community organizing, education and conservation. There are even some things I prefer about Mexico now—who doesn't like full service gas stations and more than 330 days of sunshine a year?

My relationship with my home country has changed—a lot like getting over an ex. When the U.S. broke my heart, I had to let go of her, for the most part. In having to protect my heart by not letting it hurt me, I naturally don't feel totally the same about her anymore.

If the U.S. doesn't let Margo go back, I won't have to choose between her and Mexico. I could possibly make a new peace in my relationship with her, but I wouldn't have to make the difficult decision as to where we'd be better off raising our daughter, because it would already be made for me.

One night, I was up late juggling three jobs, marveling at how all those years of essays in school had finally paid off. It surprised me how the language I spoke had equated to support for our family.

Everyone else in the house was asleep. Before going upstairs, Margo had said, in that motherly way of his, "Don't come too late." And I just nodded and kept on because I was on the first of dozens of tasks for that weekend.

By the time I reached the bedroom, Margo was fast asleep with the nightlight on. It threw gentle shadows on his square jawline, which so closely resembled our daughter's it made me catch my breath. Settling onto the bed, I noticed how rare it is for me to stop and really look at him, contemplate what we started eleven years ago, where it's taken us. Not just the heartaches, dammit, but all the love we've shared and things we've done together.

I smiled, recalling the night before when Margo confided that he could feel our bond so much stronger than ever before—that we had more good feelings and less fear.

I unclasped my necklace, an opal pendant my parents had given me on their last visit. It was my mother's birthstone, that's found here in Querétaro in *cantera* stone. Holding the shimmery brownish-pink stone in my hands, I studied the center, which held an iridescent chunk of an impossibly beautiful rose-colored gem, then looked back at Margo. I've given up a lot along this life path that's taken me far from home—and a polished rock might not seem to have a lot to do with love relationships, but somehow in that instant I felt like everything was all right.

Happy moments of inspiration are like gold to me, and so I reached over to the nightstand in the hopes of finding a notebook to jot down my thoughts. The drawer made a dragging sound and Margo snapped awake, whispering, "shhh," then groaning, "What are you looking for?"

Then he fell back asleep.

What *am* I looking for?

Politics makes the answer to that question more complex than it ought to be.

Many years ago, my partner, my husband, one of the best things to happen in my life, tried to convince me that he shouldn't be with me because he was going to ruin my life. But I couldn't accept that because I couldn't permit political reasons so beneath the realm of love to force us apart. I trusted my heart, and our love has never failed us.

I might be a better person for all that I've endured—stronger, more resilient. Margo and I have grown, and accomplished a lot. But we—and our families and friends—have also suffered needlessly, and will continue to do so, as millions of others are right now, as a result of policies that the majority of our citizenry doesn't even know exist. Policies that I'd wager aren't the best thing for the people of this continent.

In a way, Margo was right all along—my life has been ruined—not exactly in the way he predicted—but *the life I used to lead* has been lost. The same core individual remains, but I have indeed changed. One's heart can only be broken so many times before the scars obscure it irreparably.

The words of my therapist echo in my mind: *"How much can you stand?"*

"However much they give me," I think.

"But it's so much pain… when is it too much?" the words, now my own, say.

There are some ideals I may never get back. But I'll no longer live in ignorance.

One life—Margo's—was the spark that illuminated my awareness of millions of immigrants who live and work in my country everyday, to whom my own family also owes its existence. Since the beginning of time, they've only wanted to move freely on this planet that we're all citizens of.

In my mind's eye, I saw their flight filled with terror. Like an eagle from above, I watched them scurrying across the border like hunted animals, just trying to find safe refuge.

I lived that pain myself. I've seen my friends' situations. Realizing that we're in this together helped me find the courage to tell *our* story—to bear witness to the forces of our time.

To move forward out of the stalemate that threatens to strangle its very spirit, our country needs more congruency between its stated ideals and its de facto legacy. Edicts like SB 1070 and NAFTA, or terms such as "inadmissibility" or "expedited removal" just don't measure up to "*Give me your tired, your poor, your huddled masses yearning to breathe free.*" By turning a blind eye to the people who suffer from these laws, we only stand to lose camaraderie, relationships, business opportunities, wisdom, global credibility, even our own humanity.

By failing to open our doors to our neighbors—without regard to class or quota—we disregard our own history as Americans, as people. We attempt to freeze evolution. We conveniently forget that we wouldn't even exist if the first people who walked this Earth hadn't had freedom of movement over the land they stewarded.

I support some regulations. But imperialism and the unceasing profit mindset have left a heavy toll—development, conquest, extinctions, loss of knowledge, culture and deep scars on our collective psyche. Despite being a product of that legacy myself, I still believe there are other ways forward. Compassion and the long view—of seven generations—require that people's right to self-determination is respected.

In the name of love, I embraced my husband for who he really is, not what a piece of paper says he is. In order to stay with him, I had to give up a lot but I still found more. If I could do so, then surely my fellow citizens could take an even smaller step and acknowledge the presence of men and women who've taken such risks to be their neighbors, many of whom want to be their fellow citizens. I don't want to have to choose between my husband and my country, because we all deserve something so much more. Our circumstances may be different, but we're all ultimately motivated by love.

When I awake to the sun filtering in through the curtains, a warm arm is draped around my waist and my daughter's voice is coming from the room across the hall. A year after I began this mammoth task of figuring out what it is I'm looking for, I realize that I've gotten the equation about my options wrong. It's not one or the other, and it's not something I can control. Whether I end up in the U.S., live in Mexico for the rest of my life, or get to make my own choice with my family by my side, I will steer my course toward love and find more of it than ever before.

Chapter 12

Love, Marriage and the Case for Reform

~

Nathaniel Hoffman

The first time I formally interviewed Nicole for this book, she described one of Margo's most profound qualities. She was walking around a track at a park in Querétaro, talking to me on her cell phone. It was 2010—before their daughter was born, not even four years into their exile in Mexico. She recalled her first dates with Margo—her initial apprehension, their language and cultural barriers and the way that he quickly put her at ease.

And then Nicole recalled the story of her fourth date with Margo when, through the fog of Spanglish, he offered to help her. She wrote about this moment in Chapter 6. For a long time I assumed he wanted to help her speak Spanish better, or maybe help Nicole figure out what to do with her life. But both Nicole and Margo agree that he offered to help her financially, a notion that Nicole initially laughed off—what would an immigrant laborer have to offer her, a self-sufficient and independent American woman? But over the years, this brief exchange became one of the foundations of their relationship.

"I was so rude," Nicole said during that first interview. "That's all that Margo has ever done in our life is help me."

I often reflect on that moment in their relationship when I hear politicians or the news media discussing illegal immigration. It was a moment when Nicole and Margo still saw one another through larger societal lenses—after all, they had just met. Nicole could not imagine how Margo might help her. Perhaps she thought that she might be of more assistance to him than the other way around. And Margo, slyly aware that he had just uttered a classic pick-up line, knew that their chances of a next date depended heavily on improved communication—literally, in a shared language, but also in working on shared emotions, dreams, destinies.

At one point, Beth and Carlos also had a conversation around shared language and communication. In their case Carlos was seeking a leg up in English.

Susie and Roberto got together while dancing, an intense form of communication. Communication is at the center of all human interaction, and yet, too often the mass media addresses complex subjects like migration as a one-way conversation and a foreign problem.

A former colleague and talented foreign correspondent once suggested to me that a reporter's job is to describe clashing extremes, places of conflict and intransigence, just beyond the experience of the average citizen. He was not endorsing sensationalism, but arguing that a window into other people's problems is the primary focus of journalism and the reason people read the newspaper. A focus on the "other" is a hallmark of the mainstream news media.

This media obsession with other people's problems, foreign problems, diminishes the impact of terrible events on our psyche. We accept a certain level of war and starvation around the world, despite graphic reports on the nightly news. We accept a certain level of murder in our own town, comforting ourselves that it's not happening in our immediate neighborhood. It's not happening to people like us.

A sensational treatment of transnational marriage would have been easier to write. Such a book might focus on immigration scofflaws or on worst-case scenarios. People do abuse the U.S. immigration system, to be sure. "Russian brides" and women from other nations marry Americans solely to get a green card. Americans marry drug dealers and human smugglers and maybe even terrorists. Immigrants are caught up in the global sex trade, trafficked by American citizens. Abusive spouses threaten their immigrant partners with deportation on a daily basis.

But those examples strike the vast majority of Americans as extreme cases, exceptions to the rule, just beyond the grasp of our experience or imagination.

What happens instead, when the experience of the average citizen itself becomes extreme?

Ordinary Americans have lost everything fighting the immigration system. They have lost their partners, their careers, their homes, their shot at the "American Dream." They have been separated from their communities. Fathers and brothers and sons of American citizens have been deported into the clutches of street gangs in Central America and Asia. Some have even been kidnapped or shot filling out U.S. government paperwork, as we saw in Chapter 7. Jake Marlowe Reyes-Neal, the American who was killed waiting in Ciudad Juárez for his Mexican wife's waiver to come through, is a grave example. Cases like Jake's must be better investigated and documented by the media, and the role that the U.S. government played in his death should be scrutinized.

But the stories in this book are not sensational, although a hair's breadth separates them from Jake's. They are ordinary love stories whose protagonists remind us of ourselves. It's not easy to dismiss the couples we've met as outliers, as unique or extreme cases, because their stories of meeting and falling in love and starting families sound like our stories: Susie and

Roberto dancing the night away, going to yoga class together, raising rabbits. Ben and Deyanira finally finding one another after a little urging from mom, trying a long distance relationship and eventually reuniting in a romantic, colonial-era cobblestone city in Central Mexico. Nicole and Margo flirting among friends, reaching into one another's souls despite a vast linguistic and cultural gap, setting off, with reluctant determination, on a great and terrifying adventure together. J.W. and Gabriel choosing to be together despite immense societal and political pressures bent on keeping them apart.

And so, how do we comprehend the stories in this book in light of what we believe about the United States of America and democracy and freedom?

It's not easy.

Another cliché of journalism—that the truth lies somewhere in between—is relevant to this discussion. In the case of immigration to the United States, and particularly immigration from Mexico, there is a vast, unexplored middle ground. That middle ground includes the millions of American citizens who interact daily with undocumented immigrants—at their businesses and schools, in their neighborhoods, within their families.

It is there that we begin anew, with the right of the American citizen to decide with whom he or she associates.

In 2013, there is nothing surprising or exotic about an American marrying a foreigner. We constantly travel and live in a globalized world. We travel for business and pleasure and to meet people. And we do have an orderly, if somewhat overburdened, bureaucracy for bringing a foreign partner to the United States.

Most Americans know that. We know that marrying an American gives a foreigner legal status to reside in our country because we are a country that honors family. We know that because even if our immediate family members weren't immigrants, we watched shows like *I Love Lucy* or read about President Obama's parents or saw Sandra Bullock in *The Proposal* and Gérard Depardieu in *Green Card*.

Our grasp of the immigration system comes from friends and relatives who have gotten married abroad, soldiers bringing home war brides, perhaps a chance meeting on the Zócalo, the Champs Elysees, Bondi Beach. And when we hear that some half a million Americans are unable to sponsor their husbands and wives because of where and when they happen to meet, it does not square with our understanding of our immigration system, which is supposed to keep families together. It raises eyebrows.

It does not square with our modern beliefs about love and marriage either.

Americans believe we have a right to marry whomever we choose and to live together with our families. We believe in marrying for love. Since about 2010, according to many recent polls, a majority of Americans also believe that gay and lesbian couples should have the right to marry and enjoy the societal benefits of marriage. Marriage is one of the most fundamental of American rights, informed at once by our religions and our contract law, celebrated in thousands of federal and state benefits and endorsed in international law.

The vast majority of Americans view romantic marriage and the primacy of family as societal ideals. Our media, our religious institutions and even our laws reflect those ideals, establishing the importance of the family unit and the right of American families to live together.

U.S. courts have agreed, in at least one small case, that families have a constitutional right to live together. Houston immigration attorney Laurel Scott, who has written extensively on immigration waivers for married couples, pointed to the 1977 Supreme Court decision in *Moore vs. City of East Cleveland, Ohio,* as a case in point.

"I think it's a right, not a privilege to reside with your spouse," Scott said. "Residing with family is a right, not a privilege and rights can only be infringed upon for compelling state need."

In the Moore case, the City of East Cleveland cited Inez Moore for living with two of her grandsons—cousins, not brothers—in a neighborhood that was zoned for only "single family" residents. Her second grandson had gone to live with her after his mother died.

Moore challenged the citation and a judge found that her extended family did not fit within the city housing ordinance. The court fined her $25 and sentenced her to five days in jail. Moore took the case all the way to the U.S. Supreme Court, which ruled that the zoning rule violated her Fourteenth Amendment right to due process and her right to define her own family arrangement.

"This Court has long recognized that freedom of personal choice in matters of marriage and family life is one of the liberties protected by the

Due Process Clause of the Fourteenth Amendment," the court decision stated.

The Fourteenth Amendment protects the rights of all American citizens from any law that abridges, "the privileges or immunities of citizens of the United States," or deprives anybody in the United States of "life, liberty, or property, without due process of law." It also guarantees equal protection of the law to anyone in the United States—not just citizens.

Conservative Supreme Court Justice John Marshall Harlan defined due process in a 1961 case as the juncture of liberty and social order. According to Harlan, as quoted in the Moore decision, the Supreme Court views the Fourteenth Amendment as representing, "the balance which our Nation, built upon postulates of respect for the liberty of the individual, has struck between that liberty and the demands of organized society."

Certainly the demands of an organized society include control over its international borders. But where is the balance between the liberty of the individual American citizen to choose his or her life partner and the demands of the larger society in immigration policy? What is the compelling state need, as Laurel Scott put it, to separate mixed immigration status families?

Americans expect our government to defend us from those who would do us harm. This is a reasonable expectation of a citizen of any country. But does this expectation require us to put on blinders when it comes to our borders—to treat all illegal border crossings as potential threats? Or does that position—the official stance of the U.S. government since the 1990s—effectively abridge the rights of American citizens to free association?

Does the expanding security state curtail the liberties that we have claimed since even before the founding of this nation, this "land of the free and the home of the brave?" The September 11 attacks raised this question in many venues with the Patriot Act, Guantánamo, two lengthy wars, FBI scrutiny of Muslim organizations and drone warfare. But the impact on immigrants in the United States and politicians' unwillingness to address immigration has had lasting consequences. In the post-9/11 period, the families in this book and many other Americans were driven underground or into exile with their immigrant partners as our foreign and domestic policy became more exclusive and anxious.

If a national immigration system is to mean anything, it must first take into account the rights of American citizens. We have a right to safety and security, to be sure, but also a right to establish our own families and to determine where we wish to live.

This deeply American notion of liberty, rooted in American conservatism, includes the rights of employers to a stable and reliable workforce. The farm and construction industry lobbies have been a strong beachhead to the immigrant rights movement for decades, keeping conservative lawmakers from descent into full-fledged xenophobia and nativism with their legitimate workforce needs. Kendall Hoyd, former president of Idaho Truss, the Nampa company where Juan Díaz worked, wants a legitimate way for immigrants—particularly working class immigrants from Mexico—to obtain legal work in this country.

"We don't even have to talk about citizenship," Hoyd said. "It's just the right thing to do."

Hoyd has both moral and material interests in mind when he argues for more open immigration policies, including, at least, an expanded guest worker program. It's good for the economy. It's good for housing and construction. It's good for his industry. It's good for his bottom line. And it's good for his former employees.

Other American institutions would benefit from a more stable and open immigration system as well. American churches and mosques and temples certainly benefit from immigration. A 2012 gathering of evangelical Christians, from Jim Wallis of the liberal journal *Sojourners* to Jim Daly of the anti-gay Focus on the Family, testified to the biblical notion of welcoming the stranger, endorsing Obama's temporary relief for Dream Act eligible youth. Evangelical Christians have varied interests in "welcoming the stranger," from a heartfelt, moral commitment, to a drive to increase their own ranks through recruitment to right-wing political aspirations, but the Evangelical Immigration Table and the Conservatives for Comprehensive Immigration reform that proceeded it, are significant currents of support for immigration reform—including legalization of the undocumented population—from deep within the conservative movement.

The Mormon Church has also supported broadly inclusive immigration policies in recent years, though Mormon presidential hopeful Mitt Romney did not embrace those principles in the fall of 2012.

"Undocumented Americans," to use the term *Time* popularized in 2012, already inhabit all areas of American life. Tens of thousands of college students lack papers, including, in 2011, student body presidents at Miami Dade College's InterAmerican Campus in Florida and Fresno State in California. An undocumented law school graduate passed the California Bar exam and was fighting opposition from the U.S. Justice Department in late 2012, in order to practice law. Actress Salma Hayek announced that she had been undocumented for a short time. Undocumented journalist Jose Antonio Vargas worked at the *San Francisco Chronicle*, *Washington Post*, *Huffington Post* and wrote for the *New Yorker*. He shared in a Pulitzer Prize for his coverage of the Virginia Tech shootings.

In a remarkable June 2012 exchange on the Fox News media theater, conservative commentator Bill O'Reilly told Vargas that he did deserve a path to citizenship because he was dragged to the United Sates as a child and was an asset to the nation. But O'Reilly went on to insist that if a 32-year-old sneaks across the border in Tucson, tomorrow, there is no way he should be offered a path to citizenship.

"What we want is legality across the board," O'Reilly concluded, insisting on some philosophical agreement as to who is deserving of citizenship and who is not. "We do need to carve out a process for people like you," O'Reilly told him.

In a media landscape full of posturing and pretending, the interview between Vargas and O'Reilly demonstrated one of the most deep-seated American attitudes toward immigrants: As a nation, we welcome *some* strangers and not others.

O'Reilly is an unpredictable political actor who has taken hardline positions against immigration reform for years. But he was willing to give Vargas credit for his contributions to society. Vargas was innocent when he arrived in the United States from the Philippines. He studied and worked hard and made many contributions to American society. His grandparents were naturalized American citizens. He is deserving.

In contrast, an adult Mexican man who walks into the country in Tucson is not.

That is O'Reilly's philosophical line. Vargas tried to talk to the Fox News audience about context and the individuality of any one case, and O'Reilly cut him off. But here's the crux of the matter and the reason that hard philosophical lines are always flawed: If that 32-year-old Mexican man were to marry Bill O'Reilly's daughter, then all philosophical bets are off.

J.W. Lown's conservative Republican friends in Texas were willing to make exceptions to their personal philosophies and seek status for his undocumented boyfriend because Lown was, "people like them." Whenever family comes into play, our American lines in the sand tend to evaporate. Our beliefs assume as many winding contours as that 2,000-mile line in the North American desert.

In high school classes, on Fox News and even in the newspapers, debates about immigration reform take various tacks. We like to run and re-run the cost-benefit analysis of undocumented immigrants on society.

For example: Do undocumented people use more government services—hospitals, roads, schools, etc.—than they support with tax dollars and other contributions to society? That question will never be answered, nor is it even the right question. Many credible studies have shown that undocumented immigrants pay more in taxes than many people think—sales tax, fees for government services and income tax and social security taxes that they often never claim.

An ugly corollary to the services argument is the cultural debate: Are immigrants diluting American culture, debasing the English language and corrupting American children with new forms of music and dance? Or is American culture in fact immigrant culture, the steadily bubbling melting pot, the deep, rolling bass and saxophonic cries of a century of American jazz, the burrito.

The debate continues, leading us farther from actual solutions. The border. Terrorism. Overpopulation. Racism. *Reconquista*. Drug wars. Border. NAFTA. Unpicked fruit rotting in orchards. Spanglish. *La frontera*. And then a breakthrough: childhood arrivals.

Immigrant children, smuggled into these United States before they were old enough to choose, break the stalemate. Some know only our ways, while many grow up fully bicultural. They stand up in the halls of Congress in their black graduation robes and mortarboard hats and they sit down in busy intersections and the talking heads stop talking to one another and listen for just a minute. All of a sudden immigration ceases to be a metaphor and becomes a remarkable young person asking only that America live up to its own principles of justice and opportunity, as young people have asked in every generation.

And this is where the conservative and liberal arguments for more open borders merge. It starts with the heartfelt valedictorian with perfect grades and excellent diction. The Pulitzer Prize winning reporter with an earnest plea for that piece of paper that separates him from his destiny. The young computer programmer with an accent. The tattooed artist with a short rap sheet who wants to design skyscrapers. A million or two million young undocumented Americans come forward and claim their piece of paper, for just a two-year reprieve, at first.

And then a 32-year-old Mexican man with an earnest desire to find meaningful work and build a nest egg and support his family walks to Tucson and walks onto O'Reilly's Fox News set and falls in love. Where is the deferral, the loophole, the waiver for him and his American family?

Where is the land of opportunity, the streets paved with gold that O'Reilly's ancestors and my ancestors found on these shores? While the golden streets may never have existed in a literal way, there was a time when the United States rewarded hard work and creativity with expanded citizenship and opportunity for some. Migrants fleeing harsh economic conditions and religious persecution in Europe found refuge and new lives in the United States just two generations ago.

But now, when faced with similarly bleak prospects at home, economic migrants like Margo and Carlos and Juan find closed doors. O'Reilly's fictional immigrant will spend thousands of dollars on legal advice. His American spouse will learn things about her country that do not square with her patriotism. She will find, as all of the Americans in this book have learned, that she has two difficult choices: live underground with her partner or self-deport and hope the government allows them to return together.

This is not a choice that American families should have to make. There are simple steps that Congress could take to alleviate this burden. The Obama administration now allows some families to apply for their hard-ship waivers before they leave the United States. Knowing that a waiver has already been approved before visiting the U.S. Consulate in Ciudad Juárez or in another country will ease their decision to apply, but as we saw in Chapter 7, it only covers a limited group of mixed-status couples, and those already abroad are not eligible. In addition, it is an administrative fix and not a permanent solution.

Reinstating 245i and allowing the undocumented spouses of American citizens to adjust their status in the United States is a more permanent solution, but one that also cuts out a large number of couples, such as those facing permanent bans for the common practice of crossing to America more than once. But 245i and the Dream Act are two well-established ideas that would enjoy popular support. Helping the spouses of Americans and young immigrants to become full citizens are ideas that members of Congress could easily take up, with broad support from the American people.

The reason that Congress has failed to approve even a highly desirable and sympathetic fix like the Dream Act, is that any bill that opens a new pathway to citizenship has been seen as a step toward comprehensive immigration reform, which eventually requires that the vast majority of the undocumented people in this country—ten or eleven or twelve million of them—be provided with a process for earning citizenship. This large and controversial goal has frozen policy makers on both sides of the aisle, with liberals refusing to shepherd anything short of comprehensive reforms and conservatives holding piecemeal reform hostage to threats of "amnesty." In the wake of the 2012 elections, when Latino voters were credited with cementing Obama's win, Republicans seemed to finally realize they were losing a growing Latino voter base. A new version of comprehensive reform emerged that provided a path to citizenship—a long and arduous one, but one that Senate Republicans would support. The negotiations over the Senate version of reform hinged on agreements between organized labor and business interests and included new spending on security infrastructure and policing along the border.

Immigration reform does require us to consider a rational system for accommodating our future labor needs and addressing our responsibility toward changing labor markets in Mexico—as a regional trade partner—and other immigrant source countries with economies tied to our own. There are many paths to visa reform: Should we provide more temporary guest worker visas, expand the definition of immediate relatives, open up the annual ceilings or recruit highly educated tech workers? How do we address the individual needs of every other constituent group from telemarketers to poultry workers? Congress appeared to favor guest workers, tightening family immigration categories and eliminating the diversity visa. While immigrant families marched in the streets and demanded an end to family separation and a means to fully participate in American society, Congress debated the needs of the dairy and manufacturing industries.

Proposals in the first part of 2013 did address some of the needs of mixed status couples through expansion of existing waivers. A blanket waiver would cover most spouses of American citizens who were found inadmissible. Congress also floated the idea of lowering the standard for a waiver from "extreme hardship" to just "hardship" and considering the hardship to U.S. citizen children of inadmissible immigrants.

But as attorney Laurel Scott suggested, the "unlawfully present spouse of an unlawful worker" would have an easier time normalizing than the spouse of an American citizen under the initial Senate proposal.

One reform that Congress did not seem prepared to take on was repeal of the ten-year and permanent bars—something rarely discussed in the media or proposed in legislation. The bans are inflexible, unreasonable in many, many cases and punitive in a unilateral way, without consideration of mitigating factors like family and other ties to the United States. Similar to mandatory minimum sentences for drug offenses, the time bars remove the vantage of the agencies and the judicial branch in ruling on immigration cases.

The time bars, established in the 1996 immigration bill, were a direct congressional challenge to the U.S. Department of State and the former INS. Congress presented immigration officials and judges with a long list of visa ineligibilities, including certain specific criminal charges, health conditions and common immigration violations. The ineligibilities written into the Immigration and Nationality Act in 1996, took away the power of case adjudicators to weigh mitigating factors like family ties and contributions to society in visa cases and, to a lesser extent, deportation cases.

Restoring that power to USCIS, the State Department and immigration courts would help to depoliticize immigration reform by allowing trained officers in the Justice Department, State Department and Department of Homeland Security to do their jobs again. In the vast majority of cases, the bans do not reflect on an individual's fitness to immigrate to the United States—though the public assumes that they do. They merely register a person's stay in the United States, which is the very reason they may be applying for permission to re-enter in the first place. Congress could convert the inflexible language of the time bars into more flexible guidelines for prosecutorial and judicial discretion. This move would have other, positive political ramifications as well. Many people who have felt trapped in the United States, unwilling to leave for fear of triggering a lifetime ban, would be able to return home. Combined with a willingness in Congress to relax the standards for waivers, some form of time bar repeal would lessen the imperative for a mass legalization program. This move would also lessen the bureaucratic burden in foreign embassies and consulates.

Such a move would have allowed Margo and Nicole to control their own fate, and establish their family home in the nation of their choosing. It would have allowed Ben and Deyanira to demonstrate the validity of their marriage and return to Idaho together. It would have removed the fear associated with Beth and Carlos risking life and limb to cross into Ciudad Juárez in the hopes of returning together. It would have given Veronica and Juan a chance to make a case for their reunification. And it would provide Susie and Roberto with an opportunity to emerge from the shadows.

Along with repeal of the discriminatory Defense of Marriage Act, the elimination of the three-year, ten-year and lifetime bars would also provide J.W. and Gabriel a chance to return to Texas together, to attempt a second political career and to put an end to their *de facto* banishment from the United States.

Eliminating banishment as a core element of our national immigration policy is necessary for the continued development of the democratic process in the United States. Our nation was founded as a shining example of modern democracy. The roots of democracy—a system of government in which power is vested in its people—began in ancient Africa. But our understanding of early democracy comes from ancient Greece, and the writings of the great Western philosophers.

In ancient Greece, before notions of early democracy began to take root, exile was a common cure for political strife. The victor in a political struggle in any one city-state would banish his defeated opponents and all of their kin into exile, often with violent consequences.

Then, as the Greek Classical period began in about 500 BCE, a new method of political transition developed. According to Sara Forsdyke, a classicist at the University of Michigan who wrote about the roots of early democracy, the *demos*—the 99 percent in ancient Greece—took political matters into their own hands and halted the destabilizing exile of political elites. They invented a new form of exile called ostracism, in which, by a popular vote of the masses, one political player each year was expelled from the state. Ostracism replaced wide scale, unilateral deportations as a more civilized, popular form of governing.

"The moderate use of the power of expulsion, as represented by the institution of ostracism, was a potent symbol of the moderation, justice, and legitimacy of democratic rule in contrast to the forms of rule that had preceded it (tyranny, oligarchy)," Forsdyke wrote in her book, *Exile, Ostracism and Democracy.*

Though not a perfect parallel, the wide scale deportation in modern U.S. history of one political class—undocumented immigrants—is similar to the tyrannical practices of archaic Greece in several ways. American politicians, across the ideological spectrum, use the threat of deportation to solidify voting blocks, to demonstrate patriotism and for demographic control. Those who are expelled—whether immigrants or their U.S. citizen partners—have little legal recourse. And broad social stigma is attached to deportation, denying immigrant families a voice in the greater society.

The whole notion of banning large groups of people from the nation is a step backward in the march of democracy. It's even more starkly undemocratic when American citizens like Nicole Salgado and Benjamin Reed are banished from the polis, even if theirs is a *de facto* exile, born of their choice of spouse.

The ancient Greeks also had an advanced understanding of love as a journey. Orpheus, the great lyricist, crossed the ethereal border to the gates of Hades, to meet his young wife, Eurydice, after her untimely death at the fangs of a poisonous snake:

> *"O ye Deities of the world that lies beneath the earth, to which we all come at last, each that is born to mortality; if I may be allowed, and you suffer me to speak the truth, laying aside the artful expressions of a deceitful tongue; I have not descended hither from curiosity to see dark Tartarus, nor to bind the threefold throat of the Medusæan monster, bristling with serpents. But my wife was the cause of my coming; into whom a serpent, trodden upon by her, diffused its poison, and cut short her growing years. I was wishful to be able to endure this, and I will not deny that I have endeavoured to do so. Love has proved the stronger.*
> *-Ovid's Metamorphoses, Book X, translated by Henry T. Riley, Cambridge, 1893*

Love has proved the stronger across America as well. Each of the couples in this book has chosen the path of love over the path of poison, pushing back against the powerful forces of exclusion and xenophobia to embrace our new, emergent America. Will the Medusan monster, the chaos that inhabits Washington, D.C., conjure a path toward justice, toward the light? Or will our gaze fix backward—as Orpheus' did on his return from the darkness—losing our grasp on the true promise of this free nation?

A song by Conor Oberst and Bright Eyes that was produced and sold to benefit immigrant legal defense in Arizona, echoes this notion of love across time and space.

Loving you is easy, I can do it in my sleep
I dream of you so often, it's like you never leave
But you've gone below the border, with a nightmare in between
I'm sending love coyote, to bring you back to me

In the United States, in the 21st century, this exile below the border, the nightmare in between, the deep relationships that no border or border patrol can touch—this is the coming test of our modern democracy.

Epilogue

When we started writing this book, in the Summer of 2010, Barack Obama was still in the honeymoon of his first term, Mexico's drug war appeared to be peaking and binational couples remained well below the radar of the American public and the media. Three years later, Obama had captured a second chance to deliver on his hopeful message, once again courting record numbers of new Latino voters. Mexican voters had retreated to the familiar control of the PRI, the political party that ruled the Republic for 71 years. And even as the Senate proposed the most significant immigration reforms in almost thirty years, much remained the same for all of the couples in this book.

"We're doin' our regular stuff," said Susie Fischer, the American woman from Denver whose husband, Roberto, remains undocumented. In the fall of 2012, Roberto went to see another immigration attorney. A friend of his who had been in the United States for ten years and was in deportation proceedings beat the deportation and obtained a work permit. Roberto wanted to see if he could get the same deal. Roberto has been in the United States more than ten years, and it's been almost ten years since his last trip to Mexico, but the great irony of his situation is that since he is not being deported, he's not eligible for any kind of discretion or cancellation of removal.

Roberto also missed out on the Obama administration's deferred action for young arrivals program. He did not come to the U.S. as a child and he's now 34, and has aged out of the program. When he asked about a hardship waiver, the lawyer told him he would have to have a really sick child or some similar tragedy to apply.

"You have to be sick, or have immigration following you around to get a permiso," Susie said.

In 2011, Susie and her two American daughters met Roberto's mother, sister and two nieces in Puerto Vallarta, a beach resort on Mexico's West Coast. It was the first time that the girls had met their Mexican grandmother, aunt and cousins in person. They stayed at a hotel called "Friendly," spending every possible moment together at the hotel pool and at the beach. Each morning they Skyped with Roberto back home in Denver and he helped coordinate their plan for the day in English and Spanish, so everyone knew what to expect.

Susie and Roberto are still looking to Carlos and Beth's success for inspiration.

Meanwhile, Carlos and Beth have come full circle. Carlos is now a U.S. citizen and had a chance to vote, though his political views remained a point of contention until right before the election. Carlos was seriously troubled by his U.S. immigration experience, up to and including his naturalization interview, which he considered abusive and prying.

"They want people to be citizens," Carlos said. "But at the same time... they don't know how to treat people." He calls it *prepotencia*, or arrogance, a high-handed, even racist position that Carlos felt from many government officials. From his first border crossing, to his second appointment in Ciudad Juárez where he felt like he was treated as a criminal, to his recent citizenship interview, during which his marriage and commitment to the nation was questioned, Carlos is not a fan of government and is attracted by Tea Party rhetoric on government accountability.

It made it difficult for him to vote for Obama, but in the end, Carlos supported the incumbent and his piecemeal nods toward immigration reform.

Beth and their two kids also visited Mexico in 2012. Carlos could have gone—he had legal residency and was on his way to becoming a citizen—but he had to work and was not able to go. Their kids bonded with Carlos' older children and Beth enjoyed time with her mother-in-law.

"I just was thinking about how far we came, how different everything is," Beth said recently. "It feels different that I don't have to worry that Carlos is going to get pulled over for a traffic violation and not come home. Or he'd be in the wrong place at the wrong time, during a raid at work."

Still, there is insecurity. Less, now that Carlos is a citizen, but the general instability of the economy and the racial politics of immigration reform still worry Beth.

"There is insecurity in work," Beth said. "It's the economy. I think lots of people are feeling the same insecurity."

Though thwarted at every turn by the messy immigration bureaucracy, unreliable Mexican postal system and vagueness about the penalties surrounding their case, Deyanira eventually received a visa. In the fall of 2012, they flew to Ciudad Juárez for six days and applied in person for an immigration visa for Deyanira, as the spouse of an American citizen. Deyanira had a broken foot and was able to avoid waiting in lines at the

U.S. Consulate and the nearby medical clinic. Ben also arranged several meetings with other binational couples living in Juárez with whom he'd connected on Facebook over the years.

"It was surprisingly very cool," Ben said. "I was pleasantly surprised, very uneventful."

In the meantime, Ben and Deyanira underwent a spiritual transformation together, leaving the Mormon Church, which informed both of their lives for many, many years, and becoming born-again Christians.

"I was really faithful in that religion," Deyanira said. "In the beginning, it was a shock for me to know the truth… Ben shared some things with me and I said, 'leave me alone—you believe what you believe and I will stay Mormon.'"

While in Mexico, Ben studied theology at a Bible college, finally earning his bachelor's degree after many years out of school. He researched Mormon theology and loves to debate matters of faith with his former co-religionists.

Ben and Deyanira described their waning days in Mexico as *agridulce*, bittersweet. They planned to return to Idaho, but ended up in Kansas City, Missouri, where Ben is taking further religious studies. They still contemplate living in the border region some day, to be close to the land of *nopales*, *mariachi* and universal healthcare.

Juan and Veronica are still in La Virgen. They had another baby in early 2013 and remain in sporadic touch with friends and family back in Idaho. They have no landline and their pre-paid cell phone runs through minutes even when they are on the receiving end of a call. Juan is working hours away in Querétaro during the week and Veronica is home alone most of the time. Veronica's four daughters are growing up in La Virgen, experiencing a childhood that is far removed from her youth in Idaho.

Occasionally Veronica makes it to an internet café to check in on Facebook, so I left her a series of questions to answer whenever she had time.

Veronica, steadfast in her *agridulce* outlook on life, answered as best she could:

> *I'd say the best thing about being in Mexico is that I get to see where Juan is from and to experience what he did as a child, to a point. The worst or hardest thing is not being able to communicate the way I would like to with my family and friends. I'm used to being able to just pick up the phone or get on the internet whenever I feel like it and*

call or chat.

The girls. Mercedez wants to go back to the States. We will let her go after middle school. Education is not that great here in Michoacán and I can't say I blame her for wanting to go back. I want the best for my girls and the... education isn't the best or close to. Victoria just started her first of three years of kinder. She likes going. I like her going... it gets her out of the house. Sara Elizabeth, what can I say about her? She is almost two and acts it. I love her laughs and smiles. She helps me get through some rough times and she gives them to me too. She's a busy, busy bee! =)

Veronica remains ever hopeful that some form of amnesty will prevail, though the daily news from the States reaches them only sporadically.

What the U.S. government should do for us? What can they do? I'm hoping that some miracle law will pass so we can go home soon. I feel my girls are suffering and sacrificing a lot for us to be with their dad. We sure eat a lot of beans to get through it, but even those are expensive.

J.W. and Gabriel live a somewhat charmed life in San Miguel de Allende. Gabriel finished his bachelor's in international business with several job prospects at multinational companies. They had been counting on getting at least a tourist visa for Gabriel after he graduated—after three years in Mexico. But when Gabriel went to the U.S. Embassy in Mexico City for his interview, the officer bluntly told him to come back in 2019, after finishing out his ten-year bar.

J.W., counting on a tourist visa for Gabriel and new opportunities to live at least part-time in the United States with his partner, had coasted a bit on his career. But after the news from the Embassy, he redoubled his efforts at selling real estate and applied to law school in San Miguel.

In a cruel twist, Gabriel would have been eligible for a two-year deferred action visa had they stayed in the United States, since he arrived as a minor, but because they had decided to return to Mexico to "wait in line," he could not apply.

"So much for all the talk of going across the border and getting in line, which we did," Lown said. "It takes the wind out of my sail to a great degree."

Lown criticized Obama for using his executive authority to grant deferred action, rather than going through Congress, but acknowledged that they probably would have taken advantage of the program anyway, had they remained in Texas. He supported the Libertarian candidate, Gary Johnson, for president, urging Republicans to focus more on "personal liberty" and make a greater effort to understand the Hispanic population.

Some Republicans did make gestures of support toward Dreamers in the lead up to and certainly in the aftermath of the 2012 election.

"I've been pleasantly surprised watching TV that Democrats and Republicans are supportive of this group of immigrants," Lown said. "Part of me wonders if Republicans realize how long the line is and in many cases, especially in our case, the line doesn't exist. There is no line to get in."

Twenty-four hours after Obama's second presidential victory, high-ranking Republican officials were speculating about comprehensive immigration reform and finding solutions for Dreamers. The large Latino participation in the 2012 election may have turned a tide, but much work remains for a still-divided Congress and a second term President Obama.

And even if such reform includes some form of amnesty for undocumented immigrants, it is unlikely that it will embrace couples like J.W. and Gabriel, Veronica and Juan, and Nicole and Margo. When that law is signed, they will still find themselves mired in limbo outside the United States, without a line in which to stand. Unless, of course, Congress repeals the time bars or establishes a new procedure for the banned spouses of U.S. citizens living abroad.

At the tail end of Obama's second term, in four more years, Nicole and Margo will have their chance to seek reentry together to the United States. Meanwhile, they continue to seek "the place where exile ends and life begins," as Nicole describes below.

✳   ✳   ✳

Since I finished writing my last chapter for this book, life has continued mostly along the same vein—counting the blessings alongside the hardships of exile. Our daughter brings us much joy. We're lucky to have many good friends here. On occasion, we go salsa dancing or vacation with visitors.

We struggle professionally but usually make enough to cover the basic expenses. I do environmental education work and teach English for supplemental income. Margo does maintenance, remodels and carpentry work, but still longs to get back into residential construction with a crew of his own. I'd love to help him start a business building green homes, but we can't afford it. Our only real asset is the home we built, and we have yet to obtain the title since the shared property is still technically *ejido* land. We lack insurance, but are grateful for government medical services when emergencies strike.

The tail end of our own bittersweet ten-year exile is approaching. Soon, our life plans might include geographic options. But first we need to scrape up enough for Margo's visa application fees and a lawyer, not to mention relocation costs. Since our current income simply won't permit that, we need more than just a legal miracle.

When the immigration debate resurfaced in early January, I got very involved. I began organizing, created a petition and outreach materials, blogged and participated in a documentary project on families in exile in Central Mexico.

The activist group I helped start, which we called Action for Family Unity, was organized completely online. I was new at participating in the online immigration forums, so it was the first time I had mass contact with dozens of individuals whose lives had been uprooted like mine, their families torn apart. Seeing so much suffering heaped upon American families strengthened my resolve that justice be served, and provided some much-needed solidarity.

One other thing has become clear as a result of becoming part of a wider network: The many difficulties of my life in exile do not represent the full extent of disenfranchisement that other American citizens who are separated from their families and exiled abroad experience as a result of the 1996 IIRIRA law. I also became a member of American Families United, which lobbied specifically to get families like ours included in legislative plans.

It had been almost seven years since we marched to support immigrant rights in California, and our lives hung in the balance yet again. But this time we were almost 2,000 miles away. Although I did see an uptick in the amount of media attention given to families like ours, we still had to endure every last debate about the merits of further criminalizing immigrants and the border. My advocacy efforts helped meet a need I had to participate, even if it wasn't in person.

I also finally got updated legal advice. I had long assumed that we would apply for an extreme hardship waiver after a decade outside the U.S., but now I understand that our chance to return north together hinges on a different type of application, an I-212. They'll weigh all the "favorable equities" such as Margo's family ties to the U.S. (me, Bea and my family), time spent out of the country, character strengths and hardship against "adverse factors" such as deportations, entry without inspection and work without authorization. Perhaps a federal agent will consider the fact that here, we live below the poverty line, my health suffers from stress, my daughter does not know much of her U.S. family, and our safety is at risk. Or not.

That's if a comprehensive immigration bill that includes families like mine fails to pass Congress.

According to one lawyer, our case should be very easy.

Very easy. That's all relative, obviously.

I find it hard to pin all my hopes on a one-shot deal, but it is nice to have a glimmer of hope at the end of this long, dark tunnel.

The early Senate bill, floated by a bipartisan group of senators, included one clause that might actually benefit families like ours: a blanket waiver that could allow permanently barred spouses of U.S. citizens to apply immediately for a hardship waiver, as opposed to a years-long wait, even from abroad. It wouldn't result in much of a net benefit for Margo and I, already having waited out seven of our ten years, but I still felt committed to efforts to help bring home the maximum number of families like ours in whatever bill passed Congress.

When the prospect of filing immigration applications sooner than we'd expected came up, I had to deal with a lot of old fears about how to navigate the intimidating immigration system, and doubts that we could pull it off. But this time, I wasn't as "alone" with the issue as I had been before, thanks to my contacts who had gone through the same process. Margo, on the other hand, has no way of vetting his doubts except with me, and for him, picturing a life split between the U.S. and Mexico is difficult. Even to me, the logistics seem daunting, and short of getting a passport to the United States of North America, as Erika Harrsch envisioned, we just might not be able to have it both ways.

While the final outcome for many of us has yet to be written, especially for same-sex couples, spouses with criminal records or those of us unable to afford the costs of legalization, Turtle Island is awaking from its slumber. I was heartened to see the Sierra Club, a fairly mainstream environmental organization, come out in favor of comprehensive immigration reform. And even though some families may lose the battle this time around, important groundwork is being laid. In this case, a long fight is better than no fight at all.

Life in exile, as it's turned out, has as much to do with my mind as it does my location. I'm constantly resisting the chains of the exile mentality. I struggle to separate my actual physical constraints from the ones I've developed internally over the years—to protect myself from the damage wrought by pessimism, paranoia and depression.

I regard my optimism and perseverance as precious. That is what's allowed me to get to this point with Margo, twelve years after our journey began in Northern California. It's let me have a child in another country, be a model for her and become a dual citizen. It will be the saving grace that keeps my family together—wherever we all shall be.

For perspective, I need only look to nature. The regal old mesquite tree still stands alone behind our house. The ground has been razed and concrete walls and wire stand between it and other neighborhood trees. But when I look up and see the flashes of colorful wings in the branches, I'm reminded that man-made barriers will never subdue the flow of life.

Acknowledgments

Both authors would like to thank the organizations and individuals below for their support of our collaborative work.

To all of the families who shared their stories with us, and through us, with the world, we greatly admire your courage and vision for a better America. And to all of the people who have contacted us throughout this project, your spirits are part of this book, even if we could not include every story that we encountered.

Immigration attorneys Maria Andrade in Boise, Idaho, and Michael Davis in Minneapolis, Minnesota, deserve special recognition for their dialogue with us, the detailed legal review that they both provided and their insights on our draft manuscript.

Thanks to Gilad Foss for producing a cover design that was both awesome and suited two authors' tastes. Thanks to Rachael Daigle for a thorough and efficient copy edit of our manuscript. Bevan Miller, Benjamin Frieburger, David Woolsey, Liza Long, the Rev. Dr. Ellin Jimmerson and Al Greenberg provided valuable feedback and perspective in the later stages of manuscript review.

The City of Boise's Artist in Residence (AiR) program at the 8th Street Marketplace supported Nathaniel's middle stages of writing of *Amor and Exile* and also served as a space for public discourse regarding the project.

Radio interviews with Amanda Turner at KRBX Radio Boise, Gavin Dahl at KYRS Spokane, Benjamin "El Chupacabras" Reed at KFTA Rupert, and Belia Paz at KWEI Boise helped us explain our ideas and communicate our process in writing the book.

We would like to thank our agent, Robert Guinsler of Sterling Lord Literistic, for seeing the potential in our book and staying committed to the project.

Thanks to Chad Summervill who produced the video for our crowdfunding campaign to send a copy of *Amor and Exile* to every member of Congress.

We owe thanks as well to our followers for their support and for engaging in meaningful discourse about the stories we've shared on amorandexile.com, Facebook and Twitter.

Finally, we are grateful to the various free, public internet platforms that allowed us to execute our book as a team online, despite living on opposite sides of the continent. If it weren't for applications like Gmail, Google Drive, Dropbox and Skype we would have been virtually unable to carry out this project.

Nathaniel Hoffman

In order to write this book, to immerse myself in the great immigration debates and in the people and places I've described, I took a leap of faith and quit my reporter job at *Boise Weekly*. And so first and foremost, I thank my wife and life partner Tara Wolfson, for trusting me, supporting our family and gifting me nearly three years to follow my passion. Her patience, guidance and wisdom throughout the reporting and writing process leave me forever grateful. My two little girls, Petra and Mandela, have guided me along the path as well, urging daddy to finish his book and providing my muse at every turn.

The theme of patience and perseverance must extend as well to my co-author, Nicole, who answered my every prying question, rose to the challenge of our rigorous, collaborative editing process, held me to some semblance of deadline—or at least gave it her damndest—and even taught me how to make tamales from scratch. And to Margo: had only we taken to heart your perfect economy of language. Dos palabras: *El fin*.

Boise readers John McCarthy and Rich Rayhill provided enthusiastic critiques of early drafts of the book, in writing and in spirited dialogue over two seasons on the old Chair Five on the backside of Bogus Basin. Houston immigration attorney Laurel Scott provided valuable insight into the waiver process and a Golden Gate University Law Review article by Julie Mercer provided early context for *Amor and Exile*. Rosa Gaona, paralegal in attorney Michael Davis' office, shared insights from her extensive work with mixed-status couples. Political scientist Mike Touchton at Boise State University assisted with analysis of the Mexican Migration Project data.

Miles de gracias also to the entire delegation at the Mexican Consulate in Boise for your sustained interest in this project and for making Idaho an even more interesting, beautiful place to write about migration. Thanks to the Idaho Press Club, which awarded me a late-hour grant to assist in my travel to San Angelo, Texas, to meet the fascinating protagonist in Chapter 9.

Finally, to all family, friends and strangers who shall not—or cannot—be named, thank you for sharing your stories, your *luz* and your lives with me and for encouraging this work.

Nicole Salgado

I would like to thank my friend Naomi Tucker, MFT for midwifing my original vision to tell a story about migration, in 2008, and for helping me to find creative support for my memoir.

I am grateful to my coauthor Nathaniel for wanting to make these stories known and for having the idea and the faith to join forces as a team, and to his wife Tara for her support of our project. Our voices together tell a stronger tale than our voices alone could have, and both of us have grown as a result of this collaboration. Our cross-continental collaboration was challenging, but more often than not, this project was a source of great personal satisfaction and I'm so happy to have had this opportunity to work with him.

J. Nichole "Coley" Williams, marriage, family and art therapist, provided therapeutic support for the process of drafting my narrative. Delving into my past stirred many emotions, and making a public memoir leads to feelings of vulnerability and fear of backlash, but Coley served as a touchstone throughout the process. She helped to remind me of the greater reasons why I wrote our story: to share my voice when others in similar situations are unable to do so, to address the questions I've been asked for years and to bravely begin to heal myself. She helped me to stay focused, balanced and to evolve, and I thank her for that.

I would like to thank the individuals who allowed me to use their real names in the story.

Shannon Jones gave valuable feedback on my early chapter drafts in addition to the rest of our manuscript readers.

DefineAmerican.com, RestoreFairness.com and The Democracy for America Netroots Nation scholarship program allowed me to experiment with sharing my story publicly online and receive encouragement during the early phases of the manuscript.

The people I came in contact with who are working to make immigration policy more humane, or whose families are separated or in exile are too numerous to name, but I would like to thank a few in particular. The women of Action for Family Unity provided a circle of trust, support, dedication, valuable networking, as well as comic relief from frequently isolating conditions, as we took steps together to make the personal political during the 2013 immigration debate. I am also so appreciative of organizations like American Families United, which is doing vital work on behalf of families like ours, lobbying tirelessly in order to reunite and bring many of us or our family members back to the U.S.

I am so lucky to have family and friends, both in the U.S. and Mexico, who are supportive in their own ways. Some have inquired about the book and encouraged me to keep writing. Others have stayed in touch or visited us, lifting my spirits and helping us to create good memories here in Mexico. Others simply helped keep the unpolitical parts of me sane. My parents in particular have been our unfailing allies and have risen to the occasion to embrace, along with us, much of what Mexico has to offer. My experience would have been a lot different without their help.

Ultimately, my husband Margo is the reason I share our story. He opened my eyes to America's undocumented class, its complex facets and its inability to be stereotyped. My contribution to this book is for him. Thank you, baby, for being quite possibly the most grounded person I have ever known, your *apoyo moral* and your ever-distinct perspective from my own. *Gracias por ser una pareja y un padre inigualable. Te quiero, mi amor.*

I thank my sweet daughter for enduring Mama's endless typing at odd hours, never loving me the less for it, and for providing me new, unequaled life inspiration. I hope someday this book may help explain things about our family that we haven't been able to adequately convey.

Finally, I thank the creative spirit for the vision and courage to tell our story, the strength to continue beyond the fear and the energy to see this project through to fruition. I put my trust in you and you provided.

To those who may not agree with my life choices or views on immigration or the environment, may we find a way to communicate and resolve problems compassionately and effectively as we eliminate illusion from our perspectives, together as a society. Our children and our very existence as a species depend on us for this.

About the Authors

Nathaniel Hoffman has written about immigration and politics for more than a decade as a reporter and editor at newspapers in Idaho and California. Hoffman filed stories for the *Christian Science Monitor, High Country News, The Miami Herald,* AlterNet and NewWest.net and produced audio reports for KQED public radio in San Francisco and KBSU in Boise. He worked as a reporter at *Boise Weekly,* the *Contra Costa Times* and the *Idaho Press-Tribune.* His journalism has taken him to Cuba twice, to Mexico, Israel and Lebanon and deep into Oregon's Hell's Canyon. Hoffman has covered the immigration and demographics beat since he got his start in journalism in Nampa, Idaho, in 2001. In 2010, Hoffman left his post as News Editor at *Boise Weekly* to write *Amor and Exile.* Hoffman is the founding editor of *The Blue Review,* a journal of popular scholarship at Boise State University. He lives in Boise with his wife and two daughters and a large front-yard garden.

Nicole Salgado is a biologist, educator and artist based in the Central Mexican highlands. She is the author and illustrator of *The Bajío's Bounty: Home Cooking from the Querétaro, Mexico Region.* Salgado is actively involved in the environmental and education fields both in the U.S. and Mexico. Her writing and art centers on nature, sustainability, motherhood and biculturalism. Salgado is originally from Central New York and has a B.S. from Cornell University and an M.A. from San José State University. She lives in Querétaro, Mexico, with her husband, daughter, two cats and a flock of birds.

For more information, visit amorandexile.com.